Everything for Sale?

The marketisation of higher education is a growing worldwide trend. Increasingly, market steering is replacing or supplementing government steering. Tuition fees are being introduced or increased, usually at the expense of state grants to institutions. Grants for student support are being replaced or supplemented by loans. Commercial rankings and league tables to guide student choice are proliferating with institutions devoting increasing resources to marketing, branding and customer service. The UK is a particularly good example of this, not only because it is a country where marketisation has arguably proceeded furthest, but also because of the variations that exist as Scotland, Wales and Northern Ireland increasingly diverge from England.

In *Everything for Sale?*, Roger Brown argues that the competitive regime that is now applicable to our higher education system was the logical, and possibly inevitable, outcome of a process that began with the introduction of full cost fees for overseas students in 1980. Through chapters including:

- Markets and Non-Markets
- The Institutional Pattern of Provision
- The Funding of Research
- The Funding of Student Education
- Quality Assurance
- The Impact of Marketisation: Efficiency, diversity and equity

he shows how the evaluation and funding of research, the funding of student education, quality assurance, and the structure of the system have increasingly been organised on market or quasi-market lines.

As well as helping to explain the evolution of British higher education over the past thirty years, the book contains some important messages about the consequences of introducing or extending market competition in universities' core activities of teaching and research.

This timely and comprehensive book is essential reading for all academics at University level and anyone involved in higher education policy.

Roger Brown is Professor of Higher Education Policy at Liverpool Hope University, UK.

Helen Carasso is Associate Research Fellow in the Department of Education, University of Oxford, UK.

The Society for Research into Higher Education (SRHE) is an independent and financially self-supporting international learned Society. It is concerned to advance understanding of higher education, especially through the insights, perspectives and knowledge offered by systematic research and scholarship.

The Society's primary role is to improve the quality of higher education through facilitating knowledge exchange, discourse and publication of research. SRHE members are worldwide and the Society is an NGO in operational relations with UNESCO.

The Society has a wide set of aims and objectives. Amongst its many activities the Society:

● is a specialist publisher of higher education research, journals and books, amongst them Studies in Higher Education, Higher Education Quarterly, Research into Higher Education Abstracts and a long running monograph book series.

The Society also publishes a number of in-house guides and produces a specialist series "Issues in Postgraduate Education".

● funds and supports a large number of special interest networks for researchers and practitioners working in higher education from every discipline. These networks are open to all and offer a range of topical seminars, workshops and other events throughout the year ensuring the Society is in touch with all current research knowledge.

● runs the largest annual UK-based higher education research conference and parallel conference for postgraduate and newer researchers. This is attended by researchers from over 35 countries and showcases current research across every aspect of higher education.

SRHE *Society for Research into Higher Education*
Advancing knowledge Informing policy Enhancing practice

73 Collier Street   T   +44 (0)20 7427 2350
London N1 9BE   F   +44 (0)20 7278 1135
United Kingdom   E   srheoffice@srhe.ac.uk

                      www.srhe.ac.uk

Director: Helen Perkins
Registered Charity No.313850
Company No.00868820
Limited by Guarantee
Registered office as above

Society for Research into Higher Education (SRHE) series

Series Editors: Lynn McAlpine, Oxford Learning Institute
Jeroen Huisman, University of Bath

Published titles:
Intellectual Leadership in Higher Education: Renewing the Role of the University Professor
Bruce Macfarlane

Strategic Curriculum Change: Global Trends in Universities
Paul Blackmore and Camille B. Kandiko

Reconstructing Identities in Higher Education: The Rise of 'Third Space' Professionals
Celia Whitchurch

The University in Dissent: Scholarship in the Corporate University
Gary Rolfe

Forthcoming titles:
Literacy in the Digital University: Learning As Social Practice in a Digital World
Robin Goodfellow

Feminism, Gender and Universities: Politics, Passion and Pedagogies
Miriam David

Everything for Sale?

The marketisation of UK higher education

Roger Brown with Helen Carasso

 Routledge
Taylor & Francis Group

LONDON AND NEW YORK

First published 2013
by Routledge
2 Park Square, Milton Park, Abingdon, Oxon OX14 4RN
together with the Society for Research into Higher Education (SRHE)
73 Collier Street
London N1 9BE
UK

Simultaneously published in the USA and Canada
by Routledge
711 Third Avenue, New York, NY 10017 together with the
Society for Research into Higher Education (SRHE)
73 Collier Street
London N1 9BE
UK

Routledge is an imprint of the Taylor & Francis Group, an informa business

British Library Cataloguing in Publication Data
A catalogue record for this book is available from the British Library

Library of Congress Cataloging in Publication Data
Brown, Roger, 1947–
   Everything for sale? : the marketisation of UK higher education /
   Roger Brown with Helen Carasso.
   p. cm.—(Research into higher education)
   1. Education, Higher—Great Britain—Marketing.
   2. Education, Higher—Economic aspects—Great Britain.
   3. Education, Higher—Aims and objectives—Great Britain.
   4. College students as consumers—Great Britain.
   I. Carasso, Helen, 1957– II. Title.
   LB2342.82.B76 2013
   378.41—dc23
   2012028864

ISBN: 978-0-415-80979-5 (hbk)
ISBN: 978-0-415-80980-1 (pbk)
ISBN: 978-0-203-07116-8 (ebk)

Typeset in Galliard
by Swales & Willis Ltd, Exeter, Devon

This book is dedicated to Ann and Raymond Simson

Contents

Illustrations

Figures

Tables

Series editors' introduction

This series, co-published by the Society for Research into Higher Education and Routledge Books, aims to provide, in an accessible manner, cutting-edge scholarly thinking and inquiry that reflects the rapidly changing world of higher education, examined in a global context.

Encompassing topics of wide international relevance, the series includes every aspect of the international higher education research agenda, from strategic policy formulation and impact to pragmatic advice on best practice in the field. Each book in the series aims to meet at least one of the principle aims of the Society: to advance knowledge; to enhance practice; to inform policy.

Roger Brown, with Helen Carasso, puts the current English higher education policies in the broader context of this system's movement on the road towards marketisation. The book is a thorough and critical analysis of changes in policy since 1979, but also assesses their impacts. These impacts are carefully benchmarked against lessons learnt in other marketised higher education systems. We hope – with the author – that there are plenty of lessons to be learnt from this eminent contribution to the scholarly debate on the marketisation of higher education.

Lynn McAlpine
Jeroen Huisman

Foreword

The three decades covered by *Everything for Sale? The marketisation of UK higher education* saw the most rapid and radical changes in the eight-hundred-year history of British higher education. The emergence of electronic communications technology is bringing about in decades changes as fundamental as occurred over centuries, following the invention of printing. However, the changes in the system's size, shape and values, which are the main theme of the book, have been at least as far reaching.

There are two basic ways in which higher education can be organised: as a publicly provided service, free at the point of delivery, with its profile determined by politicians and planners: or as a service provided by Adam Smith's invisible hand, in which markets decide how much is provided and who reaps the benefits on the basis of choices by individual consumers. In practice, all higher education systems are a combination of the two but, as Burton Clark showed in his well-known Triangle of Coordination (Clark, 1983), the balance between them can differ radically between national systems and change over time.

After the end of the Second World War, higher education in the United Kingdom was a public service to which all school leavers were entitled, free of charge or at very low cost, if their previous educational performance demonstrated that they were likely to benefit from it. Despite considerable expansion in the 1960s and policy changes aimed at promoting equity and upward social mobility, the benefits of higher education continued for the most part to be passed down within families and social groups from generation to generation. A university education came to be considered as a social-welfare service for the upper-middle classes, who were often willing to pay large secondary school fees to increase their children's chances of obtaining a free higher education.

This public service model fell apart in the 1990s, partly because of radical changes in ideas about how public services are best provided and partly as a result of the pressures brought about by the massive expansion of student numbers in the early 1990s. Brown charts the transition in the United Kingdom from an overwhelmingly public service model of higher education in the 1980s, to a system in which market considerations had become the dominating feature a quarter of a century later.

The past twenty years have seen a global shift towards market-based provision, especially in the Anglo-Saxon world and in former communist countries but movements in this direction are becoming evident nearly everywhere. In the UK the 1988 Education Reform Act indicated that universities and colleges were no longer to be state-subsidised service providers, setting their own priorities about what to offer students; rather they were to be treated as economic organisations selling specified services to the state and to others who were willing to purchase them. Initially, the move was part of the wider 'new public management' whereby the state continued to supply a major part of the financial resources but provided them on market-like criteria, so called 'quasi-markets' (Le Grand and Bartlett, 1993). However, universities and colleges were also encouraged to sell a variety of academic services at full cost to other purchasers, including students from outside the European Union. This process received increased impetus in 1998, with the introduction of significant tuition fees for by far the largest group of higher education consumers, first-degree UK and EU undergraduates, though they still received a substantial subsidy from public funds. In 2010 the decision was taken by the Government that in all except expensive science and technology courses students should meet the estimated full costs of their courses from autumn 2012 onwards. Although loans were available to enable students to pay the fees and meet the costs out of their future higher earnings, the shift to a market-based system was almost complete. From 2012 onwards all English universities will receive much less than half their income directly from central government. Most will be paid by customers of various kinds.

However, all markets need some regulation even if, as in the drugs trade for example, much of it is self-regulation. The marketization of UK higher education has been accompanied by increased regulation, as governments have tried to moderate some of the excesses of market behaviour.

The story Brown tells is one of tension between an ideological desire to promote efficiency in resource use in universities and colleges by subjecting them to market forces, and regulatory measures to try to promote equity and to moderate producer monopoly powers. The market has brought some benefits, especially in reducing the cost of provision through weakening the monopoly power of providers, but the so-called commodification of higher education has also many weaknesses.

Roger Brown is particularly well placed to chart these tensions. He has been both gamekeeper and poacher. As a senior civil servant in the Department for Trade and Industry in the late 1980s he was responsible for promoting links between universities and business, another important policy strand for successive governments. After the passage of the 1988 Education Reform Act, Brown was appointed Secretary of the Polytechnics and Colleges Funding Council, one of the predecessors of the Higher Education Funding Councils. He then changed sides and became the first (and, as it proved, last) Chief Executive of the Committee of Directors of Polytechnics. In both these jobs he was heavily occupied with the incorporation of the polytechnics and other major institutions as finan-

cially autonomous organisations and the debates which led to the transformation of the polytechnics into universities, following the 1992 Further and Higher
Education Act.

When the CDP disappeared in 1992 he was briefly Head of Research at the
Committee of Vice-Chancellors and Principals (now UniversitiesUK) before
becoming Chief Executive of the Higher Education Quality Council (HEQC).
This gave him a ringside seat and a participatory role in the intensive delibera-
tions that led to the creation of the Quality Assurance Agency (QAA). This can
be seen as a great debate over what regulation of market behaviour was desirable
and possible in higher education. In 1998 he changed his vantage point again
and became Principal and then Vice-Chancellor of what is now Southampton
Solent University. After stepping down from there, he moved back into research
and scholarship and became Professor of Higher Education Policy at Liverpool
Hope University.

Participant observation of a complex set of social activities such as higher education has its advantages and disadvantages. Only those who have been intimately
involved can clearly understand the pressures which led to the decisions that were
made: a record of their experiences and reflections on them is of immense value
to those who come after. On the other hand, there is always a risk of partiality. Is
only one side of any story being told? Bias is a special problem in higher education
research. Most academic studies of higher education issues are by authors who are
themselves working in the area and whose livelihood depends on it. It is often difficult to distinguish disinterested academic study from sophisticated lobbying. As
an academic researcher who has known Roger Brown since the time he obtained
his PhD from London University for a study of the post-war planning of further
and higher education in London in 1978, I have always been impressed by his
perceptiveness and his determination to understand the drivers of change, as well
as making it happen. Helen Carasso complements Roger Brown's experiences.
She has a solid academic research background, having obtained an MBA from the
Institute of Education and a DPhil from Oxford University, where her thesis was
a pioneering study of the emerging student fees scheme in England in the early
years of the twenty-first century. Professionally, Helen has held senior roles in two
very different universities and draws on their distinct perspectives to inform her
understanding of developments in the sector.

Much more will be written about this eventful quarter century, but Brown and
Carasso have provided an excellent, well-informed and critically reliable foundation for later historians and policy analysts to build on.

Gareth Williams
June 2012

Acknowledgements

Although as author I take full and final responsibility for *Everything for Sale? The marketisation of UK higher education*, it is in fact the result of a good deal of collaboration.

First and foremost, I must thank my researcher Dr Helen Carasso. As well as doing a huge amount of devilling and number crunching, Helen effectively wrote Chapter 4. She also made heroic efforts to make large parts of the text more accessible or, at least, more readable. Far more important, however, has been her enthusiasm and commitment to the project, which was very necessary given both the timescale – from start to finish, the writing of the book took not much over a year – and the fact that many of the policies we were analysing were being invented, developed, and changed, as we wrote. I am profoundly grateful to her. A number of other friends and colleagues have also contributed to the book: Geoffrey Alderman, Nick Barr, Bahram Bekhradnia, Andrew Boggs, Sue Boorman, Nigel Brown, Tony Bruce, Caroline Carpenter, Tony Clark, Stephen Court, Mark Dixon, Steve Egan, John Elmes, Mark Gittoes, Ron Glatter, Stephen Gorard, Lydia Hartwig, Bill Harvey, Don Heller, Richard James, William Locke, Simon Marginson, Andrew McGettigan, Ian McNay, Philip Moriarty, Brian Ramsden, Peter Scott, Stewart Sutherland, Jane Thompson, John Thompson, Ian Warren, Gareth Williams and Peter Williams. I am also grateful to colleagues at Routledge (Philip Mudd and Vicky Parting) and to Helen Perkins at SRHE. I have particularly benefitted from the help and encouragement of the joint series editor, Jeroen Huisman. I am very grateful to Gareth Williams not only for his Foreword, but also for his help and comments as the book was being written.

Thanks are also due to former colleagues from Southampton Solent: Barbara Ebrey, who typed many of the drafts, and Lilian Winkvist-Noble, who read through the manuscript at a late stage and made many helpful points. Special thanks go to Andy Forbes and Sarah Belkacem in the Solent Library for all their help not only in locating books and articles, but also in smoothing out infelicities in the bibliography. I should also like to acknowledge Universities UK's kindness in allowing me access to past Main Committee papers.

Finally, and most of all, thanks are once again due to my long suffering wife, Josie, for putting up with both me and the book for many months.

Roger Brown

Abbreviations

ABRC   Advisory Board for the Research Councils. Representative body for the Research Councils until 1993.
BBSRC   Biotechnology and Biological Sciences Research Council.
BTEC   Business Technology Education Council. Awarding body for Higher National Diplomas and Certificates, now EdExcel.
CDP   Committee of Directors of Polytechnics. Representative body for the heads of polytechnics. Dissolved in 1993.
CNAA   Council for National Academic Awards. Awarding and regulatory body for the polytechnics and higher education colleges from 1965 to 1992. Dissolved in 1993.
CVCP   Committee of Vice-Chancellors and Principals. Representative body for the heads of universities. Renamed UniversitiesUK (UUK) in 2000.
DBIS   Department for Business, Innovation and Skills. Sponsor department for higher education since 2009.
DELNI   Department for Employment and Learning, Northern Ireland.
DES   Department for Education and Science. Sponsor department for higher education until 1992. Renamed Department for Education (DFE) when responsibility for Science was transferred to the Department for Trade and Industry (DTI).
DFE   Department for Education. Sponsor department for higher education 1992–7, when renamed Department for Education and Employment (DFEE).
DFEE   Department for Education and Employment. Sponsor department for higher education 1997–2001, when renamed Department for Education and Skills (DFES).
DFES   Department for Education and Skills. Sponsor department for higher education 2001–7, when the responsibility for science was transferred to the Department for Innovation, Universities, Science and Skills (DIUS).
DIUS   Department for Innovation, Universities, Science and Skills. Sponsor department for higher education 2007–9, when renamed the Department for Business, Innovation and Skills (DBIS).

DTI	Department for Trade and Industry.
ECU	Equality Challenge Unit. The organisation that works to support and promote equality and diversity for staff and students in higher education.
EPSRC	Engineering and Physical Sciences Research Council.
ESRC	Economic and Social Research Council.
GuildHE	Representative body for the higher education colleges since 2006, previously Standing Conference of Principals (SCOP). Contains some university members.
HEA	Higher Education Academy.
HEFCE	Higher Education Funding Council for England. Principal government agency for funding English higher education since 1992.
HEFCW	Higher Education Funding Council for Wales.
HEPI	Higher Education Policy Institute. Independent higher education 'think tank' founded in 2002.
HEQC	Higher Education Quality Council. Principal quality assurance agency for UK higher education 1993–7. Succeeded by QAA.
HESA	Higher Education Statistics Agency. The central repository of statistics for the sector since 1994–95.
HMI	Her Majesty's Inspectorate.
HMSO	Her Majesty's Stationery Office, now The Stationery Office Ltd.
HMT	Her Majesty's Treasury.
IUSSC	House of Commons Innovation, Universities, Science and Skills Committee.
NAB	National Advisory Body for Public Sector Higher Education. Principal coordinating and funding body for the polytechnics and colleges 1982–1989. Succeeded by PCFC.
NAO	National Audit Office.
NERC	National Environment Research Council.
NUS	National Union of Students.
OECD	Organisation for Economic Cooperation and Development.
OFFA	Office for Fair Access.
OIA	Office of the Independent Adjudicator. The body established by the 2004 Higher Education Act to investigate complaints concerning 'acts or omissions' by English and Welsh higher education institutions, but not those relating to academic judgments.
OST	Office of Science and Technology. The body coordinating policy between 1992 and 2007.
PCFC	Polytechnics and Colleges Funding Council. Principal funding body for the polytechnics and higher education colleges from 1989 to 1992.
QAA	Principal quality assurance body for UK higher education since 1997.

RAE   Research Assessment Exercise. Periodic evaluation of the quality
          of university research since 1986. To be succeeded in 2014 by the
          REF.
RCUK   Research Councils UK. Representative body for the Research Coun-
          cils since 2002.
REF   Research Excellence Framework. Successor to the RAE.
SHEFC   Scottish Higher Education Funding Council.
SCOP   Standing Conference of Principals. Representative body for the higher
          education colleges until 2006, now GuildHE.
SRHE   Society for Research into Higher Education.
TES   Times Educational Supplement.
THE   Times Higher Education, previously Times Higher Education
          Supplement.
UCU   University and College Union. The principal trade union for aca-
          demic staff since the merger between the Association of University
          Teachers (AUT) and the National Association of Teachers in Further
          and Higher Education (NATFHE) in 2006.
UFC   The principal funding agency for the universities between 1989 and
          1992.
UGC   University Grants Committee. Funding and coordinating body for
          the universities until 1989 when succeeded by the UFC.
UUK   UniversitiesUK. Representative body for the heads of universities
          since 2000.

Chapter 1

Introduction

Our reforms tackle three challenges. First, putting higher education on a sustainable footing. We inherited the largest public deficit in post-war history, requiring spending cuts across government. By shifting public spending away from teaching grants and towards repayable tuition loans, we have ensured that higher education receives the funding it needs even as substantial savings are made to public expenditure. Second, institutions must deliver a better student experience; improving teaching, assessment, feedback and preparation for the world of work. Third, they must take more responsibility for increasing social mobility.

(DBIS, 2011a, Executive Summary, paragraph 3)

What is at stake here is not primarily the question of whether this group of graduates will pay a little more or a little less towards the costs of their education, even though that may seem (particularly to those in marginal seats) to be the most potent element electorally. What is at stake is whether universities in the future are to be thought of as having a public cultural role partly sustained by public support, or whether we move further towards redefining them in terms of a purely economistic calculation of value and a wholly individualist conception of 'consumer satisfaction'.

(Collini, 2010, p. 8)

Introduction

The reform programme announced by the Coalition Government in November 2010 and incorporated in the subsequent (June 2011) White Paper (DBIS, 2011a) is the most radical in the history of UK higher education, and amongst the most radical anywhere. The main change is that in future most of the money universities receive for undergraduate teaching will come through the student fee, with direct state support limited to a small number of priority areas. The limit on the fee institutions can charge Home and EU students will be nearly tripled, from £3,375 in 2011–12 to £9,000 in 2012–13. There will be a partial lifting of the controls on student places to enable some more popular institutions to expand although, since overall numbers are capped, this can only be at the expense of others. Another key proposal is for the rules for market entry to be modified to facilitate the participation of private providers, as well as to encourage more further education (FE) colleges to offer higher education at much lower cost. All of this will be underpinned by a more 'student friendly' quality assurance regime with much greater information about institutional provision. Instead of being seen as a public service, higher education is now viewed as something that primarily benefits private individuals.

The Government argues that these reforms are needed to put UK, or at least English, higher education on a sustainable footing whilst reducing claims on the taxpayer. By putting 'students at the heart of the system' – to refer to the title of the White Paper – both quality and efficiency will be raised as institutions respond more effectively to students' interests and needs through greater competition and information. To quote the independent review report on which much of the reform programme is based:

> Students are best placed to make the judgement about what they want to get from participating in higher education.
>
> (Independent Review of Higher Education Funding and Student Finance, 2010, p. 29)

However, other explanations have been offered.

One is that the reforms are simply a 'kneejerk' response to the economic crisis that began in the autumn of 2008. This appears to be the view of the Official Opposition (Frankel, 2011). Another is that they are part of a wider government attack on the public sector, involving increasing privatisation and a shifting of responsibility from the state to the individual, as can be seen in the health service, local government, social care and social housing, and which goes well beyond what may be needed to respond to the crisis in the public finances (Taylor-Gooby and Straker, 2011). However, the view that is offered here is that they are the latest, but also the most significant and far-reaching, stage in a long process of marketisation under which, through the policies of successive governments of all political parties since 1979, British higher education – or at least the core functions of student education and academic research – has increasingly been provided on market or 'quasi-market' lines. This phenomenon is by no means confined to Britain but is to be found across many developed countries (Brown, 2011a and b; see also Foskett, 2011 and Hemsley-Brown, 2011).

The basic features of such a system are:

- Universities and colleges are legally autonomous entities with considerable freedom to determine their mission, employ their own staff, etc.
- Market entry barriers are low to enable the entry of new providers (and the exit of existing ones).
- There is significant competition for students, who have a real choice about what, where and how to study.

- Institutions receive all or some of the revenue for teaching in the form of a tuition fee, all or part of which students or graduates have to find from their own or their families' pockets.
- Institutions compete not only on quality, but also on price.
- Quality assurance is focussed on consumer information and support rather than on quality enhancement.

Students' teaching and living costs may still be subsidised by the state. University research is usually subsidised, but often through a 'quasi-market' where the state acts as monopoly purchaser and allocates funds with varying degrees of selectivity. Other university services may be provided on market or non-market lines. The terms 'market', 'quasi-market', 'non-market' and 'privatisation' are all defined in Chapter 2.

In Britain, this process of marketisation may be seen to have commenced with the Thatcher Government's announcement in November 1979 that, from the following academic year, students from overseas would no longer enjoy a fee subsidy. Other major steps included:

- The separation of public funding for teaching and research, and the introduction of selective research funding, from 1986.
- The increase in the level of the still-subsidised Home tuition fee in 1989, and the corresponding reduction in the institutional grant for teaching.
- The introduction of 'top-up' loans for student support from 1990.
- The abolition of the 'binary line' between universities and polytechnics in 1992.
- The introduction of top-up fees of £1,000 in 1998.
- The changes in the rules for university title in 2004 to enable institutions without research degree-awarding powers to obtain a university title.
- The introduction of 'variable' fees of £3,000 in 2006.

A chronology of key events is appended to this chapter.

The book analyses the Coalition Government's reforms and places them in a wider historical and international context. It focusses, in particular, on four major domains or sites of marketisation: the institutional pattern of provision; the funding of research; the funding of student education, both teaching and student support; and quality assurance.[1]

Chapter 2 sets out the analytical framework for the study. The two main components are (a) public and private goods and (b) market and non-market modes of production. It begins by reviewing the relevant literature, as well as offering a brief overview of the extent of marketisation amongst developed higher education systems generally.

Chapter 3 gives an account of government-led changes in the institutional pattern of provision between 1979 and 2012. These changes were designed to increase institutional competition for students and research income. Three main sets of developments are identified: a more than doubling in the number of universities; the removal or reduction of external limits on institutional development; and an increase in the number of larger, comprehensive institutions and a reduction in the number of smaller, specialist institutions. The chapter concludes by outlining the Coalition Government's plans for increasing the market participation of FE colleges and private providers, both 'not for profit' and 'for profit'.

Chapter 4 describes how the provision of public funds for research has gradually been placed on a quasi-market basis. This began in earnest with the first Research Assessment Exercise (RAE) in 1986 and was refined through successive exercises up to 2008; the next such exercise – the Research Excellence Framework, incorporating some judgement of research impact – will be undertaken in 2014. These exercises, together with their financial implications, are summarised. Chapter 4 also describes, more briefly, the parallel processes for the allocation of research infrastructure funds and public support for graduate research students. It concludes by discussing the concentration of research resources that these policies have produced.

Chapter 5 shows how both the sources and the direction of funds for student (undergraduate) education (teaching, support) gradually changed, so that an increasing proportion of funding was private and/or provided on a competitive basis. It begins with the introduction of full-cost fees for overseas students in 1980, continues with the increase in the subsidised Home/EU fee in 1989, the introduction of top-up fees in 1998, and the introduction of variable fees and income-contingent loans for both fees and maintenance in 2006. It concludes with the replacement of most direct state support for teaching by what is in effect a 'voucher' system.[2] It also describes the parallel changes in student support, beginning with the introduction of loans for maintenance in 1990, and continuing with the abolition and then the reintroduction of maintenance grants in 1998 and 2004. Chapter 5 also gives an account of the diverging policies for funding student education in Scotland, Wales and Northern Ireland since 2000.

Chapter 6 begins with an account of quality assurance in the then existing separate sectors of higher education in 1979. It tells how a unitary system of quality assurance came to supplement and eventually encompass institutions' internal quality processes. It traces the evolution of this system from one still essentially based on traditional processes of peer review to one where officially sanctioned consumer market mechanisms – league tables, performance indicators, student satisfaction surveys, published quality information, etc. – are increasingly supplementing, if not yet replacing, conventional academic judgements. It concludes with some reflections on the changes in the structure and governance of quality assurance over the period (see also Brown, submitted for review).

Chapters 7 and 8 offer an assessment of the effects of the policies described in Chapters 3 to 6. Chapter 7 begins by summarising what is known from the literature about the impact of market-based policies in developed higher education systems. It then considers how far what has happened in Britain is consistent with this picture. It looks in turn at efficiency and the use of resources, institutional diversity and stratification, and equity and widening participation. Chapter

8 looks at the impacts on educational and research quality and on the universities' ability to control the academic 'agenda'.

Finally, Chapter 9 suggests some of the messages that can be taken from this experience internationally as governments in many countries resort to various forms of marketisation, in order to obtain better value for the enormous public and private resources now invested in universities and colleges. Given the potentially far-reaching nature of the current reforms, this assessment attempts to look forward as well as back. It is necessarily somewhat provisional: it was only during the final drafting that it became known that legislation to implement some of the key elements in the Government's programme would not be introduced in the 2012–13 legislative programme. This has incidentally attracted considerable criticism not only on grounds of continuing uncertainty, but also because it is difficult to get an overall picture of the reforms (Morgan, 2012a).

This introductory chapter concludes with a 'pen picture' of UK higher education at the start and end of the period covered by the book.

It should be noted that the book is primarily about the development and implementation of public policies for higher education in England. This is partly because of the relative scale of the English system within the UK – 84 per cent of the students and 83 per cent of income (Bruce, 2012) – and partly because this is where marketisation has so far gone furthest. However, reference is made to developments in Scotland, Wales and Northern Ireland where these are relevant to the main theme.

UK higher education in 1979–80

In 1979–80 there were 777,800 students in UK higher education, including 58,900 from outside the European Community (7.6 per cent of the total). The Home participation rate was 12.4 per cent. Males were in the majority. Most students were studying full-time. The proportion from working-class backgrounds was small. Most students were studying for first degrees or diplomas: the number of postgraduate students was small. These students were studying at 48 universities, 30 polytechnics and 61 colleges, the latter two groups constituting the so-called 'public sector' of higher education. In principle, the polytechnics and colleges were supposed to be offering a more practical, applied curriculum but already arts, humanities and social science courses could be found there. Nevertheless, across the system as a whole a broad vocational/non-vocational distinction applied. Other than at the Open University (OU) and the University of London's Birkbeck College, university students were overwhelmingly full-time, while polytechnic and college students were both full- and part-time. Modular and 'joint' courses were still in their infancy.

Whilst a small part of the costs of teaching was met by fees, the amounts were nominal (and generally subsidised by the state). Most of the money for teaching came from government grants to institutions (which in the case of the universities did not yet distinguish between teaching and research). There were generous means-tested maintenance grants and significant student debt was almost unheard of: for most Home and EU students, undergraduate courses were effectively free. The universities received their funding via the University Grants Committee (UGC), which acted as a buffer body between the Government and the institutions and which covered the whole of Great Britain. Research was still a secondary activity in most institutions and departments. Research funds were distributed to universities pro rata to student numbers: external quality judgements for research were mostly confined to Research Council grants. The public sector institutions received their funding from their local authority, although there had long been collective pooling arrangements and a national planning and coordinating mechanism had lately been mooted. They received no public grants for research. The OU and a small group of specialised providers received their funding direct from the Department for Education and Science (DES). The great bulk of institutional funding came from the state, although some universities received a modest income from endowments.

Whilst the universities had their own degree-awarding powers, the public sector institutions offered the awards of the Council for National Academic Awards (CNAA), or the Business and Technology Education Council (BTEC); some also offered external University of London External degrees. Together with Her Majesty's Inspectorate (HMI), CNAA regulated the quality of courses and awards in the polytechnics and colleges. There was no comparable supervision of the universities, although by convention HMI were 'invited' to inspect courses of initial teacher training. Tenure still existed as a bulwark of academic freedom, and the great majority of academic staff were on full-time, permanent contracts. Whilst the universities were self-governing, the public institutions were mostly subject to local authority control, although they had developed academic boards. Overall, and bearing in mind the fact that its universities enjoyed greater legal, financial and operational autonomy than elsewhere in Europe, the UK system was seen as occupying an intermediate position between the non-market, state-supervised continental systems and the more diverse, open and market-driven US one.

UK higher education in 2011–12

In 2010–11, the most recent year for which there is data, there were 2.5 million students. The participation rate in England was 47 per cent. Women are in the majority. There have been huge increases in the numbers of part-time and mature students, and also in the numbers of students from ethnic minorities. There are many more working-class students than before, although they are still seriously underrepresented; however, a greater proportion of the overall population is now 'middle class'. There are now significant numbers of postgraduate students (19 per cent of the total) and many universities have developed graduate schools. 14.5 per cent of students are from outside the EU and many institutions are effectively dependent on their ability to attract such students. There are 165 higher education institutions, of which 115 are universities. These include one non-state-funded private university, one non-state-funded private university college, and three non-state-funded private colleges with degree-awarding powers. The range of subjects studied is now far wider and large numbers of students are now studying subjects that could broadly be described as 'vocational'. With the exception of the OU (and Birkbeck), most of the students at the pre-1992 universities are still full-time, but so are many of the students at the post-1992 ones. Modular and joint courses are now the rule in many institutions. There are now separate policy and funding regimes in each country of the UK.

Institutions continue to receive funds for teaching from a combination of grants and fees, but from 2012 fees will constitute the great bulk of their income for teaching (in England). Whereas the introduction of top-up fees in 1998 and variable fees in 2006 saw few variations in institutional charges, the increase in the cap in 2012 is expected to see significant variations in both gross and net charges, with some universities charging the maximum £9,000 for all their courses. Universities and higher education colleges are also anticipating price competition from 65 FE colleges, including four sixth-form colleges. Whilst maintenance grants still exist, many students enrolling after 2012 can expect to graduate with debts of over £30,000. There are also more 'hidden' costs such as laboratory fees. Universities and colleges have substantially reduced their dependence on state funding and this will accelerate further after 2012.

As well as competing for students and income, universities are competing for research funds, research performance having emerged, as in the US, as a major signifier of institutional value. At the same time, the proportion of research funding allocated selectively has increased so that by 2010–11 three-quarters of Higher Education Funding Council for England (HEFCE) research funds went to just 23 institutions; Research Council funds and public funds for postgraduate research students are similarly concentrated. The UGC has long been replaced by funding agencies more directly accountable to the Government: the Universities Funding Council (UFC) and the Polytechnics and Colleges Funding Council (PCFC) from 1989, the HEFCE, the Scottish Higher Education Funding Council (SHEFC) and the Higher Education Funding Council for Wales (HEFCW) from 1992. Tenure having been abolished for new university staff since 1988, the vast majority of staff are on conventional employment contracts but a significant proportion are on short-term, teaching- or research-only, and/or part-time terms, again as in the US.

Although academic staff continue to play an important part in the governance of the pre-1992 institutions, even there a corporate model – small governing councils with external 'lay' majorities, the norm for the polytechnics since 1989 – is gaining ground, as is the concept of the vice-chancellor as chief executive as well as leader of the academic community (Brown, 2012a). Overall, although subject to the Bologna process,[3] and in spite of the significant (and growing) funding and policy differences that now exist between England and Scotland, Wales and Northern Ireland, the UK as a whole now has far more in common with the US than with any other European system.

Chronology of key developments in the marketisation of UK higher education 1979 to 2012

1979   The Government announces that from October 1980 the remaining sub-sidies for overseas students will be ended so that they would have to pay full-cost fees.

1980   Education (No. 2) Act gives the Secretary of State the power to cap the Advanced Further Education Pool so that overall expenditure on public sector institutions is brought under national control.

1981   National Advisory Board for Public Sector Higher Education (NAB) cre-ated to coordinate policy on non-university higher education provision.

1983   University College Buckingham becomes the University of Buckingham, the first wholly privately funded university in Britain.

1984   In *A Strategy for Higher Education into the 1990s* the UGC announces research selectivity policy.

1985   Green Paper *The Development of Higher Education into the 1990s* sets out a government 'agenda' for higher education, with the greatest emphasis being on the need for universities to serve the economy. *Report of the Steering Group on University Efficiency* (Jarratt Report) marks the first step towards the corporatisation of university governance and the devel-opment of sector-wide performance indicators.

1986   The UGC separates institutional funding for research and teaching. The first RAE is conducted (subsequent exercises in 1989, 1992, 1996, 2001 and 2008).

1987   White Paper *Higher Education Meeting the Challenge* announces the Government's intention to incorporate the polytechnics and other major public institutions and create new national funding agencies for them and for the existing universities.

1988   Education Reform Act. Abolition of tenure (protection from dismissal for redundancy). The UFC and PCFC replace the UGC and NAB and apply 'contractual' funding of teaching. Consultative paper on top-up mainte-nance loans for undergraduate students.

1989   Speech at Lancaster University by the Secretary of State (Kenneth Baker) setting out the Government's vision of an expansion of higher education on the American model, with greater engagement of private resources.

1990   Increase in the undergraduate fee level and reduction in the level of teaching grant to institutions (though both continue to be paid in full by the Government). Introduction of student loans for maintenance, supple-menting grants: Education (Student Loans) Act.

1991   White Paper *Higher Education: A New Framework* announces the Gov-ernment's intention to abolish the binary line and enable the polytechnics and certain other institutions to obtain a university title.

1992   Further and Higher Education Act and Further and Higher Education

(Scotland) Act. Creation of a new single funding council in England (HEFCE). Establishment of funding councils in Scotland and Wales for the first time. Incorporation of further education colleges.

1993 Introduction of Teaching Quality Assessment (Subject Review) as intended complement to RAE. Establishment of the Higher Education Quality Council (HEQC) as a sector-owned quality assurance body.

1994 Introduction of Maximum Aggregate Student Numbers (quotas) for undergraduate places at individual institutions.

1996 Following the Vice-Chancellors' revolt in late 1995 threatening to levy additional top-up fees, the Government establishes the Dearing Committee with all-party support to investigate alternative funding schemes. Second private institution receives degree-awarding powers (Royal Agricultural College, subsequently HEFCE-funded)

1997 Dearing Committee recommends significant undergraduate fees to help meet institutions' teaching costs, along with the retention of maintenance grants. New Labour Government emphasises universities' role in social mobility. Government announces intention to introduce means-tested top-up tuition fees and abolish maintenance grants. New regime introduced the following year in the Teaching and Higher Education Act.

1998 Quality Assurance Agency takes over the functions of HEQC and the Funding Councils' assessment units.

1999 Scotland and Northern Ireland obtain powers to determine some elements of higher education policy. Publication of Performance Indicators Steering Group First Report which leads to the production and publication of a set of indicators of institutional performance for the entire sector across the UK for the first time, including statistical benchmarks.

2001 Prime Minister announces review of student support. Reforms to quality assurance regime. Teaching Quality Information in effect replaces Subject Review.

2003 White Paper *The Future of Higher Education* announces the Government's intention to introduce variable tuition fees supported by income-contingent loans.

2004 Higher Education Act. Partial reintroduction of maintenance grants. Modification of rules for university title. Extension of Foundation Degree-awarding powers to FE colleges.

2005 First National Student Survey.

2006 Introduction in England of variable fees capped at £3,000 and income-contingent fee and maintenance loans for full-time Home and EU undergraduates. New Office for Fair Access (OFFA) to monitor institutions' widening participation plans. More private institutions gain degree-awarding powers. New Office of the Independent Adjudicator (OIA) to handle student complaints not resolved through institutions' procedures. Wales gains control of some aspects of higher education policy.

2009   White Paper *Higher Ambitions: The Future of Universities in a Knowledge Economy* proposes closer links between institutions and skills needs in the economy, as well as an amplification of information for students. Establishment of the Browne Committee to review the impact of the 2004 legislation.

2010   Government accepts recommendation of the Browne Committee that in future most teaching in English universities should be funded through the tuition fee, with direct funding to institutions confined to a small number of priority areas. Fee cap to be raised to £9,000 from 2012. Proposed modifications to the fee and maintenance loan regimes.

2011   Government publishes a White Paper *Higher Education Students at the Heart of the System* also proposing changes to the rules for degree-awarding powers/university title to facilitate the market entry of private providers and FE colleges.

2012   Introduction of new regime for funding student (undergraduate) education. Further concentration of public funding for research. Reduction in numbers threshold for university title.

Chapter 2

Markets and non-markets

The general message I offer is that most of the significant developments of the decade happened in piecemeal and pragmatic fashion. There were certainly some overall trends of policy, though these could by no means be assembled into any kind of grand strategy ... an even less realistic target was a cohesive policy, or set of policies, across the whole of education and training ... However, perhaps there was a guiding philosophy ... The obvious candidate for consideration is promotion of some sort of 'market' whose functioning compels greater attention to the customer. For my own part, I have always found it hard to discern any clarity of theme or practice which would justify an assertion that a 'market approach' (never mind just who are the customers!) was being pursued. In detail, there was not always consistency.

(Bird, 1994, p. 83)[1]

This chapter is in two parts. The first reviews existing explanations of government policies towards higher education since 1979. The second introduces the analytical framework that will be used in the study.

Explaining government policy

Somewhat echoing Bird's comments, Kogan and Hanney (2000) professed to see no underlying threads:

We therefore look for no single factor affecting change but for the interaction of actors and their historical contexts, and a constant reiteration or connection between them. Intentions were forged partly by belief systems, partly by the power of circumstances, and partly by opportunistic reactions to what might not have been planned or even rationally contemplated.

(Kogan and Hanney, 2000, p. 35)

Policy-making followed no rational model. Policies were created largely on the hoof and were, as we have said, the product of a complex interplay of context, ideologies, ministers and bureaucracies.

(Kogan and Hanney, 2000, p. 235)

However, Kogan and Hanney also noted that as a result of government policies and institutional leadership, there was a shift from academic control towards both the incorporation of the universities in the generality of state control, and the introduction of market-based policies. These indeed are the two themes of most attempts to explain the evolution of government policies towards higher education over the period. Let us consider them in turn.

Increased state control

Perhaps the dominant theme in the literature to date has been that of growing state, and reducing academic, control over the universities. This reflected the increased importance of economic competitiveness and the view of successive governments of all parties that, left to themselves, universities would make a sub-optimal contribution to national wealth. The two earliest statements of this theory were Halsey's *Decline of Donnish Dominion: The British Academic Profession in the Twentieth Century* (Halsey, 1995) and Tapper and Salter's *Oxford, Cambridge and the Changing Idea of the University: The Challenge to Donnish Domination* (Tapper and Salter, 1992). But perhaps the classic statement is the same authors' *The State and Higher Education* (Salter and Tapper, 1994).

Salter and Tapper argued that higher education offers a unique blend of two resources essential for economic and social development: knowledge and status. In its dealings with higher education, the state is obliged to recognise that universities perform a key social function by controlling the individual and occupational mobility necessary for social change. But in addition, the universities' monopoly of the union of high-status knowledge and culture endows them with a third kind of socio-political power: the authority to promote particular sets of values. Hence the growing exercise of state power in relation to higher education is inevitable.

Salter and Tapper (1994, p. 16) quoted the 1972 White Paper *Education: A Framework for Expansion* as an early manifestation of this view:

> At the same time they [the Government] value its [higher education's] con-tinued expansion as an investment in the nation's human talent in a time of rapid social change and technological development. If these economic, personal and social aims are to be realised, within the limits of available resources and competing priorities, both the purposes and the nature of higher education ... must be critically and realistically examined. The con-tinuously changing relationship between higher education and subsequent employment should be reflected both in the institutions and in individ-ual choices. The Government hope that those who contemplate entering

higher education, and those advising them, will the more carefully examine their motives and their requirements; and be sure that they form their judgement on a realistic assessment of its usefulness to their interests and career intentions.

(DES, 1972, paragraph 34)

Accordingly, students should base their decisions about their higher education on how it will contribute to their future employment and not, for example, on whether they would find it intrinsically interesting. This will enable them to become part of the efficient distribution of human capital and so facilitate the linkage between economic demand and human supply. Equally, institutions should assist the process through the selection of appropriate students, by the manipulation of entrance requirements for particular courses, and by internal restructuring.

Salter and Tapper noted the Secretary of State for Education, Sir Keith Joseph, writing to the UGC in July 1982 requesting the development of a strategy for higher education into the 1990s. A further letter the following year set out what was wanted, using the now familiar terminology of the economic ideology of education: more efficient use of resources and a shift towards technological, scientific and engineering courses and other vocationally relevant forms of study. The subsequent Green Paper *The Development of Higher Education into the 1990s* (DES, 1985a) stated:

> The economic performance of the United Kingdom since 1945 has been disappointing compared to the achievements of others. The Government believes that it is vital for our higher education to contribute more effectively to the improvement of the performance of the economy ... The Government is particularly concerned by the evidence that the societies of our competitors are producing, and plan in the future to produce, more qualified scientists, engineers, technologists and technicians than the United Kingdom.
>
> (DES 1985a, paragraphs 1.2–1.3)

It was this concern with the need for higher education to contribute more effectively to the economy which led to increasing government controls, especially over research policy. These began with the Science and Technology Act 1965, and continued with changes in research funding from 1984, the transfer of responsibility for research policy from the Education Department to the Office of Science and Technology (OST) in 1993, and the replacement of the University Grants Committee (UGC) and the National Advisory Body for Public Sector Higher Education (NAB) by the UFC and the Polytechnics and Colleges Funding Council (PCFC) in 1989, and then the Higher Education Funding Council for England (HEFCE) from 1992.

Although by the time of publication Salter and Tapper felt that the control framework was reasonably stable, they also noted that:

There are continuing pressures within the Conservative Party to dismantle this institutional structure, and for the state to encourage a much closer relationship between the universities and their clients. On the teaching front, this could mean giving student vouchers with which they would purchase directly their higher education. On the research front, the state's resources could be allocated entirely to the research councils which would then distribute them to deserving applicants – from the universities or elsewhere. Whereas research quality could be ensured by appropriate processes of evaluation, teaching quality could be measured by the changing pattern of student demand.

(Salter and Tapper, 1994, p. 201)

This seems remarkably prescient in view of the recent funding changes described in Chapter 5.

In what was in part an update, Tapper (2007) noted that whereas the Education Department was at the centre of these efforts to increase government or state control, after 1992 policy formation became fragmented even though the overall thrust of policy remained the same. Tapper also located what has happened in higher education within the broader arena of public policy, seeing it as an 'issue that needs to be analysed with reference to the wider debates that have surrounded the delivery of British public policy' (Tapper, 2007, p. 4). He also gave greater recognition to the market as a factor in institutional behaviour:

We are now entering an era in which market forces (including the power that students can exercise as consumers) will have a more significant part to play, in which British higher education will find itself increasingly in a competitive global environment …, in which a regulatory framework appears to be emerging – the Bologna Process – at the European level, and in which missions will be more sharply differentiated with universities aspiring to be both international players and/or significant local institutions. These are forces that will inevitably act upon the manner in which systems of higher education are governed.

(Tapper, 2007, p. 8)

A writer with a broadly similar perspective is Shattock (2008). Shattock argued that in moving from being 'self-governed' to 'state governed', the policy drivers for higher education were no longer those of the system itself but were derived from broader policies for the reform of the public sector – often called New Public Management (Ferlie et al., 1996) – of which marketisation is one, alongside modernisation and minimisation. 'Modernisation' is 'bringing in faster and more flexible ways of budgeting, managing and accounting for the delivery of services'; 'minimisation' is 'outsourcing' or 'hollowing out', pushing decision-making downwards to smaller units, under the semblance of giving them greater autonomy' (Shattock, 2008, p. 190; see also Pearce, 2004).

Higher education policy is thus an adjunct of public policy as well as of wider changes in government itself. So:

Although the structures of a former self-governed, self-managed, sector remain largely in place, such as the so-called 'buffer' machinery intended to protect institutional autonomy, they no longer have substance but rather serve to conceal the state's control of policy … The institutions themselves may still retain legal autonomy and a freedom of decision-making that is qualitatively different from the experience of institutional autonomy in most European countries but the individual policy choices are heavily constrained by policies initiated in the heart of Whitehall.

(Shattock, 2008, p. 182)

Again:

Whereas in the past the university sector had dominated its own reform processes, now reforms were directed from outside and were dictated by considerations that derived from an external perception of how state-funded institutions should operate … . This reflected the fact that the nature of higher education and its importance to the modern state had drawn it into national politics in a way that before 1980 could not have been conceived.

(Shattock, 2008, pp. 186, 199)

Other writers with this perspective of growing state control at the expense of the academy include Henkel and Little (1999), Henkel (2000), Scott (2001) and Deer (2002).

The market

In his review of the Halsey and Tapper and Salter books, Johnson (1994) commented:

What [the Thatcher and Major Governments] have done is to treat university education as a marketable product and to insist that its delivery is subject to the same output and performance assessment criteria as might be applied to the production of goods and services in a real market.

(Johnson, 1994, p. 375)

But the writer who has most clearly and consistently depicted the marketisation of British higher education is Gareth Williams. In a 1992 book, *Changing Patterns of Finance in Higher Education*, he remarked that the case for market approaches to higher education funding was based on three main propositions:

One is the belief that the private sector can relieve governments of some of the cost burden. The second is that many of the benefits of higher education accrue to private individuals and they should be prepared to pay for them. However, private finance is not necessary for market mechanisms to operate and the third premise is that both external and internal efficiency improve if government agencies buy services from universities rather than make grants to them. More efficient institutions offering better value for money flourish while those that are less efficient lose out. Markets put the power in the hands of purchasers of higher education services, so the system has to be responsive to their demands. Advocates of markets define efficiency as the satisfaction of consumer wants at minimum costs.

(Williams, G., 1992, p. 138)

In a 1995 essay, Williams reviewed changes in higher education financing in a number of advanced countries. He noted that:

A marked shift is occurring from input-based budgeting whereby the state supplies educational services, either directly or indirectly, and the main criterion determining what is provided is knowledge and expertise, towards output and performance-based budgeting, in which suppliers receive resources to the extent that they provide services that satisfy consumers.

(Williams, G., 1995, p. 174)

This shift was not confined to higher education but was occurring in many public services.

Williams suggested that there were two criteria by which we should judge the extent to which marketisation was actually occurring: the source of funds and the funding mechanisms. An increasing share of private financing was an indicator of increased marketisation. Within public funding, a shift towards output-oriented programme budgets would similarly be a move in a market direction, although a real market system of finance was still some time away because education was still being provided to students free, or at a price well below cost. Finally, Williams suggested three criteria by which market-based funding approaches should be judged:

Does response to market indicators bring about a satisfactory level of total expenditure? Are resources used effectively and efficiently within institutions? Is the pattern of resource allocation brought about by the market socially acceptable in other ways?

(Williams, G., 1995, p. 191)

In a 1997 article, Williams described the progress of marketisation in Britain. He noted the crucial importance of the expenditure cuts brought in by the Thatcher Government in 1980–81 (see Chapter 5). Because of their private legal status, British universities were always prone to market-like behaviour. But it was their response to these cuts – with the universities intensifying their recruitment of overseas students after the removal of the subsidy, then declining to expand numbers when their general funding was cut as the polytechnics did the opposite – which showed the

Government that the universities would respond like any other organisation to market and quasi-market incentives.

It was in this context that the 1988 Education Reform Act provided for the abolition of lifetime tenure for new academic staff, the abolition of local education authority control of the polytechnics, and the creation of two new funding councils more directly answerable to the Secretary of State. But the key step was the introduction of the principle of contractual funding, as stated in the Secretary of State's guidance letter for the new funding agencies:

> I shall look to the Council to develop funding arrangements which recognise the general principle that the public funds allocated to universities are in exchange for the provision of teaching and research and are conditional on their delivery ...
>
> (DES, 1988 b and c, quoted in Williams, G., 2004, p. 246)

Williams commented that the letter:

> was quite explicit that higher education institutions were henceforward to be seen as selling teaching (and, in the case of universities only, research) services to the government which was the near monopsonistic purchaser of these services. This transfer of financial power from the suppliers of academic services to a proxy consumer was extremely far reaching. Henceforward, the only way universities (and now polytechnics) could make much effective use of their cloak of legal autonomy was by continuing to diversify their funding sources.
>
> (Williams, G., 1997, p. 283)

Williams (2004) again emphasised the importance of the 1988 legislation which 'transformed [the universities] from partners of the state in the provision of high level teaching and research into audited vendors of academic services to the state' (2004, p. 246). However, he also stressed the importance of the enhanced regulation which greater competition was thought to require, notably quality assurance. He also reviewed the consequences of the new funding mechanisms for institutional decision-making, taking in income for teaching, income for research and income for other services, with nearly all universities now having resource allocation models; these he described as:

> essentially a set of formulae that constitutes a planning and management tool for allocating resources on a systematic basis to each cost centre in a university. Departments and centres which are not financially viable within their allocation must reduce their costs, raise income from other sources, seek subsidies from the rest of the university because of their non-financial contributions to its well-being, or become candidates for closure.
>
> (Williams, G., 2004, p. 251)

By this time marketisation had taken a further significant step with the introduction of top-up fees in 1998 and the announced intention in 2003 to introduce variable fees. Williams found that the main effects of marketisation in the UK had been:

1) much greater efficiency as measured by most quantitative indicators.
2) much expanded and less distinct boundaries of both 'the university' and 'higher education'.
3) diversification with standardisation of processes and outcomes within similar categories of activity.
4) radical changes in management arrangements within higher education institutions.

(Williams, G., 2004, p. 258)

Williams concluded:

The important issue for public policy purposes is not the existence of a market but the extent and the way markets are regulated. What are providers and purchasers allowed and encouraged to do, how are they regulated and how are the regulations enforced?

(Williams, G., 2004, p. 265)

His answer was that:

A market that was once generously financed from public funds and very lightly regulated has become one that is parsimoniously financed and subject to very many more conditions on the receipt of public funds.

(Williams, G., 2004, p. 265)

Another early exponent of the markets argument was Walford (1988). Walford saw the Education Reform Act changes as part of a wider process of privatisation. This could also be seen in the changes proposed for the schools, notably the possibility that individual state schools could opt out of local authority control to become directly government funded, semi-independent, grant-maintained schools run by charitable trusts. Such privatisation might not literally be a transfer of the ownership of public enterprises to the private sector but 'the reduction in the activities of the state and the replacement of the "welfare state" systems of collective provision and finance by more privatised systems' (1988, p. 50).

In higher education, privatisation could be seen most obviously in the Thatcher Government's early decision that students at what was then University College, Buckingham (founded in 1976 but originally proposed in 1967) should be eligible for local authority mandatory grants. However, it could also be seen in government attempts to make the universities more entrepreneurial and competitive, to be more diverse, and to provide a variety of services to a range of customers.

The particular instances included the removal of the subsidy for overseas students' fees, the abolition of tenure, the Jarratt Report on university efficiency, the creation of the new funding councils, the introduction of contractual funding, research selectivity and the subsequent proposals for institutional rationalisation, and the introduction of student loans, where:

> the aim is not just the reduction of government expenditure, but there is also the desire to make individuals recognise the costs of higher education and make some financial commitment to it, and for institutions to become more responsive and accountable to student demands.
>
> (Walford, 1988, p. 60)

State versus market?

In a 1994 article, Pritchard queried the assumption that the state and the market were necessarily alternatives. She reviewed the progress of marketisation in Britain in very similar terms to Williams and Walford. She saw the same dangers, as well as the transactions costs of operating a 'managed market'. However, she also noted the continuing evidence of strong government control; at least in such areas as higher education, 'the market economy can only be maintained by strong state intervention' (Pritchard, 1994, p. 263). Her conclusion was that governments should stop pretending that they were not intervening and instead try to make those interventions more efficient by improving their planning:

> In order to avoid 'stop-go' recruitment policies and financial lurches from one year to the next, ideally, [government] interventionism should be moderated by a consciousness that university autonomy also serves to defend and champion values which, although periodically unpopular in government circles, are of lasting worth to the whole community.
>
> (Pritchard, 1994, p. 264)

In another important analysis, Middleton saw three models as potentially implicit in the 'modernisation' of higher education:

> The first treats marketisation and state intervention as incompatible strategies for reform, the second argues that state intervention may contribute to the success of a higher educational market economy (thus subordinating the state to the market), while the third proposes that market relations are mobilised in the cause of centralised policy objectives.
>
> (Middleton, 2000, p. 537)

The 'essential claim' of the third model was that government support for market relations in higher education was not a policy sufficient to itself. On the contrary:

it has an ulterior political objective: specifically, the enhancement of graduate skills and employability ... Similarly, the attack on professional 'monopolies' can be re-evaluated as involving the use of market competition to fragment opposition to centrally defined curriculum objectives, rather than as the use of regulatory mechanisms to make markets work more effectively. The development of a customer mentality among students is also designed to promote more robust instrumental attitudes, encouraging students to view higher education as an investment rather than a 'right' to a free service.

(Middleton, 2000, p. 549)

More recently, Naidoo (2008) has also queried the notion that state regulation and market forces are incompatible. On the basis of a study of higher education policy reform in Britain between 1980 and 2007, she argued that while there were certainly cases where an increase in market coordination leads to a reduction in state regulation:

there is also increasing evidence that higher education can be increasingly regulated by the state whilst simultaneously opening up to market forces. Furthermore, rather than pulling in different directions, increasing articulation between the two modes of coordination may occur. State intervention may help establish the conditions for the operation of a quasi higher education market.

(Naidoo, 2008, pp. 2–3)

As well as the abolition of the overseas subsidy and the funding changes following the 1988 Education Reform Act, and the introduction of top-up and then variable fees, examples have included the use of earmarked grants to reflect specific government priorities (widening participation, links with business, specialist subjects). However, she extended the analysis not only into quality assurance (where university staff were incorporated into the state accountability function), but also into teaching and learning with the 'active reconceptualisation of students as consumers of higher education' ((Naidoo, 2008, p. 15). This in turn has led both students and institutions to respond in a more market-oriented way:

One simple measure is the rise of centres within universities which have the sole function of marketing university programmes to potential students (customers). Universities also appear to be paying greater attention to choice and quality in relation to non-academic aspects such as accommodation, shopping, sport and leisure facilities. The rise of formal student complaints in the sector has also increased markedly. Performance indicators and league tables which have become part of a higher landscape to provide students with information and choice also function as powerful market currencies. There are indications that universities invest valuable resources in attempting to move up rankings, as the development of an 'industry' of consultants selling their services to institutions to help them 'pass' Quality Assurance Agency 'tests' such as institutional review indicates.

(Naidoo, 2008, pp. 17–18)

Like Pritchard and Middleton, Naidoo noted that for all the rhetoric about flexibility, diversity and responsiveness, there remained a strong emphasis on bureaucratic control. However:

> what is also true is that the market mode of coordination, however restrained, managed and controlled, has its own logic and power and may establish changes in culture and path dependencies which are likely to impact on the future functioning of the higher education system. Some elite universities, for example, having had a 'taste' of the market, may be willing to decrease their financial dependence on government and move over to the market, thus rejecting state administered forms of accountability. In addition, policy changes have not been unidirectional and linear. There has been considerable regulatory oscillation and an overload of different initiatives.

(Naidoo, 2008, pp. 23–24)

We shall revert to the changing identity of the student as consumer (in Chapter 8). In the meantime we may note the irony of the fact that under the new funding regime from 2012 (described in Chapter 5) the institutions that might be thought suitable candidates for leaving the (so-called) state system, the pre-1992 universities and especially the elite Russell Group (see Chapter 3), will continue to receive large amounts of direct state funding for both teaching and research, whilst those that were previously 'public sector' institutions, the post-1992 universities and colleges, will be receiving hardly any direct public financial support for either teaching or research!

Other theories

Drawing on some well-established theories of public policy making, Brown (2009a) discussed major policy changes between 1985 and 2005 in terms of two 'policy drivers' – effectiveness and economy – where 'effectiveness' referred to the aim of meeting specified societal needs, whilst 'economy' referred to the need of the system to (a) make as little demand on public resources as possible and (b) make the best possible use of those public resources. Thus the 1985 Green Paper, the 1987 White Paper, Kenneth Baker's 1989 Lancaster Speech and the 2003 White Paper were all about effectiveness, whilst the 1991 White Paper, the introduction of Maximum Aggregate Student Numbers in 1994 and top-up fees in 1998 were mainly about economy.

In a not dissimilar approach, Carpentier (2010), drawing on data from several systems, including the UK, posited a cyclical process where levels of public expenditure on higher education oscillate in line with long economic cycles. He found that in the UK (and to a lesser extent, France), private funding has generally substituted for public expenditure; this was not the case in the US, at least up to 2001.

Markets and non-markets

Middleton (2000) also noted that:

> Models are abstractions from reality that, whether invoked by the policy-maker, the policy analyst or the casual observer, are characterised by their claim to make rational sense or coherent order out of complicated reality.
>
> (Middleton, 2000, p. 540)

Against this background, we now set out the analytical framework for the study. This has two sets of components:

- Public and private goods, where a 'good' is a value of the consequences of an activity.
- Market and non-market means of production.

The social character of goods

> Knowledge is the unique claim of higher education. It is at the core of every public and private good that is created in the sector.
>
> (Marginson, 2012, p. 9)

The classic economic definition of public and private goods is that of Samuelson (1954). Public goods (and services) are ones that are non-rivalrous and non-excludable. 'Non-rivalrous' means that they can be consumed by any number of people without being exhausted. 'Non-excludable' means that the benefits cannot be confined to individual buyers. In contrast, private goods are both rivalrous (exhaustable) and excludable. Sandler (1999) developed the notion of 'club goods' for products that are not rivalrous but are excludable, e.g., patents, copyright, etc.

The two principal products of higher education are education and research. Taking education first, Marginson (2011a) notes that teaching can be a predominantly public or a predominantly private good, depending upon which aspects of teaching and learning are uppermost in its social organisation:

> Teaching and learning contain public good aspects: the knowledge learnt; general education unrewarded in labour markets that contributes to a shared knowledge base; education understood as a citizen entitlement to the common culture and to social opportunity; and the contribution of higher

education to social tolerance and international understanding.

However:

> Teaching and learning also carry private good aspects: scarce credentials, from exclusive higher education institutions, providing entry to income-generating professions.
>
> (Marginson, 2011a, p. 426)

In another study, Marginson (2011b) distinguishes four forms of research – new knowledge at the point of creation, knowledge held within the academic community, knowledge published in commercial journals, and knowledge circulated freely in social communications. The last of these is a pure public good, being both non-rivalrous and non-excludable (which makes it especially unsuitable for market production). Knowledge held within the academic community and knowledge published in commercial journals are part public goods: they are non-rivalrous but can be club goods, access to which can be policed by rules or price. New knowledge at the point of creation, being both rivalrous and excludable, is a private good being confined, at least initially, to the creator or owner. Marginson (2007) extended these notions to higher education goods traded internationally.

Forms of production

> [The] coordination of human activities not by central command [but] by mutual interactions in the form of transactions.
>
> (Lindblom, 2001, p. 4)

In economic theory, a market is a means of social coordination whereby the supply and demand for a product are balanced through the price mechanism. Consumers choose between the alternatives on offer on the basis of suitability: not only price, but also quality and availability. Suppliers adjust their product to accommodate consumers' preferences or lose money and/or go out of business. Markets are usually held to offer both greater 'static efficiency' (the ratio of outputs to inputs at any one time) and greater 'dynamic efficiency' (sustaining a higher rate of growth over time through product and process innovation and better management) than any alternative.

If student education were to be supplied according to pure market theory, institutions would have full legal, financial and operational autonomy. Market entry would be lightly regulated, if at all. Institutions' funding would depend entirely on the ability to attract (and retain) students. There would be no controls either on the prices charged (tuition or fees), or on the numbers of students enrolled. The costs of teaching would be met entirely from fees, set usually at a level to at least cover costs, and students would meet these (as well as their living costs) from their own or their families' or employers' resources. Students' choice of what, where and how to study would be based on valid, reliable and accessible information about the price, quality and availability of relevant subjects, programmes and institutions, and their suitability for them. Regulation would be minimal, in effect limited to the protection of contracts. Research funding would depend on the interests of research sponsors but again there would be no subsidies for either suppliers, or purchasers.

In contrast, in a non-market system, institutions' autonomy would be limited. Market entry and student choice would be heavily constrained. There would be no, or minimal, fees. Both institutions and students would be heavily subsidised. There would be no competition on price. Information would be limited. There would be little student choice of provider. Regulation would in effect protect suppliers rather than consumers. Table 2.1 sets out two 'ideal types' of higher education provision, market and non-market (for a fuller discussion, see Brown, 2011a).

Finally, two further definitions are needed. 'privatisation' and 'quasi-markets'.

Marketisation is often confused with privatisation, but conceptually they are distinct. Privatisation is defined here as the penetration of private capital, ownership and/or influence into what were previously publicly funded and owned entities. 'Quasi-markets' differ from conventional markets in three ways:

> non-profit organisations competing for public contracts, sometimes in competition with for-profit organisations; consumer purchasing power either centralised in a single purchasing agency or allocated to users in the form of vouchers rather than cash; and, in some cases, the consumers represented in the market by agents instead of operating by themselves.
>
> (Le Grand and Bartlett, 1993, p. 10)

In other words, the state, rather than the consumer, provides all or most of the finance, with purchasing agents (funding councils, research councils) being used to act on behalf of the consumer.

Higher education markets in practice

The fact that both student education and research are subsidised in nearly every system takes us to the subject of 'market failure'. The main market failures relevant to higher education are externalities/public goods, monopoly powers and information (a further factor is the difficulty which institutions face in moving rapidly in response to market signals by virtue of the length of the life cycles of their 'products': 'stickiness').

Public goods will by definition be unattractive to private market providers because of their non-rivalrous and non-excludable nature. Monopoly, or at least some degree of oligopoly, may be justifiable or unavoidable because of the role which universities play in producing, allocating and regulating knowledge and

Table 2.1 Market and non-market models of higher education systems

Market	Non-market
1. Institutional status Institutions self-governing, independent entities with a high degree of autonomy to determine prices, programmes, awards, student numbers, admissions, staff terms and conditions, etc.	1. Institutional status Institutions either not independent entities or independent but with little ability to determine prices, etc.
2. Competition Market entry and exit. Low barriers to entry. Lots of competing suppliers. Significant private and/or 'for profit' providers offering serious competition to public institutions. Wide student choice. Funding linked to enrolments. Some degree of product/price innovation.	2. Competition High barriers to entry. Little market exit. Few suppliers or little competition. Few or no private or 'for profit' providers. Little student choice. Funding not linked to student numbers. Little product/process innovation.
3. Price Competition on price of tuition. Fees cover all or a significant proportion of costs and may vary between subjects as well as modes of attendance. Students meet costs of tuition from own or family resources ('cost sharing'). As a result of competition plus price liberalisation, considerable variations in price for comparable programmes that cannot be explained by local cost factors.	3. Price Teaching funded mainly through grants to institutions. No or purely nominal tuition fees. Because of subsidies and/or cross-subsidies, fees bear little or no relation to costs. Fees do not vary between subjects or even modes of attendance. Tuition fees (and sometimes student living costs) heavily subsidised. No cost sharing. Few or no variations in charges for comparable programmes.
4. Information Students make a rational choice based on information about price, quality and availability. Such information plays an important part in their choice of programme and supplier.	4. Information Limited information about price, quality or availability. Information plays little or no part in student choice of programme and supplier.
5. Regulation The state facilitates competition whilst providing basic consumer protection. Important role in information provision or brokerage (unless left to commercial agents), and dealing with consumer complaints.	5. Regulation Protects standards and constrains competition that may threaten standards.
6. Quality Ultimately determined by what the market will pay for, which often comes down to what students, employers and the media value (high student entry scores, high post- graduation earnings, etc). Subsidiary roles for state and academy.	6. Quality Usually determined through a combination of state and academic self-regulation, with the state laying down broad frameworks and the key decisions about applying those frameworks being taken by the academic community.

(Brown, 2011a)

status, including the knowledge required for professional occupations and practices, as well as information problems. Information is a special problem in higher education, as we shall see in Chapter 8.[2]

All this means that we can nowhere find a higher education system that exhibits pure market features.[3]

Nevertheless, some systems exhibit more market features than others. For the purposes of this section of our discussion, a marketised system is one with:

- A significant amount of institutional autonomy.
- A liberal system of market entry, including usually both private 'not for-profit' and 'for-profit' participants.
- A significant amount of competition between institutions for students, with students having a genuine choice of provider.
- Tuition fees which represent all or a significant share of the costs of teaching.
- Private support for those costs which represents all or a significant share of institutional funding.
- A substantial proportion of students' living costs are met privately.

Research is nearly everywhere funded on non-market or quasi-market lines but with increasing amounts of private funding and support.

Developed systems which merit this description include the United States, the United Kingdom, Australia, New Zealand and Canada. Amongst continental European systems, the Netherlands and some German Laender display some market characteristics, although recently there has been some rowing back so that tuition fees now exist only in Bavaria and Upper Saxony (Lydia Hartwig, personal communication). Japan and Korea both have substantial private sectors and high levels of private expenditure on both tuition and support. Many other systems are moving in this direction (for a fuller discussion, see Brown, 2011b; see also Foskett, 2011 and Hemsley-Brown, 2011).

Market production and the supply of public goods

We can now see whether there are any relationships between the products of higher education and the means of producing them. Figure 2.1 suggests that there may be a natural association (a) between market production and the supply of private goods and (b) between public or non-market production and the supply of public goods.

But there is not a complete synergy. Public or non-market provision can produce some private benefits, thus justifying a private contribution to costs. Marketised systems can produce some public benefits, thus justifying some subsidy. But how to determine the relative values or proportions?

MEANS OF PRODUCTION

	MARKET	NON-MARKET
PRIVATE	Natural fit.	Non-market provision will produce some private benefits: even with public provision and no fees, a substantial proportion of the goods produced will be private ones e.g, credentials.
PUBLIC	Marketised systems will produce some public benefits e.g., an educated labour force.	Natural fit.

NATURE OF PRODUCT

Figure 2.1 The production of higher education goods

McMahon (2009) has produced some estimates of the relative value of the private market, private non-market, and direct social benefits of higher education in the US. Private market benefits equate to graduates' additional earnings, which are estimated at $31,174 per annum. The private non-market benefits include own health benefits, own longevity, spouse's health, child's health, child's education and cognitive development, management of fertility and lower family size, and better consumption and saving patterns. McMahon estimates that these average $38,020 per graduate overall. There is also a range of unquantified effects related to job conditions and location amenities, more sophisticated tastes, less obsolescence in skills due to better general education, greater well-being through enhanced income, etc. The direct collective non-market benefits average $27,726 per graduate. These wider benefits include democratization and political institutions, human rights and civic institutions, political stability, community life expectancy, reduced inequality, less crime, lower health and prison costs, and a better environment. Other unquantified social benefits relate to higher tax receipts, social capital and the dissemination of the outcomes of research (see also HEFCE,

2001b). The estimation of wider benefits is of course bedevilled by the problem of selection effects (Carasso, 2010). However, McMahon's is a timely reminder of the need to consider the entire range of products and outcomes if appropriate policies are to be considered, a point we shall return to in Chapter 9.

Against this background, we can now address the first field of marketisation since 1979, the institutional structure of the UK higher education system.

Chapter 3

The institutional pattern of provision

We want a diverse, competitive higher education sector that can offer different types of higher education, giving students the ability to choose between a wide range of providers. Unless popular institutions and courses can expand, and new providers, including those who offer different models of higher education, can enter the market, the concept of student choice cannot become a reality.

(DBIS, 2012c, paragraph 2.2.38)

The taste now is for 'market' solutions, even within state systems of government. This 'market' approach is difficult to reconcile with structured binary systems which assign missions to classes of institution. Instead it encourages much finer-grained and more flexible differentiation between and within institutions regardless of their formal nomenclature.

(Scott, 1995, p. 43)

Introduction

The lowering of entry barriers to facilitate supply side competition between institutions is a cardinal feature of a market-based approach to the provision of higher education (Hare, 2002). Over the period since 1979, three particular sets of developments can be identified:

- An expansion in the number of institutions with a university title.
- The removal or reduction of formal limits on institutional development.
- An increase in the number of larger, comprehensive institutions and a reduction in the number of smaller, specialist institutions.

On top of this, the 2011 White Paper *Higher Education: Students at the Heart of the System* (DBIS, 2011a) and the subsequent Technical Consultation Paper *A New, Fit-for-Purpose Regulatory Framework for the Higher Education Sector* (DBIS, 2011b) pave the way for more providers, including more 'for profit' organisations, to enter the market in student education. Each of these developments will now be described.

It should be noted that there has also been some blurring of the boundary between higher education delivered in higher education institutions and higher education delivered elsewhere (Pritchard, 1994). Validation, franchising and other forms of partnership under which a non-higher education institution – typically a further education college or a private college – offers programmes leading to a university or university college award have long been a feature of UK higher education (in Scotland, further education colleges offer a significant proportion of HE awards under articulation arrangements with universities). The Coalition Government has given this a boost by allocating more than half of the marginal places under the new post-2012 funding methodology described in Chapter 5 to FE colleges (HEFCE, 2012g), although it appears that these may be offset by places being withdrawn by universities under partnerships (Matthews, 2012c; Lee, 2012b). Nevertheless, as a result of these decisions 65 FE colleges, including four sixth form colleges, will have direct funding agreements with HEFCE for the first time (Lee, 2012a).

We should also note that, alongside what Scott (1995, p. 13) has called the 'progressive integration' of the system, there has also – largely because of research selectivity – been some differentiation, what Scott, in another felicitous phrase, has called 'differentiation by stealth' (2011, p. 9) whereby certain highly selective institutions have been implicitly, and sometimes explicitly, favoured by government policy decisions. This issue will be explored in Chapter 9.

The expansion in the number of universities

The number of universities increased from 48 in 1979–80 to 115 in 2011–12; part of the increase has been due to many of the constituent colleges of the federal universities of London and Wales obtaining university titles in their own right. There were two main waves of expansion. The first was in 1992, following legislation to permit the polytechnics to obtain a university title. The second was from 2004, with legislation to permit colleges without research degree-awarding powers to obtain a university title.

The abolition of the binary line

The White Paper *Higher Education: A New Framework* (DES, 1991) began by stating that UK higher education was 'more efficient and more effective' than it had ever been. More young people than ever before were staying on in full-time education after the age of 16. One in five of all 18- to 19-year-olds now entered higher education compared with one in seven at the time of the last White Paper in 1987. The polytechnics and colleges had led the expansion, achieving considerable improvements in efficiency as capacity 'at the margin' had been taken up. Moreover, this had been achieved without any loss of quality, the proportion of first and second class degrees awarded by universities, polytechnics and colleges having steadily increased during the 1980s.

At the same time, the latest projections of student numbers indicated that participation rates would continue to increase. By the year 2000 it was expected that approaching one in three of all 18- to 19-year-olds would enter higher education. There would also be increased demand from adults and for part-time study. Increasing national wealth could be expected broadly to match these increases. But the general need to contain public spending, the pattern of relative costs in higher education, and the demands for capital investment, all meant that a continuing drive for greater efficiency would be needed. The Government believed that:

> the real key to achieving cost effective expansion lies in greater competition for funds and students. That can best be achieved by breaking down the increasingly artificial and unhelpful barriers between the universities, and the polytechnics and colleges.
>
> (DES, 1991, p. 12)

The Government therefore proposed to end the distinction between universities and polytechnics in terms of degree-awarding powers and the channels for funding teaching. The polytechnics and colleges would also be included in the dual support system for funding research (see Chapter 4). Legislation to allow the polytechnics and certain other colleges to adopt a university name, or include it in their titles, received the Royal Assent in March 1992 as the Further and Higher Education Act. As a result, an additional 41 institutions – the 34 polytechnics in England and Wales, the five Scottish Central Institutions, and two English colleges (Derby and Luton) – obtained a university title.

The creation of 'teaching only' universities

One of the main themes of the 2003 White Paper *The Future of Higher Education* heralding variable fees (DFES, 2003) was the need to raise the profile of teaching in higher education. A series of proposals was made. These included one that university title should no longer require the right to award research degrees. This was on the basis that:

> The right to award research degrees requires that the institution demonstrate its strength in research. This situation is at odds with our belief that institutions should play to diverse strengths, and that excellent teaching is, in itself, a core mission for a university ... It is clear that good scholarship, in the sense of remaining aware of the latest research and thinking within a subject, is essential for good teaching, but not that it is necessary to be active in cutting-edge research to be an excellent teacher.
>
> (DES, 2003, p. 54)[1]

As a direct result of the Higher Education Act 2004, ten new universities were created, most being diversified teacher training institutions in cathedral cities.[2]

Since 2005 a further eleven institutions have received a university title.[3] The 2004 legislation also made two important changes in the rules for obtaining degree-awarding powers.

First, it brought to an end the provision in the 1992 legislation in England and Wales that degree-awarding powers could only be awarded indefinitely. This would continue to be the case for 'organisations in the publicly-funded higher education sector'. However, other institutions – i.e., private, non-HEFCE-funded providers – would be granted the powers for a fixed period of six years, after which they would be reviewed. Four such providers now have such powers (alongside the University of Buckingham, which obtained its powers when it received a university title in 1983): the College of Law (which is undergoing its six-year review at the time of writing, June 2012); the ifs School of Finance; Ashridge Business School; and BPP University College (owned since 2009 by the US Apollo Group). Another, Regent's College, is in the wings. After Buckingham the first private provider to receive degree-awarding powers was the subsequently HEFCE funded Royal Agricultural College in 1996 (this was on condition that it became a subscriber to the Higher Education Quality Council (HEQC) and underwent periodic audits). Second, the Act enabled further education colleges to apply for powers to award Foundation Degrees. Three colleges now have such powers: Newcastle College, New College Durham and West Lancashire College.

The abolition of formal categories of institution

In 1979–80 there were three quite distinct categories of institution: universities, teacher training colleges (colleges of education), and polytechnics and technical colleges. There was also a small number of institutions directly funded by the Department (including the College of Guidance Studies, Cranfield Institute of Technology, the Open University (OU) and the Royal College of Art). These formed quite separate sectors, the universities being funded through the UGC, the colleges of education through the local education authorities, and the polytechnics and other colleges, also funded by their sponsoring local education authorities but also part of a national funding system through the Advanced Further Education Pool and soon to receive a new national coordinating body, the National Advisory Board for Public Sector Higher Education (NAB). Whilst the universities were free to offer what programmes and awards they wished, the public sector institutions awarded the degrees, diplomas and certificates of one or more universities, the Council for National Academic Awards (CNAA) and/or BTEC (now EdExcel). They were also required to obtain permission for new advanced courses from the Department in the shape of the Regional Staff Inspector, after advice from the relevant Regional Advisory Council (of local education authority representatives), a regime that lasted until incorporation but which has now been completely forgotten.

There was a clear government rationale for these distinctions. There were concerns on the part of the Department that if the polytechnics became universities they might lose their distinctive mission of providing mainly vocational and 'applied' higher education to students attending in a variety of modes. Because of the Secretary of State's responsibilities for teacher supply, the Department was always keen to retain close control over teacher training, something which was reinforced with the creation of the Council for the Accreditation of Teacher Education in 1984 and the Teacher Training Agency ten years later. At the same time, the local authorities were anxious to retain some hold over institutions they had founded and/or nurtured, even though many of these now played a regional or even a national role.

All this was to change in the 1980s. Following the policy announced in the 1972 White Paper *Education: A Framework for Expansion* (DES, 1972) most of the teacher training colleges either diversified as colleges of higher education, or were incorporated into larger, multi-campus institutions in, usually, the public sector (Furlong *et al.*, 2000); this followed extensive rationalisation in the previous decade (Hencke, 1978). The polytechnics and major colleges were incorporated in 1989. In the author's view, this made it inevitable that at some point they would become universities. It should be borne in mind here that the polytechnics were never as different from the universities as their analogues in most other European binary systems: the German Fachhochschulen, the Dutch hogescholen, the French Instituts universitaires de technologies, etc. Moreover, over the period since the first polytechnic designations in 1970 a significant degree of convergence had taken place with the universities (Scott, 1995, 2009; Pratt, 1997, 1999). By 1988, 13 polytechnics had powers to register students for PhDs and 22 had set up their own research degree committees (Henkel and Kogan, 2010).[4,5]

The actual trigger for the decision to ennoble the polytechnics appears to have been the reluctance of the universities to expand their numbers and reduce their costs in response to the UFC's bidding competition (see Chapter 5). This mirrored their behaviour in the previous decade: Pratt (1999, p. 263) quoted departmental estimates that between 1980–81 and 1984–85, unit costs in the universities dropped by only 3 per cent whereas those in the public sector institutions fell by 16 per cent. Kogan and Hanney (2000, p. 88) described the universities' attitude to expansion and cost cutting as 'a major strategic error', not only because it made them unpopular with the Government, but also because the 'displaced' students were absorbed by the polytechnics. Pratt (1999) believed that the deciding factor within the Government was the support for the change of the Prime Minister, John Major, on egalitarian grounds. This was stated in Major's memoirs (Major, 1999, p. 212) and was confirmed to the author by a senior civil servant involved in the decisions.

We note in Chapter 4 Sir Peter Swinnerton-Dyer's (1991) comment about the way in which the polytechnics were allowed to enter the 1992 RAE, and the extra twist this gave to the research selectivity 'ratchet'. It is a nice question whether, even if the Government had decided to abolish the binary line, this should have applied immediately and to all the institutions, without any further filtering process. There might, for example, have been an argument for restricting at least some of the aspirant institutions to taught courses, at under- and postgraduate level, until they had built up their research. The decision not to do so seems to have been the product of two factors.

First, shortage of time: the civil servants concerned had only six weeks to produce the White Paper.[6] Second, the advice given to the Department by the CNAA Chief Executive, Malcolm Frazer. Frazer's view was that whilst only about a third of the polytechnics had research accreditation from CNAA (as we have just seen), they would all get there eventually, so there was little point in distinguishing them. Ironically, it was this advice that led to the Council being abolished, on the basis that there was little case for continuing with the significant costs of the organisation when it would only be dealing with a relatively small number of institutions.

The American political scientist David Easton (1965) coined the term 'breeder demand' to describe a policy decision which, once made, leads inevitably to another which might not have been foreseen at the time of the previous decision. The decision to allow the public sector higher education providers to incorporate was a classic breeder demand. It seems to have been a combination of a long-standing desire on the part of the Department to exercise a greater degree of central control – or at least coordination – over the institutions, and the intention of the Thatcher administration to cut local government down to size.

The former can be seen in the Department's intention in 1979, following the Oakes Report's recommendation that a UGC-like body should be set up to advise the Secretary of State on the funding and planning of public sector higher education, that the institutions should be taken out of local government and placed under a central agency. This proposal was withdrawn when there was a strong reaction against it and instead the NAB was created (Kogan and Hanney, 2000).[7] Jones (1984) argued that the push for greater national coordination became irresistible once the Advanced FE Pool – the mechanism whereby 'providing' local authorities like Inner London were able to recoup most of the costs of their institutions from 'exporting' authorities – was capped, by general agreement; the legislation was enacted in 1980, the cap took effect from 1980–81.

As a senior member of the team of Department of the Environment officials who worked on the legislation to abolish the Greater London Council and the Metropolitan County Councils in 1984–86, the author can certainly attest to the strength of the Thatcher Government's animus against local government. Heavy lobbying of key ministers by polytechnic directors with lurid tales of local authority interference may also have played its part. In his history of the polytechnics, Pratt (1997, p. 274) argued that it was the difficult relationship with the local authorities that 'perhaps more than any other issue' led to incorporation. Kogan and Hanney (2000, p. 135) quoted a polytechnic director as follows:

> The main change was not so much the change of title from polytechnic to university but releasing the polytechnics from local authority control and making them independent bodies in law. Then their governing bodies ... were responsible ... for what went on and were able to bring, particularly as most

of the governing body were connected with the employing side of industry, a sense of purpose which hitherto, to some extent, had been much weaker in the polytechnics simply because the local authorities were in control and they were a dead hand, without any doubt, and not least because, for example ... the County Council retained £1m a year of our budget ... supposedly for services rendered, but I could never understand what those services were.

As a result of these various government decisions, all universities and higher education colleges are now formally equal, with no government-imposed limits on their development: Watson and Bowden (2005, p. 2) even wrote of the 'destratification' of the polytechnics, central institutions and large colleges. We should, however, note that the period since 1980 has also seen attempts – in at least partial response to this gradual liberalisation, and of differing degrees of explicitness – to create 'sub-sectors'. The two most important were the proposals from the Advisory Board for the Research Councils (ABRC) for 'R, X and T' universities in the mid-80s (described in Chapter 4), and the Government's and the Funding Council's attempts in the early 2000s to get institutions to focus their missions to a much greater extent, described here.

Focussing institutional missions

In a section headed 'Diversity and mission', the 2003 White Paper *The Future of Higher Education* (DFES, 2003) raised the question of whether it was reasonable to expect all higher education institutions to embrace lifelong learning, research, knowledge transfer, social inclusion and economic development:

> No higher education system in the world is organised in this way. Rather, scarce resources are applied in such a way as to produce a focus on comparative advantage: individual institutions focus on what they do best, while the sector as a whole achieves this much wider range of objectives.
>
> (DFES, 2003, paragraph 1.37)

Accordingly, whilst:

> Government will continue to be the principal funder of higher education ... we need to move to a funding regime which enables each institution to choose its mission and the funding streams necessary to support it, and to make sure that our system recognises and celebrates different missions properly.
>
> (DFES, 2003, paragraph 1.39)

The White Paper also made use of terms like 'research-intensive', 'more focused on teaching and learning', 'engaged in serving local and regional economies', etc. (see also Watson and Bowden, 2005).

The draft HEFCE Strategic Plan for 2003–8 two months later proposed that:

a. All HEIs should aim for excellence in all that they do.
b. While it is right to expect the sector to strive for excellence across the full range of activities envisaged in our plan, individual institutions should be more selective. All HEIs should develop missions which focus upon achievable individual chosen areas of strength, and which provide for collaboration across a broader range of activity.
c. Within this distribution there will be activities which all HEIs are expected to undertake, and areas in which some have elected to specialise.
d. Our funding arrangements should recognise and advance this pattern of activity, with targeted funding made available to support focused excellence in activities underpinning each of the four core strategic aims.[8]

The paper concluded:

> This approach to funding will enable and encourage institutions to develop distinctive missions building on their areas of relative strength. It will enable them to choose the areas in which they plan to achieve particular excellence – within a coherent national framework.
>
> (HEFCE, 2003a, pp. 35–36)

The final Strategic Plan adopted the same wording.

Scott, who was a HEFCE Council member for part of this period, has described (2009) the steps taken by the Funding Council to give effect to this agenda, which was also being espoused by the HEFCE Chief Executive, Howard (later Sir Howard) Newby (e.g., 1999). There were three main vehicles: funding mechanisms, targeted initiatives and strategic development, some of which pre-dated the White Paper.

As Scott noted, more than 90 per cent of the Funding Council's funding was allocated on common criteria. The largest targeted initiative was the premium for widening participation, originally introduced in 1999–2000. This provides for the additional costs of educating students from less favoured backgrounds, supports success in widening participation, and offers an incentive for institutions to make additional efforts. It is distributed by formula and the largest allocations naturally go to those institutions with the largest numbers of disadvantaged students. It is worth £140 million in 2012–13. Another high-profile initiative, already referred to in Note 1, was the £315 million Centres for Excellence in Teaching and Learning (CETLs) programme between 2005–6 and 2009–10 (see also Chapter 6). Other initiatives focussed on links with business and the community: the Higher Education Reach Out to Business and the Community; the Higher Education Active Communities Fund; the Knowledge Transfer Capability Fund; Business Fellowships; and the (still current) Higher Education Innovation Fund (where 'innovation' refers not to the curriculum but to work with business). Finally, the Strategic Development Fund (before 2003, the Restructuring and Collaboration Fund) has been used to support institutional restructuring, collaboration and employer engagement and the development of 'business facing' universities.

It can of course be argued that in seeking to introduce some categorisation into the system, the Government and the Funding Council were only imitating the behaviour of most universities and colleges in forming or joining mission groups. The Russell Group was formed shortly after 1992, and there are now also the 1994 Group, Mission+ (originally, the Coalition of Modern Universities), and the University Alliance – alongside Universities UK and GuildHE, the latter (previously called the Standing Conference of Principals) representing (mostly) the remaining higher education colleges.[9]

The trend to comprehensive institutions

As well as the demise of the teacher training colleges as separate specialist institutions, two further waves of institutional rationalisation have occurred, and a third (in Wales) is apparently imminent.

In the 1990s, most of the London medical schools became part of larger London institutions. In the 2000s, many of the other specialist institutions were absorbed into larger ones. The reasons in both cases were various, but a common theme was the greater resources, protection against competition, and spreading of risks which being part of a larger and more diverse institution afforded. This was both a response to market competition and, arguably, a reduction in market choice.

In June 2011, the Higher Education Funding Council for Wales (HEFCW) issued a consultative document proposing a substantial rationalisation of the sector, with the ten existing separate institutions being reduced to six (HEFCW, 2011b). In November 2011 the Higher Education Minister, Leighton Andrews, announced that he had accepted the Council's advice about mergers involving the University of Wales Trinity St David, Swansea Metropolitan University, the University of Wales, the University of Glamorgan, Cardiff Metropolitan University and the University of Wales, Newport. There would be a review of provision in North East Wales. Cardiff and Swansea universities are to remain separate and Aberystwyth and Bangor will continue with their strategic alliance (Welsh Government, 2011). It is not yet clear whether and how this will be effected, although the Minister was earlier reported as threatening to legislate if necessary (BBC News, 2010).[10] The March 2012 HEFCW Remit Letter (Welsh Government, 2012) referred to the Council reporting back on progress in March 2013. In the meantime, the University of Wales has suffered a humiliating demise following damning criticism of its management of its overseas partnerships over many years (Matthews, 2012a).

In Scotland, a pre-legislative agenda document *Putting Learners at the Centre: Delivering our Ambitions for Post-16 Education* published by the Scottish Government in September 2011 noted that there was some room for consolidation in the university sector, with particular overlaps in provision around the urban areas.

The document stated the Government's intention to require the Funding Council periodically to review the number and pattern of 'fundable bodies' (colleges and universities) and make recommendations on implementing changes, including mergers, new providers or transfers of provision, the aim being to improve coherence and value for money. Following such a review, ministers would have the power to require institutional governing bodies to work with the Funding Council to respond to and implement the recommendations (Scottish Government, 2011).

Overall, in a recent report for the Higher Education Policy Institute on institutional diversity, Ramsden, B. (2012) estimates that over the sixteen-year period since 1994–95, there have been 40 institutional mergers in UK higher education, the large majority involving the 'takeover' of a smaller specialist institution by a larger, comprehensive one.[11] Also taking into account new entrants to the sector, there has been a net decrease of three general institutions and fourteen specialist ones. This has led to a reduction in institutional diversity, at least as indicated by the number and range of institutional types. There has also been a substantial rationalisation of provision in some subjects. Overall, there has been some degree of institutional convergence, an issue that will be explored further in Chapter 7.

After 2012: new providers?

Another important aspect of this enhanced competition, if the present Coalition Government has its way, will be from new providers. The June 2011 White Paper *Higher Education: Putting Students at the Heart of the System* (DBIS, 2011a) contained a number of proposals for changing the rules for degree-awarding powers and university title, in order that more private and smaller providers could enter the market. The stated rationale was to improve the student experience by increasing competition and extending the diversity of provision: 'we want a diverse, competitive system that can offer different types of higher education so that students can choose freely between a wide set of providers' (DBIS, 2011a, paragraph 4.6).

The main proposals (DBIS, 2011a, paragraphs 4.10 to 4.34) were:

- To extend to all providers (in due course) access to public student financial support on the same terms as existing HEFCE-funded institutions, subject to placing themselves within the same regulatory framework for access, price and student information.
- Making available a margin of 20,000 places – some 8 per cent of the total new entrants in any one year – for which private providers accessing public support could bid where their average charge (after fee waivers had been taken into account) was £7,500 or less.
- Making changes to the rules for degree-awarding powers. Possibilities included the removal of the requirement that an applicant organisation must have at least a four-year track record of offering degrees, and allowing organisations that did not themselves teach to award degrees.

- Reviewing the requirement that an applicant should have at least 4,000 full-time equivalent (FTE) students before they could apply for a university title.

The White Paper also indicated the Government's intention to consult on ways of encouraging private investment in HEFCE-funded institutions by making the process of changing institutions' legal status easier (DBIS, 2011a, paragraphs 4.35–6).

Some of these proposals were fleshed out in the Technical Consultation Document *A New, Fit-for-Purpose Regulatory Framework for the Higher Education Sector* published in August 2011 (DBIS, 2011b). New or enlarged proposals included the following:

- HEFCE would become the 'Independent Lead Regulator' for the sector (DBIS, 2011b: paragraph 3). It would have a 'new specific remit to champion the student interest, where appropriate with competition' (DBIS, 2011b, paragraph 1.1.2). The HEFCE Business Plan 2011–15 (HEFCE, 2011d) explained how the Council means to go about this.
- In future, the HEFCE remit would also include giving advice to ministers on applications for degree-awarding powers and university title, a function previously exercised by the Quality Assurance Agency for Higher Educaiton (QAA) and HEQC. This will presumably include advising ministers on the possible suspension or removal of degree-awarding powers 'where quality or standards fall below acceptable thresholds and efforts to improve the position have proved unsuccessful' (DBIS, 2011b, 4.1.1 and 4.2.18).
- The process for changing the corporate status of institutions would be simplified, presumably to facilitate the acquisition of the assets, including where relevant the university title and degree-awarding powers, of an existing institution.

As we noted in Chapter 1, the timing of the legislation to implement these proposals is unclear, but it appears that much of what the Government wishes to do can be done under existing legislation (Morgan, 2012a). In June 2012 the Government announced that with immediate effect the minimum number threshold for university title would be lowered to 1,000 FTE students, of whom at least 750 should be studying at degree level (DBIS, 2012c). It also appears that a 'for profit' organisation can already acquire a 'not for profit' provider with degree-awarding powers without having to make a fresh application. This happened when Apollo Inc. acquired the then BPP College in 2009 (BPP has since become a 'not for profit' subsidiary of Apollo). It also seems to be true of the recently announced acquisition of the College of Law by Montagu Private Equity, a transaction welcomed by the Higher Education Minister (College of Law, 2012); in the US, if a college or university changes ownership, its regional accreditation is automatically withdrawn (see Brown and Alderman, 2012). As a result of these changes, and without fresh legislation, over 400 private providers now (July 2012) have courses with 'designated' status compared to 157 in 2009–10 (Morgan, 2012d). This means that their students will be able to borrow up to £6,000 towards the cost of their fees. Maintenance grants and loans will also be available to such students on the same terms as those at HEFCE-funded institutions.[12]

Conclusion

The Coalition Government's planned changes in the market entry rules are fully in line with, but significantly extend, the initiatives of previous governments to remove or reduce the formal distinctions between institutions, and encourage the participation of new providers, all with the aim of increasing competition for existing institutions. Although entry restrictions remain, this is a particularly clear instance of marketisation. Another of the aims of successive governments has been to increase consumer – student, employer and research funder – choice. It is therefore somewhat ironic that there has at the same time been some reduction in institutional diversity. This is discussed more fully in Chapter 7, where we conclude that the removal of formal distinctions between institutions has led to an informal reputational hierarchy which is at least as strong as the formal distinctions that existed previously, and with a far weaker rationale (see also Locke, 2011).

Chapter 4

The funding of research

We propose to adopt a more selective approach in the allocation of research support among universities in order to ensure that resources for research are used to best advantage.

(UGC, 1984, paragraph 1.9)

Introduction

This chapter describes the creation of a quasi-market in university research in the UK. The main developments were:

- The separation of research and teaching funding in universities from 1986.
- The introduction of selectivity in 'core' research funding through the Research Assessment Exercise (RAE), also from 1986.
- The introduction and operation of selectivity in the funding of research infrastructure from 1995.
- The introduction and operation of selectivity in the funding of postgraduate research students from 1998.

Together, these strands of selectivity led to greater concentration of research funding at both department/unit and institution levels, the wider consequences of which will be discussed in Chapters 7 and 9 (for a recent parallel survey, see Henkel and Kogan, 2010).

To set the context, it should be noted that, historically, under the so called 'dual support' system, public support for university research has been given through two channels:

- Core funding of research facilities and infrastructure – the 'well-found laboratory'– through grants from the funding councils.
- Support for the costs of specific projects through the research councils.[1]

University research is also funded by other government departments and local authorities, UK-based charities such as the Wellcome Trust, companies and EU institutions. Table 4.1 gives universities' sources of income for research in 2010–11.

Table 4.1 Sources of research income for UK universities 2010–11

Source of income	Income (£m)	% total research income
Recurrent FC grant (QR)	1952	30.6
Research grants and contracts:		
BIS RCs, RSoc, BA, RSoc of Edinburgh	1558	24.4
UK-based charities	921	14.4
UK cent govt bodies/LAs, health & hosp authorities	808	12.7
UK industry, commerce and public corps	294	4.6
EU sources	513	8.0
non-EU sources	291	4.6
other sources	47	0.7
Total:	6384	

Source: HESA

While this chapter will mainly consider aspects of research policy (notably funding through the research councils) which have remained a UK-wide responsibility, there have been a number of initiatives in Scotland and Wales, which will be briefly described at the end of the chapter.

The separation of research and teaching funding

The allocation of the block grant that UK universities received – which in 1979–80 made up 63.3 per cent of their total income (Shattock and Rigby, 1983), but by 2010–11 made up 31.4 per cent of total income (HEFCE, 2012a) – was, before 1986, not directly associated with particular aspects of academic activity. Furthermore, the formula that the UGC used to calculate the distribution of grants to individual institutions was not published. This was desirable, it was argued (Walne, 1973), as it avoided the possibility that the block grant would simply be allocated internally in line with the basis on which it was calculated; this, it was thought, would have created a 'circularity' in the allocation of future funds, rather than encouraging universities to evolve as they considered appropriate.

The UGC's approach to the allocation of its grants up to 1986 therefore reflected and respected the traditional collegial view of a university as an independent, self-governing community of scholars, best able to make appropriate decisions about its teaching and research. This position was reinforced by the fact that the committee took the view that the basis on which its grants were distributed within each institution was legitimately distinct from any principles on which those resources had been allocated to it.

This stance on the distribution of grants greatly reduced the potential for funding to be used to facilitate the 'political' direction of academic activities within individual institutions, in support of the Haldane Principle (Haldane, 1918); this stated that public funds for research should be allocated on the basis of academic criteria, and not political considerations. This principle has been regarded, both in the academic world and more widely, as a key tenet upon which to ensure the integrity of academic endeavour. We shall come back to this in Chapter 8.

Nevertheless, when considering the future financial sustainability of research within the sector after the sudden and significant cuts in public expenditure on higher education in the early 1980s, the UGC identified the need to take a more strategic approach to the allocation of those funds that were available. Without this selectivity, the committee argued, the quality of the research carried out in universities was at risk, and this in turn could have consequences for what it described as 'the nation's future well-being' (UGC, 1984, paragraph 5.2).

This strategic approach would be informed by the results of the first selectivity exercise (described below), which provided the basis for the distribution of a new, distinct stream of block grant support for research in relation to its assessed quality. But even though the UGC had identified a need to move to reflect research and teaching activities separately within an institution's grant, it remained clear that it was not its role to become involved in managing or overseeing the details of the expenditure of that grant once it had been received.

The origins of research selectivity

Given its importance, it may be worth looking a bit more closely at the origins of research selectivity.

As so often happens, the policy appears to have had a number of sources, and the relationships between them are not easy to disentangle. What seems clear is that although selectivity received its main impetus from the funding cuts in the 1970s and 1980s, there had always been a view, driven very largely by the sciences (Kogan and Hanney, 2000), that some degree of concentration in strong units was desirable on grounds of both efficiency and quality. But the level at which such selectivity should apply, how extensive it should be, and how it should best be achieved, consistent with the principles of peer review and institutional autonomy, were all major issues. As we shall see, these were all to be resolved in the mid-1980s, with far-reaching consequences.

Adams and Gurney (2010, paragraph 12) say that after it moved from Treasury to the Board of Education (later, the Ministry of Education) in 1945, 'the UGC seems always to have operated some level of selective funding'. Kogan and Hanney (2000) traced the research selectivity debate as far back as 1965, when the Department for Scientific and Industrial Research came out in favour, and then in 1967 the Council for Scientific Policy had stated 'there will have to be further progress towards specialisation at selected centres together with concentration of resources in some fields of science' (Council for Scientific Policy 1967, paragraph 57, quoted in Kogan and Hanney, 2000, p. 93). However, senior policy makers remained concerned to sustain a broadly based system. Hence the policy of the research councils throughout the 1970s and into the 1980s was to fund the best proposals whatever their origin. Nevertheless, a joint UGC/ABRC report (the Merrison Report), responding to concerns about the health of the dual support system, and finding these concerns legitimate, recommended that 'universities will need to concentrate funds into selected areas'. The research committee of the university 'would come to the conclusions about the areas on which the university should concentrate' (Merrison, 1982, pp. 27–28, quoted in Kogan and Hanney, 2000, p. 95).

These demands for explicit selectivity were triggered by the progressive reduction in the units of resource allowed by government, a policy already set in train by the cuts in the 1970s; the selective allocation of the 1981 spending cuts (described in Chapter 5) was another factor. This led to the statements about selectivity in the UGC's 1984 strategy document already quoted. As an initial attempt to collect evidence on which to distribute research funds selectively, the UGC launched a series of subject reviews. The first of these, conducted by a panel of subject specialists and chaired by the Rector of Imperial College, Ronald (now Lord) Oxburgh, looked at Earth Sciences. Their report was published in 1987 (UGC, 1987).

The review looked principally at whether there was any link between size of department and excellence of outputs within UK universities; it also considered the position in the US. It recommended that there should be 10 to 12 Level 1 centres (with 30 or more academic staff, offering postgraduate teaching); up to 12 Level 2 centres (with at least 15 staff, offering teaching at honours level); and Level 3 centres which would have no more than six academics and primarily offer teaching as an adjunct to courses in related disciplines.

However, the UGC had decided on a two-stage process, and the Oxburgh recommendations were forwarded to a further national UGC committee (Shattock, 1994). This advocated four categories of provision, clearly distinct from the Oxburgh recommendations:

- Type M – medium-large departments, active in teaching (including the provision of single honours degrees) and research in mainstream Earth Sciences, housing some major items of research equipment that would be available for use more widely.
- Type I – medium-large departments or clusters of departments in which Earth Sciences contribute to interdisciplinary activity, as well as mainstream subject-specific activity. These units would be of equivalent academic status to those in Type M.
- Type J – small-medium departments or groups, teaching joint honours and as part of other courses, but without their own expensive research equipment.
- Other institutions may also teach Earth Sciences, but from another appropriate department, and may, or may not, also conduct research in Earth Sciences from that department and focus (UGC, 1987).

This second proposal was adopted by the UGC physical sciences committee, which allocated student numbers accordingly. To support the changes, the UGC set aside £17 million for the consequent equipment requirements and further funds to cover the costs of staff movements. Thus a review that was principally designed to consider research activity also influenced the future teaching profile of Earth Sciences within universities.

As reported by Evidence Ltd (2003), the 1987 report contained what may be seen as a classic argument of the case for the concentration of research resources and expertise in large departments:

> First, the intellectual environment created by a larger group of researchers may add to overall vitality, through the opportunity to exchange and develop ideas and to be spurred by visible achievement. Second, the per capita marginal costs of research (administration, clerical support, etc) could be reduced. Third, this could be accentuated by the scale of cost of major equipment and facilities in the natural sciences. Fourth, larger groups might make possible the simultaneous and parallel development of research themes, leading to an overall acceleration. Larger group size might also contribute to diversity of thought and of sub-discipline, increasing intellectual spillover and cross-fertilisation. Finally, larger groups of research students may provide a supportive atmosphere for research training. The realisation of such potential benefits would depend, however, on appropriate management.
>
> (Evidence Ltd, 2003, p. 22)

However, it was not obvious that subject reviews were necessarily the best means of achieving this concentration. Such a level of detailed scrutiny would not be suitable for all subjects. It was very resource intensive. There was also the question of the locus of responsibility. Whilst based on peer review, subject reviews placed the responsibility, and the potential opprobrium, for the consequences – departmental closures, restructuring, and perhaps even redundancies – on the central agency. They could also be seen as interfering with institutional autonomy. By contrast, as we shall see shortly, the approach incorporated in the RAE was for the responsibility for the outcomes of the peer judgements to remain with the institutions, in other words, the vice-chancellors and governing councils. In this way, peer review and institutional autonomy could both be employed to serve the overall objective of rationalisation.[2]

The concept of the three categories of departments that Oxburgh had proposed was reflected in a much wider, institution-level proposal that was advocated by the Chair of the Advisory Board for the Research Councils, David (later Lord) Phillips, in 1987. The proposal was laid out in *A Strategy for the Science Base* (Advisory Board for the Research Councils, 1987). This advocated three types of institution: R (research intensive, across a wide range of fields, teaching at all levels); T (teaching only – no research students, staff conducting only the research necessary to support their teaching); and X (mixed, with a broad range of teaching and at least some world-class research). The report also supported Interdisciplinary Research Centres as a focus for high-quality research in emerging areas.

However, both the three types of centres outlined by Oxburgh and the

R-T-X categorisation of institutions raised the spectre of centralisation. Robert (now Lord) Jackson, who was Higher Education Minister at the time, is reported to have thought:

> Part of the culture of the top-down planning: let us grade universities so that you are for all time a category X, R or T. I was instinctively opposed to that on my autonomous grounds, it was too inflexible, and gave no scope for aspirations and achievements of a particular university, but, nevertheless, you could achieve the same results on an organic and revisable basis through the means we adopted (i.e. research selectivity), to some extent under my influence.
>
> (Kogan and Hanney, 2000, p. 100)

It is not clear how far it was appreciated at this time that selectivity and concentration at department level might mean concentration at institutional level:

> In 1986 selectivity in the distribution of HE research funds changed from an underlying principle to an overt methodology. Research was to be funded differentially, based on quality wherever it was located, but this selectivity was to be exercised at roughly the level of the discipline or department. There was no overt policy to concentrate research funding at institution level. However, because a relatively small number of universities contained a large number of units judged to do outstanding research, the policy of selectivity had as a consequence the concentration of research funds in these universities.
>
> (Adams and Gurney, 2010, paragraph 8)

As we shall see, the selectivity with which public funding for university research is allocated has increased steadily since the first RAE in 1986. A similar pattern can be seen in the distribution of other sources of research income, even though the processes for the allocation of these other sources of institutional research income are independent of those that apply to recurrent grants from the funding councils (Adams and Bekhradnia, 2004).

The Research Assessment Exercise

> The RAE supports the policy goal of selectivity, ensuring that scarce resources are directed towards those with the capacity to produce research of the highest quality. The RAE makes it possible for funding bodies to discriminate in their funding (this is done in a transparent way by formulae related to quality and volume). At present, the principle which underpins research funding is that of selectivity based on quality, wherever it is located, not explicit concentration of funds in a selected number of institutions.
>
> (Roberts, 2003, paragraph 67)

The RAE must wait in the wings no longer. The first RAE was carried out in 1986.[3] It was intended to assess the quality of the research carried out in individual universities across the country; this information could then be used as the basis on which to distribute a proportion of the core public funding for research in relation to the quality of the work carried out in each institution. In the words of a subsequent review, the objective was to introduce: 'an explicit and formalised assessment process to standardise the information received from existing subject-based committees' (Roberts, 2003, paragraph 62).

The 1986 exercise was conducted from within the UGC. It ranked 37 cost centres within 55 universities on the basis of four categories: 'outstanding'; 'above average'; 'about average'; or 'below average'. The membership of the 37 panels making the assessments was not published and the process by which they operated evolved as the exercised progressed:

> By any test [the methodology of the 1986 RAE] was a pretty rough and ready lash-up of techniques. As the exercise proceeded it was frequently amended as new problems arose. Sir Peter Swinnerton-Dyer took a direct, regular and personal interest partly because it was his brainchild but also because the UGC's statistical branch was stretched to breaking point ...
>
> In addition to the problems posed by the very experimental nature of its statistical methodology were those deriving from the differences in the workings of the different sub-committees, the tasks they had to perform, the modes of working they adopted and the responses they received to their enquiries from different universities.
>
> (Smith 1987, p. 309)

These concerns and other criticisms of the 1986 RAE were voiced by a number of groups and individuals looking at the outcomes for individual subjects (e.g., Smith, 1986; Minogue, 1986). Furthermore, although the UGC made it clear that the outcomes of this first exercise could only form a legitimate basis for comparison of departments teaching and researching the same subject at different universities, there was concern that university policy makers would want to use them to make comparisons of different departments within the same university (Smith, 1987).

In 1986–87, only 14.2 per cent of the money distributed to universities by the UGC (representing just over 40 per cent of its total research grant) was allocated on the basis of the RAE results. It was nevertheless highly significant because it established the principle of quality-related funding for research. This evolved into the QR stream, which now accounts for two-thirds of HEFCE's annual grant to fund research in English universities (£1050 million in 2012–13). It also became, as we shall see, the basis for a clearer 'pecking order' of departments and institutions. Since that initial RAE, there have been five more – in 1989, 1992, 1996, 2001 and 2008. Each was intended to be more comprehensive and more transparent than its predecessor. From an institutional perspective, each exercise represented an increasing administrative load and hence cost; equivalent burdens were placed on members of the peer review panels (senior academics) and, in administering the whole process, on HEFCE itself.[4]

We now summarise the main principles behind the subsequent exercises and then how the judgements were translated into funding.

1989

The processes used for this RAE were developed from those applied in 1986; because of its recent detailed scrutiny Earth Sciences was omitted. Subjects were assessed within 152 'units of assessment'; these had been identified through a process of consultation with universities and subject or professional bodies, with the objective of reflecting more closely than had the 37 cost centres used in 1986, the organisation of research within institutions. Universities could select which units they wished to enter, but the research of all academic staff had to be entered. Institutions' submissions in each category were then assessed by a panel to which the academic members could co-opt appropriate experts (e.g., from charities, government bodies, research councils). But, in contrast to the 1986 exercise, panel memberships were published.

Perhaps most significantly, however, the 1989 RAE introduced a standard 5-point rating scale, to be used by all subject panels, with the intention of achieving consistency in evaluation across disciplines, as well as within them. This principle has been adhered to in all subsequent exercises; the evolving definitions used until 2001 are shown in Table 4.2.

1992

The 1992 exercise was brought forward by one year, to enable assessment of the research of the former polytechnics. With these institutions included, the panels found themselves considering around 2,700 submissions, covering the work of some 45,000 staff. Due to the research profiles of the former polytechnics (with, for example, significant activity in education and very little in clinical medicine), the additional submissions and staff were not evenly distributed across all units. 1992 was also the first time universities could decide which departments and staff to submit – introducing tactical decisions concerning whom to include, and establishing the principle that not all academics were necessarily 'research active'. To recognise this element of submissions, the results of the RAE included a letter to designate the proportion of staff submitted, as well as a numerical indicator of the assessed quality of the research submitted.

1996

For the 1996 exercise, those academics submitted by their institutions were judged on the basis of a maximum of four 'outputs', which they themselves identified. There was no consideration of the quantity of papers produced, quality

Table 4.2 Definitions of research quality required to obtain ratings in RAE exercises 1989–2001

1989& 1992 point	1989 & 1992 definition	1996& 2001 point	1996 definition	2001 definition
		5*	international excellence in majority of sub-areas and national excellence in all others	international excellence in more than half activity submitted and national excellence in the remainder
5	international excellence in some sub-areas and national excellence in virtually all others	5	international excellence in some sub-areas and national excellence in virtually all others	international excellence in up to half activity submitted and national excellence in virtually all the remainder
4	national excellence in virtually all sub-areas, possibly some international excellence	4	national excellence in virtually all sub-areas, possibly some international excellence	national excellence in virtually all activity submitted, with some evidence of international excellence
3	national excellence in majority of sub-areas or international level in some	3a	national excellence in substantial majority of sub-areas, or international level in some + national in others, together making a majority	national excellence in over two-thirds of activity submitted, with possibly some international excellence
		3b	national excellence in majority of sub-areas	national excellence in more than half activity submitted
2	national excellence in up to half sub-areas	2	national excellence in up to half sub-areas	national excellence in up to half activity submitted
1	national excellence in none, or virtually none, of sub-areas	1	national excellence in none, or virtually none, of sub-areas	national excellence in none, or virtually non of activity submitted

(Source: HEFCE, 1994, 2001d)

being the only concern of the assessors. The scale of the exercise had expanded to the point that HEFCE judged: 'The RAE is the largest single research assessment exercise in the world, involving over 55,000 academics, around 3,000 departments and almost 200 institutions' (2000, paragraph 61). Of the staff submitted, 32 per cent were working in departments rated in the top two categories (5 and 5*). Over the five years following the exercise, a total of over £4 billion QR funds was distributed on the basis of its results.

2001

The 2001 exercise was conducted on broadly the same lines as its immediate predecessor: panels operating in 69 units of assessment considered almost 2,600 submissions, from 173 institutions, covering nearly 50,000 researchers. However, the perceived status of the exercise, and hence the effort devoted to it within the sector, had grown to the point where, at the start of his subsequent review of the process, commissioned by the UK funding bodies, Gareth (later Sir Gareth) Roberts, President of Wolfson College, Oxford and former Vice-Chancellor of Sheffield, judged that:

> The … RAE in 2001 was the most rigorous and thorough exercise to date. It had by then become the principal means by which institutions assured themselves of the quality of their research. It had also evolved into an intense competition in which HEIs strived not only for funding but also for prestige.
>
> (Roberts, 2003, paragraph 63)

Of the staff submitted for the RAE in 2001, 55 per cent were working in departments rated in the top two categories (5 and 5*). Of the departments assessed, 38.4 per cent were in these two bands, compared to 19.8 per cent in 1996 and 12.8 per cent in 1992 (Sharp, 2004). These figures are an indicator possibly of increased quality within the national research base, or of grade inflation, or of more strategic submissions, or a combination of all three. Sharp (2004) considered possible explanations for this clear move towards higher overall RAE outcomes, and concluded that it was not possible to identify any specific causes from his data analysis alone. He did, however, highlight some areas where the process could be improved:

> If one of the aims of the RAE is the establishment of a rating scale which can be accepted as an absolute measure of research quality, then measures must be put in place which help promote this. Essentially, these are the same measures used to promote consistency of awarding standards in undergraduate programmes: clearly defined and publicised assessment criteria, a healthy separation between the assessors and the assessed, and an avoidance of unduly large shifts in award distributions. Past RAEs have scored highly on the first of these: progress remains to be made on the second and third.
>
> (Sharp, 2004, p. 217)

However, for institutions where teaching was the primary activity, there was another issue; even the most strategic of submissions would yield limited returns on the effort and cost required to enter an RAE:

In 2002–3 there were 40 out of 132 English HEIs for whom R/(T+R) came to less than 2%. These institutions received a total of £566 million in teaching funding and only £6.7 million in research funding. They made 240 submissions to RAE2001 which yielded an average of £27,580 in funding in 2002–3, compared to an average across the exercise of over £455,000 per submission. For these institutions, therefore, and for the panels and administrators tasked with their assessment, the RAE is over 16 times less efficient than the norm. This seems to us to make a strong case for assessing such institutions in a different way.

(Roberts, 2002, paragraph 144)

The Review therefore concluded that: 'The least research intensive institutions should be considered separately from the remainder of the HE sector' (recommendation 4b), but that it was a matter for the funding councils to decide how they should be assessed outside the main RAE. This proposal, which would have reduced the burden on the RAE panels, was not adopted; in Chapter 7 we give it as one of several illustrations of the 'competition through emulation' that is a characteristic feature of market-based systems.

2008

As a result of the Roberts Review, and a subsequent Funding Council consultation with higher education institutions and other interested bodies, the 2008 RAE was significantly different to its predecessors. Results were published as a graded profile rather than a fixed points system, to allow the funding bodies to identify 'pockets of excellence' and reduce the abrupt grade boundaries which had previously had significant funding impacts. A two-tier panel structure was used to ensure greater consistency across subjects, with 67 sub-panels of experts, one for each unit of assessment, working under the guidance of 15 main panels. Finally, to meet previous criticisms, explicit criteria were used in each unit to enable appropriate assessment of applied, practice-based and interdisciplinary research.

At publication of the results, the criteria for each of the quality profiles used were explained as: 'The RAE quality profiles present in blocks of 5% the proportion of each submission judged by the panels to have met each of the quality levels defined below. Work that fell below national quality or was not recognised as research was unclassified' (RAE 2008, paragraph 40).

The distribution of the profiles used is shown in Table 4.3.

After 2008: the Research Excellence Framework

The RAE is to be succeeded in 2014 by the Research Excellence Framework (REF), and its results will be used to inform the distribution of QR funds from 2015–16. The REF was developed as the result of a consultation process which was conducted under a clear policy steer from the Government in March 2006.

Table 4.3 Quality profiles used in RAE 2008

4*	Quality that is world-leading in terms of originality, significance and rigour.
3*	Quality that is internationally excellent in terms of originality, significance and rigour but which nonetheless falls short of the highest standards of excellence.
2*	Quality that is recognised internationally in terms of originality, significance and rigour.
1*	Quality that is recognised nationally in terms of originality, significance and rigour.
Unclassified	Quality that falls below the standard of nationally recognised work. Or work which does not meet the published definition of research for the purposes of this assessment.

Source: RAE 2008

From the Government's perspective, the RAE had played an important role in increasing the quality of research conducted in the country's universities:

> Over the years since the RAE was introduced, research quality has risen significantly, as the RAE has acted as a driver of competition, focusing institutions on delivering high quality outputs. Following the 1996 RAE, 32 percent of staff submitted worked in departments rated as 'excellent'. In 2001 the figure was 55 percent. This improvement was validated by international experts.
>
> (HMT *et al.*, 2006, paragraph 4.6)

The report gave its explicit support to the principles of the dual support system; however, it criticised the RAE for the costs to institutions; perverse incentives in publishing patterns; disincentivising interdisciplinary research; and favouring pure research over applied.

The Government recognised that preparations for the 2008 RAE were well under way, and that any substantive changes to the process by which QR funds were allocated could not be introduced until after that exercise. It therefore proposed running a shadow exercise to the 2008 RAE, based on its preferred future methodology of a metrics-based system for evaluation of research quality. It cited the principles against which a new system for evaluation of research quality should be judged as:

- Efficiency of operation and reduction of the administrative burden on institutions.
- Rewarding excellence in all types of research (from 'blue skies' to 'applied') and encouraging collaboration and interdisciplinary projects.
- Preserving the dual support system, to secure a funding stream which allows institutions to make strategic decisions about their own research priorities and profile and plan effectively.
- A transparent and simple assessment process which is open to all HEIs.

(HMT *et al.*, 2006, paragraph 4.10)

The resulting REF, the outline of which was announced by the Secretary of State, Alan Johnson, in December 2006, was described by the funding councils (HEFCE, 2011d, paragraphs 17–18) as 'having developed through an evolutionary process, building on previous RAEs', and as operating under three core principles:

- Equity across the assessment of all subjects and within each subject so that the exercise can be conducted: 'without distorting the activity that it measures or encouraging or discouraging any particular type of research activity, other than providing an overall stimulus to enhancing the overall achievements of the UK research base.'
- Equality in the academics eligible for submission, so that limited numbers of outputs eligible do not preclude the inclusion of excellent researchers.
- Transparency in the criteria and processes used for assessment (to be published well in advance of deadlines for universities to submit their entries), with the ultimate publication of results to include an explanation of decision-making processes used. Both these measures are intended to reinforce the credibility of the REF.

Key differences between the REF and the 2008 RAE will include:

- The introduction of the consideration of the non-academic impact of research outputs and the removal of 'esteem' as a distinct element within the assessment.
- Retaining the two-tier panel structure but reducing the 67 sub-panels of experts to 36. These, in turn, will work under the guidance of four main panels, as opposed to 15.
- greater consistency will be introduced in the processes used across all units of assessment when evaluating submissions. Specifically, standard weightings will be applied to all three strands of assessment: outputs, impact and environment.
- The introduction of stronger measures designed to promote equality and diversity within research careers (for example, by reducing, from four, the required number of outputs to be submitted for an academic by one for each period of maternity leave during the assessment period).

Furthermore, to address concerns raised in the main by those working in the humanities, publications of significant scale and scope (generally books) will carry weighting equivalent to two of the four outputs to be submitted for each individual.

The general expectation in the sector was that the 2008 RAE would be the last such exercise. The changes to the RAE which resulted in the creation of the REF were the result of business lobbying of the Chancellor, Gordon Brown, in the run-up to the 2006 budget statement, about the apparent privileging of 'pure' over 'applied' research. Neither the Education Department, nor the Funding Council was consulted. Whilst it was recognised that the details of the new process would take some while to settle, £60 million was transferred to the budget for industrially relevant research from the main HEFCE research budget. This seems ironic given the poor record of British firms in investing in R&D, where we lag behind all our main OECD competitors, as the OECD figures given in Table 4.4 show.

The financial significance of the assessments

We turn now to the financial implications of selectivity. The formula by which the Funding Council distributes its core QR funding has been published only after each RAE has been conducted. Thus – even if it were deemed desirable – it was impossible for institutions to make tactical decisions about their submissions, informed by a clear anticipation of the impact these might have on subsequent funding. Furthermore, this formula has, with increasing frequency, been modified between RAEs, usually at the Government's behest. Hence the way in which achieved assessments of quality translate into QR funding has also changed unpredictably, even though the ratings on which this funding was based were not reassessed. By increasing the multipliers relating to higher quality assessments, and reducing or removing entirely those for lower quality assessments, these changes generally served to increase the selectivity of funding, as we shall now see.[5]

The weightings used for the outcomes of the 1996 RAE, when calculating the annual QR element of the Funding Council grant are shown in Table 4.5.

Table 4.4 Proportion of national R&D expenditure by 'business enterprise'

Country	Percentage	Year of statistics*
Australia	62.0	2008
France	51.0	2010
Germany	66.1	2009
Japan	75.3	2009
UK	45.0	2010
USA	61.6	2009

Source: OECD

*Most recent available from OECD.

Table 4.5 Weightings used in QR allocation following the 1996 RAE

Quality rating (with abbreviated description)	Funding weighting
5* (international excellence in majority of sub-areas)	4.05
5 (international excellence in some sub-areas)	3.375
4 (national excellence in all sub-areas)	2.25
3a (national excellence in substantial majority of sub-areas)	1.5
3b (national excellence in majority of sub-areas)	1
2 (national excellence in less than half of sub-areas)	0
1 (national excellence in virtually no sub-areas)	0

Source: HEFCE, 1997

These multipliers remained constant throughout the period in which the *1996 RAE* was used to determine QR. However, the position changed when the results of the *2001 RAE* placed many more departments in the higher quality bands. In response, and bearing in mind the total funds available for distribution, HEFCE decided to retain the QR funding for departments rated 5*, scale down the funding for those rated 5, 4, or 3a, and remove any funding for departments that had been rated 3b or below (HEFCE, 2002a, p. 5). These changes were implemented in 2002–3, the first year in which 2001 RAE results were available to inform grant allocations.

This adjustment in weightings resulted in a clear shift in the focus of QR funding towards those departments that had been assessed to be of the highest quality, at the expense of others that might have had the potential to develop their research and increase its quality over time. This policy of increased selectivity was echoed the following year, 2003–4, when QR funding was also removed from those departments rated 3a. At the same time, the funding allocated for departments rated 4 reduced from £139 million in 2002–3 to £118 million in 2003–4. These weighting changes are shown in Table 4.6.

In financial terms, the application of these multipliers resulted in 85 per cent of the QR funds distributed on the basis of the 2001 RAE being awarded to departments rated 5 or 5* (Henkel and Kogan, 2010). However, it still remained up to the individual institutions to decide whether to allocate these funds internally to mirror the formula which the Funding Council had used to allocate them.

The 2003 White Paper *The Future of Higher Education* (DFES, 2003) can be read as advocating a further concentration of R funds in the most highly rated departments, whilst celebrating the UK's excellent research performance:

> to maintain and strengthen our position in the face of increasing global competition, we also need to review how research is organised to ensure the increased funding supports our most talented researchers and our most effective research institutions and departments.
>
> (DFES, 2003, paragraph 2.1)

Table 4.6 Weightings used in QR allocation 2001–4

RAE rating	Funding weights		
	2001–2	2002–3	2003–4
5*	4.05	2.71	3.357
5	3.375	1.89	2.793
4	2.25	1	1
3a	1.5	0.31	0
3b	1	0	0
2	0	0	0
1	0	0	0

Source: HEFCE, 2002a, p. 5 and HEFCE, 2003d, p. 6

Already about 75 per cent of HEFCE research funding went to 25 institutions, with research council funding following a similar pattern. But a further 52 institutions had at least one department rated 5 or 5* in the 2001 RAE, and departments rated 4 were yet more widespread. The Government believed that the position needed to be improved further by focussing resources more effectively on the best performers. Accordingly, the Government intended to ask HEFCE, using the 2001 results, to identify the 'very best' of the 5* departments with a critical mass of researchers – a 6* – and to give them additional resources over the next three years (DFES, 2003, paragraph 2.15).

Following the White Paper, HEFCE conducted a major review of the way that it funded research (HEFCE 2003c). This was also a response to the findings of the Roberts Review of Research Assessment (Roberts, 2003), and its own Strategic Plan 2003–8 (HEFCE, 2003a). The outcomes were reflected in the allocations for 2004–5. Average units of resource for departments rated 5 or 5* in the 2001 RAE would be at least maintained, while the resource for departments rated 4 would be capped in real terms. At the same time, an additional £24 million would be distributed among 'the best 5*-rated' departments: those that had received a 5* in 1996 and 2001 or those that had been rated 5* in 2001 on the basis of a constant or increased number of staff submitted to the RAE (HEFCE, 2004b, pp. 6–7).

The weightings used by HEFCE for the distribution of QR funds in the light of the RAE were then adjusted marginally in each of the following four years, as Table 4.7 shows; further funds were also allocated to the 'best 5*-rated' departments, with the sums remaining fairly steady through this period. The small shifts collectively, however, continued to focus QR funds in those departments with the highest RAE ratings, ignoring completely those in the lower three of the six bands.

The year 2009–10 was the first one in which the outcomes of the *2008 RAE* were used to inform the distribution of QR funding, of which mainstream QR amounted to £1,074 million (HEFCE, 2009, pp. 13–14). The 2008 RAE found that high-quality research was spread more widely across the sector than had previously been supposed. As Adams and Gurney (2010) noted:

> An immediate shift in the distribution of funding at institutional level was apparent. An additional 25 universities and colleges were now in receipt of

Table 4.7 Weightings used in QR allocation 2005–9

RAE rating	Funding weights			
	2005–6	2006–7	2007–8	2008–9
5*	3.7552	3.9478	4.036	4.036
5	3.0059	3.1198	3.175	3.180
4	1	1	1	1
3a, 3b, 2, 1	0	0	0	0

Source: HEFCE, 2006b, p. 10 and HEFCE, 2008b, p. 14

core research funding. In terms of mainstream QR cash, in 2008–09 about 90 percent of it was shared by 38 universities but from 2009 some 48 institutions were sharing this slice. There are two main reasons for this shift. First, under the previous scoring arrangements pockets of mediocre research might have become subsumed in an otherwise excellent and high-scoring department whilst, conversely, pockets of outstanding research might not have been recognised in a low-scoring department. Second, the weighting factors used in the 2009 funding formula provided a greater reward for moving from the modest plains of 2* research quality to 3*quality than from 3* to the far more challenging peak of 4*world-leading excellence, whereas in the previous scoring arrangements the step from a 4 to a 5 rating or from a 5 to a 5* rating provided a far greater reward than the step from a 3a to a 4.

(Adams and Gurney, 2010, paragraph 5, original footnotes deleted)

However, almost certainly after vigorous lobbying by the most research-intensive institutions, the weightings were changed to provide for greater relative reward for high scores. Table 4.8 shows the weightings actually applied over the period.

As the table shows, from 2012–13 there is no QR funding for activity rated 2*. The removal of this stream of funding was in response to direction from the Secretary of State in the annual grant letter (DBIS, 2012a, paragraph 13). The £35 million released will be used to increase funding for the supervision of postgraduate research (PGR) students (HEFCE 2012b, p. 10). This shift in the allocation of QR funds since the 2008 RAE has, yet again, increased selectivity at departmental and institutional level.

The funding of research infrastructure

A problem that was increasingly apparent during the 1990s – that institutions could no longer find the full costs of setting up and running a 'well-found laboratory' from within their core grants – was most noticeable in areas of science which required increasingly sophisticated equipment (with resulting costs of operation, staff training, etc). However, there was also a wider problem in that many institutions had been subject to long-term under-investment in their estates.

Table 4.8 Weightings used in QR allocation 2009–13

Quality rating (with abbreviated description)	Funding weights			
	2009–10	2010–11	2011–12	2012–13
4* (Quality that is world-leading)	7	9	9	3
3* (Quality that is internationally excellent)	3	3	3	1
2* (Quality that is recognised internationally)	1	1	0.294	0
1* (Quality that is recognised nationally)	0	0	0	0
Unclassified (Quality that falls below the standard of nationally recognised work)	0	0	0	0

This was an issue picked up by the Dearing Committee. Paragraph 11.37 of their report (National Committee of Inquiry into Higher Education, 1997) read:

> Without a major injection of funds to improve the infrastructure of the UK's top quality research departments, we do not believe the future competitiveness of the UK research base can be secured.

The committee recommended (Recommendation 34) the establishment of a fund to provide loans at very low interest rates for research infrastructure.

The 1998 Spending Review earmarked additional public funds to be spent on the sector's research infrastructure. These were allocated, on a competitive basis, through a series of schemes managed by the Funding Council, introducing a form of market for these funds. However, this was an unusual market in that the suppliers of research (the universities) were, in effect, bidding to the purchasers of that research (the major grant-awarding bodies collectively through HEFCE) for capital investment that would ultimately make them more competitive suppliers. Again, this was a classic quasi-market.

The first of these schemes was the Joint Research Infrastructure Funding (JREI), which operated from 1995 to 2000. JREI distributed a total of £161 million, with the money coming from the funding councils, the Office of Science and Technology (OST) and the research councils; under the terms of the JREI, funds were allocated competitively 'to purchase equipment for advanced research programmes' as an addition to core grants.

From 1999, JREI was complemented by the Joint Infrastructure Fund (JIF), an initiative funded by the Department for Trade and Industry (DTI), the Wellcome Trust and HEFCE, with the objective of financing essential building, refurbishment and equipment projects to ensure that UK higher education would remain at the forefront of international scientific research. Speaking at the announcement of the first round of JIF grants in May 1999, the Science Minister, Lord Sainsbury, said: 'Without this injection of funds we would have soon seen a disastrous decline in the excellence of the UK science base' (HEFCE, 1999). In total, between 1999 and 2002, £750 million was allocated through JIF.

When the JREI ended in 2000, it was replaced by the Science Research Investment Fund (SRIF). This initiative was co-funded by HEFCE, the OST, and the Wellcome Trust, with an initial budget of £1 billion, to be spent over three years (although some was to be used to support national laboratories outside universities).

A report to the OST in 2001 (JM Consulting, 2001) confirmed the need for these substantial levels of investment in university infrastructure; it concluded that about half of the higher education estate was not up to standard. This was partly because a significant amount of the estate had been built in the 1960s and 1970s, with relatively low and inflexible specifications, meaning that it had reached the end of its expected life. At the same time, the growing volume of, and rapid developments in, scientific research – particularly during the 1990s – were putting additional pressure on already overworked buildings.

The report concluded that a further £2.7 billion was required for remedial work on research buildings, with an additional £0.5 billion to be spent on equipment essential to the 'well-found laboratory'. Looking forward, it estimated that at least an additional £1 billion would need to be invested in national facilities, with a similar sum from institutions' own budgets locally, to ensure that the country retained 'leading-edge research capability' (JM Consulting, 2001, p. 14). However, the benefits that the consultants suggested would result from these levels of investment went much wider than physical facilities alone: by using a strategic approach to the allocation of funds, researchers' time could be used more productively, working conditions would improve, and the UK would be able to train, or attract and then retain, leading scientists.

While a large part of the focus for investment in facilities for research was, and remains, in science and technology, in 2002 HEFCE commissioned a report from the same firm on the requirements for research infrastructure for the arts and humanities. The report (JM Consulting, 2002) observed that for these subjects there was a significant overlap between the use of facilities for research and for teaching; however, it also noted that methods were evolving in these subjects, taking on some of the structural features of science-based research including team working (both within and between institutions) as well as the use of advanced IT. These changes, the consultants commented, were accompanied by increased expectations of, and by, research-active academics in the arts and humanities, who in the past had been used to fitting in their research around their teaching, with limited dedicated infrastructure. The report attributed these changes primarily to the impact of the RAE and to work done by the Arts and Humanities Research Board to support this research. But it also noted the problems created by the lack of integrated strategies for research and resource allocation within institutions.

The consultants recommended that investment was needed in three areas: £0.5 billion for generic institutional infrastructure; £50 million for the well-found laboratory or equivalent; and £100 million for advanced or specialist facilities. In part addressing the issues highlighted in the study, HEFCE established the Research Capability Fund: between 2003 and 2009 this distributed £125 million to support emerging research in art and design; communication, cultural and media studies; dance, drama and performing arts; nursing and other studies and professions allied to medicine; social work; and sports-related studies.

Two further rounds of SRIF – in 2004–6 and 2007 – subsequently distributed £1 billion and £903 million respectively for the funding of research infrastructure (including contributions from the Wellcome Trust and the OST). Both SRIF2 and SRIF3 followed a formula funding model, along the same lines as that used for SRIF1. While this method of allocation had the advantage of reducing the administrative burden placed on institutions to access funds, it reflected QR and external research funding already received by an institution; this inevitably reinforced the position of already successful institutions and further concentrated resources with them.

Considered as a whole, the dedicated funding of laboratories and other scientific facilities within universities in the first decade of the twenty-first century has, as one report observed, become a significant source of revenue for the sector:

> in the preceding decade, investment in research infrastructure has emerged as a major funding stream in its own right, with an annual spend of around £500 million to complement the funding bodies' institutional block grants and the research councils' project-based awards.
>
> (Technopolis, 2009, p. 7)

However, the way in which the allocation of these sums has been structured – through a series of schemes that were both defined and finite – emphasises that there is no guarantee that they will continue, or be succeeded by equivalent funds. The potential uncertainty for universities has though been removed for the four year period 2011–15: through the research stream of its Capital Investment Fund 2 (CIF2), HEFCE will be distributing a total of £549 million, a reduced figure which reflects wider national restrictions on public funding. Furthermore, in the Budget in March 2012, the Chancellor announced that an additional £100 million was to be made available to support investment in major capital projects for research facilities within universities; a bidding process is operating for these funds during 2012–13, and those projects which are successful in obtaining public money through this route will be expected to demonstrate how they will also be attracting capital from other sectors (such as business or charities).

The CIF2 funds are allocated to each institution using a formula linked to its income from the research councils and the quality of its research (as measured by QR) – with the highest award being £47 million, while 68 institutions are receiving less than £1 million each. Thus, the 'major funding stream' observed by Technopolis (above) has already, and perhaps not surprisingly, started to run dry. Those capital funds that are available are being allocated on a formula basis which mirrors the public research funding (in the form of QR and research council grants) that each institution already receives; thus CIF2 can be seen as a yet further move towards concentration of government support for university research, based on long-established, and seemingly well-accepted, criteria of selectivity.

Research students

It has long been recognised that a key role of any university department is to train, support and develop the next generation of researchers, through the supervision of doctoral students. These students are also a vital link in the innovation chain. This view was endorsed by the UGC in 1984 when presenting its strategy for higher education in the 1990s:

There is one aspect of research which is virtually a university monopoly: the development of the scholars and research workers of the future, through the training in research methods of postgraduate research students. Good research students are an asset of great value to their departments, stimulating and challenging the research interests of the staff, and contributing practical and tutorial teaching. They include some of the most able young minds in the country, many of whom will go on to strengthen the national research base or make a vital contribution to innovation in industry.

(UGC, 1984, paragraph 5.23)

As well as contributing to a department's research effort, research students can be used as teachers, so giving academic staff more time for their research. Supervision and support may be funded from a number of sources, including: university or charitable scholarships; within a larger research grant; from elements of the core grant; employer sponsorship; privately; or through research council studentships. However, writing in 1984, the UGC was concerned that cuts in research council budgets were creating serious problems:

> In the social sciences, in particular, the funding of the ESRC is now inadequate to enable it to play the proper role of a Research Council in the support of research training, and the need to make short-term economies has led to an excessive reduction in the number of students supported.
>
> (UGC, 1984, paragraph 5.23)

Overall, the committee noted, UK research student numbers had fallen by around 15 per cent between 1972–73 and 1982–83: the restoration of postgraduate studentships would be a speedy and effective way to address a wider erosion of the research base within the universities. This situation in fact improved over time, so that by 1994–95 there were 58,100 postgraduate research students in UK universities. However, the rate of expansion that had achieved this number of postgraduate students – between 1979–80 and 1994–95 the total number of postgraduate (taught and research) students more than tripled, from 100,900 to 315,400 – raised concerns about quality and funding. HEFCE therefore commissioned Martin (later Sir Martin) Harris, Vice-Chancellor of Manchester, to chair a review of postgraduate provision. This recommended (HEFCE, 1996a, paragraph 1.16) that: 'PGR students should normally only attract HEFCE research grants in subject areas within institutions which have a pervasive research culture, and can deliver excellence in research education.'

It also said that there should be a Code of Practice for PGR education covering (paragraph 4.49):

- Quality of research – with PGR students generally only expected to be supervised within departments ranked 3 or above in the RAE.
- Quality of supervision – with PGR supervisors generally research active and trained in supervision, with appropriate back-up arrangements in place.

- Quality of environment – with PGR study offered where there is a supportive environment (ie other researchers with whom to interact) and infrastructure, creating appropriate social and working conditions.
- Regular progress monitoring and assessment.
- Access to relevant facilities throughout the year.

The universities and the research councils were to be expected to endorse and monitor, with the Higher Education Quality Council (HEQC), adherence to this Code within institutions (HEFCE, 1996b). This recommendation was endorsed the following year by the Dearing Committee (National Committee of Inquiry into Higher Education, 1997).

At this time, funding for the supervision of research students awarded to departments (as opposed to studentships awarded to individuals) was not an explicit element of the annual funding council grant; instead supervised students were included in the volume measure for each department (as a proportion of the weighting attributed to academic staff). However, following the Harris Report, for the first time, funding council support was only to be given to students in departments that passed a quality threshold, as measured by RAE ratings. This policy took effect in 1998.

In spite of the expectation that departments supervising research students would adhere to the Harris Code, there was still concern about the variability of the experiences of PGR students. At the time of the 2001 Budget, the Government (Treasury, with the DTI and the DFES) commissioned Sir Gareth Roberts to consider the country's supply of high-quality scientists and engineers. His report (Roberts, 2002) – the recommendations of which were subsequently applied to PhD students in all disciplines – highlighted the importance of providing PGR students with the opportunity to acquire transferable skills (in addition to their in-depth subject knowledge), and also of offering a career development path for their post-doctoral researchers. The Government responded by allocating £20 million annually to Research Councils UK (RCUK, the lineal successor to the ABRC), between 2003 and 2010. This would be distributed to institutions to spend on career development and training in transferable skills for doctoral and post-doctoral researchers, funds which became known within institutions as 'Roberts money'.

Following its review of the research funding method in 2003 (HEFCE, 2003c), HEFCE amended its funding model so that institutions would only receive support for PGR students who were working in departments rated 4 or above in the RAE. Money awarded on this basis would, for the first time from 2005–6, be identified as a separate stream, rather than falling within the overall block grant for research. It would cover both training and supervision.

This policy has received some criticism. Powell and Green (2006) argued that using a measure of research quality to distribute funds for supervision of doctoral students did not necessarily ensure that those students were in an environment where they would receive the best quality supervision; they might indeed be at greater 'risk' in a research-intensive department where supervision might not be a high priority for established researchers. They also highlighted the lack of any proven correlation between RAE ratings and completion rates, an issue highlighted very recently in relation to a number of elite institutions (Jump, 2012b). They suggested that this rationing of HEFCE support for doctoral supervision could, over time, reduce the nation's research capacity. It would certainly, they argued, limit the development of a research base in academic departments that were rated below the funding threshold of 4.[6]

Whether in response to these criticisms or not, a subsequent review (HEFCE, 2011a) took a more nuanced approach. It has resulted in a new method for the calculation of HEFCE funds for the supervision of research students which is weighted in line with the 'quality' of the department in which a student is working. This is judged on the basis of the proportion of activity of 4* and 3* standard, within all work of 2* or higher within the department. Some moderation is applied to ensure that the range of funding available to support individual students does not vary too greatly (HEFCE, 2012b) However, this still results in wide variations in the funds available. Thus there remains a clear financial incentive – in addition to any academic drivers – for a PGR student to seek to work within a highly rated department.[7]

In 2012–13, £240 million will be distributed by this method, an increase of £35 million on the previous two years' total allocations, to support the supervision of research degree programmes. Only departments that follow Section One of the Quality Assurance Agency's Code of Practice (QAA, 2004), covering the supervision of graduate students, will be eligible to receive these funds.

Finally, it should be noted that some of the research councils have also adopted a selective approach to the funding of research students.[8] This is important because over the period since Harris's report in 1996, the councils have played an increasingly significant role in funding full-time UK-domiciled doctoral students, as Table 4.9 shows.

Funding from the research councils is therefore a significant factor in determining where and what UK full-time students at least will study for their doctorates;

Table 4.9 Primary source of funding for UK full-time doctoral students

Major source of tuition fees	1996–97	2007–8	2009–10	% Change 1996–97 to 2009–10	% Change 2007–8 to 2009–10
Research Council	2,400	2,965	3,255	36	10
Charity/British Academy	380	300	320	–16	6
Institution	1,105	1,560	2,415	118	55
Government	425	450	665	56	47
UK industry	440	240	270	–38	13
Overseas	95	165	125	37	–22
Other	300	515	615	104	19
No financial backing	860	1,620	1,755	104	8
Total	6,005	7,815	9,420	57	21

Source: HEFCE, 2011f, p. 47

it is, however, worthy of note that between 1996–97 and 2009–10 institutions themselves increased their support to include more than double the number of students. This may reflect attempts to support PhDs in those subjects where research council funding is scarcer.

Research concentration

We now consider the inevitable concomitant of selectivity, concentration.

As well as restructuring the sector, the abolition of the binary line in 1992 (described in Chapter 3) played an influential role in the move towards selectivity. According to the by then Chief Executive of the Universities Funding Council (UFC), Sir Peter Swinnerton-Dyer, in anticipation of this change:

> Some front-rank institutions are already finding that the research support they get from the UFC is not enough to underpin their earmarked research income, and the fact that UFC grant is growing more slowly than other sources of research support can only make matters worse.
>
> Even the least distinguished university gets a substantial amount for research within its block grant. Polytechnics, on the other hand, get next to nothing for research; and the main reason why polytechnics have campaigned for the abolition of the binary line is that they wish to be funded for research on the same basis as universities … . However, the Government will certainly not regard the abolition of the binary line as a reason to provide more research support for higher education as a whole. If the polytechnics are to gain, who should be the losers?
>
> (Swinnerton-Dyer, 1991, p. 212)

For Swinnerton-Dyer, political realities meant that the former polytechnics would become eligible for the research component of the block grant from 1992, resulting in an inevitable further increase in the selectivity with which this would be allocated between institutions. In this situation, he argued, it would be more logical for the research component of the block grant to be administered and distributed by a Research Funding Council, distinct from a new Higher Education Funding Council with the responsibility for teaching grants. This was canvassed in the 1991 White Paper *Higher Education: A New Framework* but the 1993 White Paper *Realising Our Potential: A Strategy for Science, Engineering and Technology* (Chancellor of the Duchy of Lancaster, 1993) ruled it out.

A study commissioned by HEFCE to inform its 1996 consultation on research funding found that there was a wide acceptance within the sector of the need for some selectivity in research funding. This, it argued, was based on two considerations:

- an acknowledgement that it would not be feasible to return to the earlier funding model, which had been based on the number of staff and students engaged in different types of research.

- a recognition of the benefits that had arisen as a result of quality-based allocations of funding, in terms of both the management and the efficient conduct of research.

(SQW Ltd, 1996, p. 40)

The report also cited clear evidence of economies of scale within research to support increased selectivity of funding, while recognising that increased investment in those research units that had been rated most highly in the RAE would inevitably come at the expense of others. Specifically, it described the potential impact of such a funding policy on two types of institution which could expect this to reduce their research income from HEFCE:

- institutions with few areas of leading research, but which were research-active in a wide spread of subjects; the reductions in their research outputs created by more selective distribution of funding could be compensated for by the use that research-intensive universities could be expected to make of the additional funds they would receive under such a model.
- institutions that were working to develop and establish their research strengths, in many cases in specialist (and possibly applied) areas of inquiry. Streams of research funding such as DevR[9] might have been as important as the selective QR to these institutions in the past, but the particular contribution that their research could make (for example, to inform teaching or because it had a strong regional focus) could be lost if a highly selective model were to be introduced for future funding of research.

(SQW Ltd, 1996, p. 42)

The consultants therefore highlighted the need, were selectivity of funding to increase following the 1996 RAE, for HEFCE to consider ways in which it would respond to three possible outcomes of such a move:

- reduced competition within the sector as concerned research activity.
- the need for ways to fund new approaches to research, where these were identified.
- the possibility that able research staff would wish to conduct research at institutions with higher ratings than their own.

(SQW Ltd, 1996, p. 46)

As the graph in Figure 4.1 shows, HEFCE's allocation of QR after 1996 did indeed increase the selectivity with which those funds were distributed across the sector. However, in its 2000 review, HEFCE was conscious that any further significant increase in selectivity following the 2001 RAE could result in a level of concentration that would reduce the country's research-intensive institutions to a small number clustered around the south-east. Further selectivity would also, HEFCE judged, create instability for those institutions that, as a result,

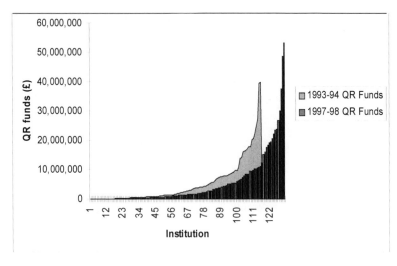

Figure 4.1 Distribution of QR funding between institutions following the 1992 and 1996
RAEs

Source: HEFCE, 2000, Annex E

Note: Each point on the x-axis represents a separate HEI with its total HEFCE grant for research on
the y-axis. The graph highlights the fact that a small proportion of universities receive the great majority of this grant. In 1997–98, 75 per cent of QR went to 28 of the 105 institutions that received more
than £250,000 of QR. These 28 universities also account for 68 per cent of the staff submitted for the
1996 RAE.

experienced significant fluctuations in their grant allocations. Thus it concluded
that 'the present level of selectivity is about right, and leads to an appropriate
spread of research funds between institutions' (HEFCE, 2000, paragraph 89).

Writing in the light of the outcomes of the 2001 RAE, the Roberts Review also
considered that this process had struck the right balance:

> By any measure, the RAE has been extremely successful. It has evolved from
> a quality assurance process to a competition for funding, while successfully
> retaining its original function of driving up standards through reputational
> incentives. At the same time it has enabled funds to be concentrated in those
> departments best able to produce research of the highest quality. It has
> helped to drive up research quality, transformed the management of research
> within institutions, and gained the acceptance of the research community
> and its stakeholders.
>
> (Roberts, 2003, paragraph 71)

Nevertheless, as we saw earlier, the 2003 White Paper envisaged further selectivity. This raised concern within the sector. A report for Universities UK *Funding
Research Diversity* (Evidence Ltd, 2003) found that there was no evidence for

concern about national research performance on grounds of lack of concentration. It argued that it was important to continue to support departments rated 4 in the RAE – which had the potential to grow into higher-rated units themselves and also often provided a base for the development of individual academics – and that selectivity was not the same as concentration. It concluded that, if there was a problem with performance, concentration of funding would not be the solution, and also that greater concentration would exacerbate existing regional differences.

A later report by Evidence Ltd, this time for HEFCE and the DFES, also suggested that the benefits of selectivity were evident not only in the highest rated departments:

> Data demonstrate that successive RAE cycles (and a period of increasingly selective funding) are associated with a progressive improvement in the performance of, and a concentration of, resources among the more research-intensive universities. More recent analyses show that improvements in research were not limited to the top performers, however, but could be found at all grades and across all subject areas. Analysts point out that continued improvement under assessment and selectivity is uncertain, but so is the maintenance of performance if the regime is significantly altered.
>
> (Evidence Ltd, 2005, pp. 6–7)

As we have seen, though, during the 2000s, the weightings used by the Funding Council when allocating QR funds on the basis of RAE outcomes have shifted, so that increasing proportions of the total allocation have gone to those departments with the highest grades. When the REF was being designed, Universities UK commissioned a research study (UUK, 2009) to evaluate the extent to which research funding within the sector was concentrated and to consider the implications of its findings. Looking at six representative sample units of assessment, it concluded that the system was already highly concentrated in terms of the distribution of both research funding and activity, as Table 4.10 demonstrates.

The study attributed this shift in part to the changes in weightings given to each RAE rating during this period discussed above. But it pointed out that this was not the only cause – income from research grants and contracts had also increasingly been found in the higher scoring units. Only research grants from industry did not follow this trend – with units with an RAE score of 4 increasing their share of this pool of income from 15 per cent in 2000–1 to 27 per cent in 2006–7. This, the report suggested, might be because these units put extra effort into obtaining research contracts from industry to make up for reduced levels of QR; this explanation assumes though that QR is distributed within institutions on the basis that it was allocated as part of the Funding Council's block grant, and so may not be correct. An alternative interpretation could be that the RAE's parameters do not favour research units which have a focus that makes them effective in competing for research contracts from industry, as industry critics of the exercise have long maintained.

Table 4.10 Distribution of research activity by grade for all six sample disciplines 2000–1 and 2006–7*

Rating	Total R		QR		RGCI		RC RGCI		RGCI industry		R active staff		PhDs		Articles	
	00/1	06/7	00/1	06/7	00/1	06/7	00/1	06/7	00/1	06/7	00/1	06/7	00/1	06/7	00/1	06/7
1	0.0	0.0	0.0	0.0	0.0	0.0	0.0	0.0	0.0	0.0	0.0	0.0	0.0	0.0	0.0	0.0
2	0.0	0.0	0.0	0.0	0.0	0.0	0.0	0.0	0.02	0.0	0.03	0.02	0.01	0.01	0.0	0.0
3b	0.01	0.0	0.0	0.0	0.01	0.0	0.0	0.0	0.0	0.01	0.04	0.03	0.01	0.01	0.01	0.01
3a	0.03	0.02	0.03	0.0	0.03	0.03	0.03	0.01	0.04	0.03	0.13	0.13	0.06	0.04	0.05	0.04
4	0.13	0.11	0.18	0.12	0.12	0.11	0.12	0.12	0.15	0.27	0.22	0.22	0.16	0.18	0.18	0.17
5	0.48	0.49	0.46	0.52	0.49	0.48	0.50	0.50	0.47	0.35	0.40	0.43	0.46	0.47	0.42	0.43
5*	0.34	0.37	0.33	0.36	0.34	0.37	0.35	0.36	0.31	0.34	0.18	0.17	0.31	0.30	0.34	0.35
5+5*	0.82	0.86	0.78	0.88	0.84	0.86	0.85	0.86	0.78	0.69	0.58	0.59	0.76	0.77	0.77	0.78

Source: UUK, 2009, p. 9

Note: *RGCI is research grant and contract income.

In conclusion, the report (UUK, 2009, p. 18) noted that 'different disciplines have reached different levels of "maturity" in terms of the development of the research base' and also that 'Data produced for this report have highlighted the way QR – often cited as a funding stream which spreads resource around – has contributed to the increase in concentration over the last six years'. It also commented, however, that vice-chancellors had, in the way that they distribute their QR funds internally, the potential to contribute to the maintenance of research diversity.

Scotland and Wales

As already noted, whilst the research council arm of the dual support system remains a UK-wide responsibility, core funding has been devolved. Nevertheless, the higher education institutions in Scotland, Wales and Northern Ireland have continued to participate in the RAE. In the earlier period following devolution, the funding agencies there distributed their funding less selectively than in England, as Table 4.11, comparing England and Scotland based on the successive annual funding allocations, shows.

More recently, however, there has been greater selectivity. The former policy may have reflected the relatively poorer performance of the local institutions; the latter may reflect the need to secure appropriate shares of UK and European research funds (Bruce, 2012, p. 88). In Scotland and Wales the devolved administrations have also taken a number of initiatives to strengthen research collaboration, beginning in Scotland in 2004 with pooling of research capacity in physics, economics, art and creative design, and biological and life sciences; other subjects have since been added. In Wales, the emphasis has been on creating research centres in areas of national priority (Bruce, 2012).

Conclusion

This chapter has described the development of a quasi-market in the funding of university research, with selectivity through the RAE since 1986 as the principal

Table 4.11 Weightings applied following 1996 and 2001 RAEs in England and Scotland

RAE rating	HEFCE		SHEFC	
	RAE1996	RAE2001	RAE1996	RAE2001
1	0	0	0	0
2	0	0	0	0
3b	1.00	0	1.00	0
3a (unchanged)	1.50	0.31	1.55	0
3a (improved)	1.50	0.31	1.55	1.00
4	2.25	1.00	2.40	1.55
5	3.375	1.89	3.72	2.80
5*	4.05	2.71	3.72	3.20

Source: Hare, 2002, p. 8

policy instrument. As good a summary as any of the effects has been provided by Henkel and Kogan:

> There is little doubt that as far as the academic research enterprise is concerned, the Funding Council has been responsible for the most effective instrument of change in terms of, first, the achievement of a policy goal of growing importance to government: research selectivity and concentration; and second, its influence on institutional and individual behaviour. The funding council's research funding is distributed to universities by an increasingly competitive formula-driven resource allocation system, based on the RAE. Its power lies in several factors; most important is the magnitude of the impact it has had on both universities' finances and their reputation. Second is the degree of the internal as well as external credibility of the RAE; third is its longevity.
>
> (Henkel and Kogan, 2010, p. 361)

In fact, the impact of research selectivity has gone far wider than research, an issue we shall return to in Chapters 7 and 9.

Chapter 5

The funding of undergraduate education

But there is also a third challenge. To make the system for supporting students fairer. Having a university education brings big benefits and while the Government will continue to pay most of the cost involved in studying for a degree, it is also reasonable to ask students to contribute to this.

(DFES, 2003, p. 2)

Currently, one of the barriers to alternative providers is the teaching grant we pay to publicly-funded HEIs. This enables HEIs to charge fees at a level that private providers could not match, and so gives publicly-funded HEIs a significant advantage. Our funding reforms will remove this barrier, because all HEIs will – in future – receive most of their income from students via fees. This reform, of itself, opens up the system.

(Willetts, 2011, p. 2)

Introduction

The costs incurred in studying for a degree are conventionally considered as falling into two categories: the funding of teaching and the funding of student support, i.e., living costs (what in the United States is called 'aid' and what is here called 'maintenance'). These distinctions will be used here as we consider both the marketisation of the funding of undergraduate courses (fees – paid directly by the student or from a scholarship fund – have always been a major means of funding postgraduate study), and changes in the funding of student support. Most of this chapter will refer to the situation in England, but we will also look more briefly at changes in the funding of undergraduate education in Scotland, Wales and Northern Ireland since these began to diverge from England after 2000. Except where indicated, no distinction is made between full- and part-time courses. Historically, the main difference has been that subsidies for part-time courses have usually been lower than those for full-time ones. However, the new student funding regime from 2012 extends income-contingent fee loans to part-time students for the first time, although the terms are not quite the same.[1]

The main issues in the funding of teaching include:

- The balance between tuition fees ('fees') and government grants ('grants' or 'block grants') as the means by which institutions fund their teaching.
- (Linked to this) the proportion that fees represent of the cost of provision.
- Whether the fee varies by provider.
- The extent to which the student is required to meet the fee costs (a) from his/her own pocket and (b) up-front, in advance of embarking on the course.
- The balance between public and private contributions to tuition and maintenance costs, what has become known internationally as 'cost sharing' (Johnstone, 1986).

In the funding of student support the main issues include:

- The extent to which non-repayable means-tested support (whether through grants, the new National Scholarship Programme or institutions' own bursaries) is available to cover costs, and thus reduce any financial barriers to participation.
- The basis on which loans for student support are subsidised and the terms on which they are to be repaid – with the principal contrasting models often referred to as 'income contingent' and 'mortgage-style'. Within this debate, there is particular interest in the extent to which different models of subsidy may, or may not, be considered regressive (i.e., favouring those who are already better off, possibly at the expense of those from lower-income groups).

Historically, British universities received a significant proportion of their income from fees. But with the post-war expansion, block grants came to replace them. By the 1960s, fees represented only a small part of institutions' income for teaching, and there was no fee competition. Moreover, the fee was usually paid by the Government: Halsey (1995, p.12) even described full-time university students at this period as 'state pensioners'. In the case of maintenance also, the UK has historically had one of the most generous regimes, especially for those not studying from home (Johnstone, 1986). Following the 1960 report of the Anderson Committee (Anderson, 1960), a means-tested maintenance grant payable by local education authorities to students on most full-time courses was introduced in place of the previous mish-mash of county and state scholarships. Half a century later, the position has changed almost completely. Fees and maintenance continue to receive a subsidy but this is much reduced and is mainly delivered indirectly, through favourable terms offered for student loans. Fees are intended to cover all or most of the cost of teaching most subjects, and the level of fee varies by provider.

The key developments that took place between 1979 and 2012 to achieve this significant shift in the sources of funding for the teaching of undergraduates and for their living costs were:

- The Government's decision in 1979 that fees for overseas students should no longer be subsidised, so that in future they should be charged full-cost fees.
- The Government's decision in 1989 that the fee level for Home/EU students should be substantially increased, so that a higher proportion of the cost of teaching would be met from the (still subsidised) fee.
- The freezing of the student grant in 1990, and with this the introduction of subsidised, mortgage-style loans to cover an increasing share of living costs.
- The introduction in 1998 of a means-tested, up-front, fee of £1,000. In parallel, although generating surprisingly little comment at the time, the abolition of maintenance grants, so that even those from the lowest income families had to fund their living costs through student loans, albeit operating under a subsidised, income-contingent scheme. Grants were reintroduced in a more limited form in 2004.
- The introduction in 2006 (in England) of a variable fee regime under which institutions were allowed to charge up to £3,000, with the fee backed by a government-subsidised, income-contingent loan (so that the cost of the fee would not need to be found initially from the student's own resources). Block grants linked to student numbers continued to be available towards teaching costs, but now represented only about 60 per cent of the institutions' funding for teaching, compared with nearly three-quarters before 2006. Institutions charging the full £3,000 – which turned out to be the vast majority – were obliged to make at least £300 available in the form of annual bursaries for students from low-income households; this and other measures to increase participation were included in institutional Access Agreements, policed by a new regulatory body, the Office for Fair Access (OFFA). The means tested grant scheme was also enhanced.
- The introduction in 2012 (in England) of a variable, full-cost fee regime under which institutions are allowed to charge up to £9,000; at the same time block grants for teaching will be removed for all but the so-called SIVS ('strategically important and vulnerable subjects' – laboratory sciences, mathematics, quantitative social sciences, area studies and modern foreign languages) and a number of other priority areas. Income-contingent loans to cover fees and maintenance continue to be available at subsidised rates, although for high-earning graduates the rates of subsidy are lower.

The rest of this chapter considers these milestones and the wider context in which they occurred in more detail, beginning with the introduction of full-cost fees for overseas students in 1980.

Overseas student fees

As far back as 1963, the Robbins Committee had drawn attention to the historic subsidies for overseas university students as a form of foreign aid. It recommended an increased fee for both Home and overseas students as well as a fund to help needy overseas students (Committee on Higher Education, 1963).

In December 1967, the Labour Government did introduce a differential fee for overseas students, but one that was still well below cost. Then, in 1969, as one of Mrs Williams's '13 Points' (see p. 78), the Government proposed a more restrictive admissions policy for overseas students; yet in spite of government requests to universities and education authorities to stabilise recruitment, numbers continued to grow.

With this pattern of admissions nationally, it seems almost certain that any administration after 1979 would have returned to the issue, although the complete removal of the state subsidy does not appear to have been contemplated until then (Williams, P., 1981). In November 1979 the new Conservative Government published *The Government's Expenditure Plans for 1980/81* (HMT, 1979). Given the overriding need to reduce public expenditure and the political pressure to give priority to Home students, the Government considered it right to remove progressively the subsidy in the education budget of around a £100 million a year on provision for overseas students. From the start of the academic year 1980 81, all overseas students beginning courses of higher and further education in Great Britain would be expected to pay a fee covering the full cost of tuition (Williams, P., 1981). Accordingly, the 'minimum recommended' fees for new overseas students were raised from £940 (undergraduate) and £1,230 (postgraduate) to £2,000 for arts courses, £3,000 for science courses and £5,000 for medicine (the same fees applied to both under-and postgraduate courses). This was an average increase of nearly 300 per cent (Williams, L., 1987).

The November 1979 announcement was criticised by a wide range of bodies, the main concern being that the wider educational, commercial and political benefits of an open policy towards overseas students were being put at risk. There were also protests from overseas governments and their local representatives. In response, the Government made a number of concessions, excluding EU students (other than Greece before September/October 1981) and introducing an overseas postgraduate research scheme for students of high calibre to enable them to study at the same fee level as British ones. However, the full-cost fees regime remained in place. Overseas student numbers fell for a few years but then resumed their upward trajectory (Greenaway, 1995).

Commenting on institutions' responses to the new regime a few years afterwards, Peter Williams wrote:

> For almost the first time British public education institutions had been aware of being in a market in which the customer calls the tune. Instead of the selective supply-oriented system in which institutions would choose from a queue of applicants, the course designers have had to look hard at what students want.
>
> (Williams, P., 1984, p. 271)

He speculated on the strains that might arise from a dual pricing system:

In an essentially competitive situation, can competition be confined and differential costs and quality be glossed over by maintaining the present regime of minimum recommended fees? Or are we about to see a disintegration of the long-proclaimed uniformity of quality and standards in the UK higher education system? The fact that all of these questions are increasingly being asked underlines the point that overseas student policy, while ostensibly primarily a dimension of overseas relations, has profound implications for the operation of the domestic education system, particularly where – as in the British case – an attempt is made to run a dual regime, with all its inherent contradictions.

(Williams, P., 1984, pp. 273–274)

The increase in the overseas fee was a harbinger of further changes in university funding. The March 1981 Public Expenditure White Paper (HMT, 1981) proposed a sharp reduction in public expenditure on institutions. There was to be a 15 per cent cut in current higher education expenditure between that year (1980–81) and the final year of the planning period (1983–84). Whilst university capital expenditure would continue almost unchanged, other funding for the sector would be reduced by 35 per cent. Johnes and Taylor (1990) estimated that there was an 8.7 per cent cut in Exchequer funding of universities (real recurrent income) between 1980–81 and 1984–85. Almost as significant as the scale of the cuts was the fact that the UGC applied them selectively. At one extreme, Salford suffered a real terms cut in funding of 36 per cent between 1980–81 and 1984–85; Keele (26 per cent), Bradford (24 per cent), UMIST (22 per cent) and Aston (20 per cent) were the other principal sufferers. However, York received 8 per cent more funding and Cardiff 4 per cent more. There can be little doubt that, although highly controversial at the time, the selective application of the cuts reduced the difficulties associated with selectivity and thus helped to pave the way for research assessment.[2]

Sir Keith Joseph and student funding

In 1984, wanting to protect the science budget from further cuts, the Secretary of State, Sir Keith Joseph, decided that the minimum student grant of £205 per year, awarded to those from the most affluent families, should be scrapped. The contributions to maintenance due from others 'in the middle and upper reaches of the income scale' would be increased, and the richest would have to pay up to £520 per year towards tuition. This breached the long-standing principle that teaching should be provided free of charge whatever the parental contribution toward living expenses. The overall saving was estimated at around £40 million. Half of this would be put towards protecting the worst-off students from earlier grant cuts, with the rest going to science.

Perhaps unsurprisingly, the package was agreed with Treasury without much difficulty. But there was Conservative backbench fury as soon as the changes were announced, on 12 November 1984. A motion deploring the new policy was tabled, and eventually signed by 180 Members, more than half the Parliamentary party. There was a difficult meeting with the Backbench Education Committee where matters were not helped when Joseph told them, in an aside, that in his view the way ahead lay in partial loans for maintenance. The Prime Minister and the Chancellor, Nigel (now Lord) Lawson, were prepared to come to terms (Joseph privately offered his resignation, which the Prime Minister declined). At a meeting at Number 10 on 5 December a face-saving formula was devised. As a result, Joseph told the House later that day that the proposal to charge tuition fees would be withdrawn, at a cost to the Treasury of £21 million. But he stood by the rest of his package, and more than half of the cost of his concession would be covered by additional cuts: the scientific community would lose £3 million from their augmented research budget (Denham and Garnett, 2001; Lawson, 1992).[3]

The raising of the Home/EU fee

In April 1989, the Government proposed that the by now £607 tuition fee should be raised to £1,600 with effect from the 1990–91 academic year, and that from 1991–92 a system of differentiated fees should be introduced which reflected the costs of teaching different subjects (Baker, 1989). The fee would continue to be met from public funds. The differentiated fees, announced in November 1990, were from £1,725 for classroom-based subjects to £2,650 for laboratory and workshop-based subjects, and £4,770 for medicine, dentistry and veterinary science. In order not to increase total direct public expenditure on teaching, corresponding transfers would be made from the moneys given in block grant to the funding councils. This would mean that by 1991–92 about 30 per cent of each university's income would come from fees, compared with only 8 per cent in 1989–90. The block grant share would fall to 70 per cent, compared with 92 per cent previously (DES, 1989).

The Government saw two advantages in increasing the fee. First, by making institutions' income dependent in large measure on their ability to attract and satisfy student demand, it would improve the effectiveness of marketing and teaching. Second, to the extent that the higher fee income covered marginal costs, it would encourage institutions to exploit spare capacity by taking in additional students, increasing participation while reducing unit costs. The Government also wanted to see the universities becoming more independent of the state by diversifying their sources of income.

The rationale for these changes – and so far as can be seen, the first explicit government reference to a market in higher education – was set out in a speech by the Secretary of State, Kenneth (now Lord) Baker, at Lancaster University in January 1989. After unfavourably contrasting the British system with American diversity, flexibility and accessibility, Baker said that we might be approaching 'a fundamental choice between two different patterns of evolution':

One route towards mass higher education could be through an increasingly state funded and therefore state organised 'system' of higher education. There is a real possibility that this will be the course followed on the Continent. If this is the path we follow, the difficulty which the institutions of higher education will face is that the expansion of provision by the State – with taxpayers' money – will be expected to take place without substantially increasing the burden of public expenditure and taxation, and in the absence of mechanisms for engaging private funding. The other route, which I have already indicated that I would prefer, would see the movement towards mass higher education accompanied by greater institutional differentiation and diversification in a market-led and multi-funded setting ...

In the first scenario, the structures of mass higher education will tend to be increasingly rationalised, under pressure to stretch public funding as far as it will go. The effect will be to offer a limited variety of institutional structures and missions, providing a range of broadly similar experiences to all, and producing a range of similar outcomes for all. In the second scenario, the structures of mass higher education will be much more diversified, as they are in the United States. The traditional modes of provision will still, of course, be cultivated: but there will be a much greater emphasis on the variety of approaches better able to meet the needs of different types of students.

Why do I prefer that we in Britain should take the second of these two routes, that of expansion through diversification and differentiation? Most profoundly, because it seems to me to be the one which is natural to us. Historically, traditionally, Britain is a bottom-up, not a top-down society. We should build on our national genius, and what comes naturally to us.

(Baker, 1989, pp. 11–12)

Even with a tuition fee of £607, institutions had some incentive to recruit 'fees only' students because the £607 represented a cash bounty over and on top of the block grant, perhaps equating to marginal cost in some institutions. At £1,600 and above, institutions had a still greater incentive to do so. Thus, in the early 1990s, a number of former public sector institutions effectively gorged themselves on 'fees only' students, demand having increased chiefly as a result of changes on the supply side, notably the integration of GCE O Levels with the Certificate of Secondary Education to form the new GCSE (ironically, under threat at the time of writing this book from one of Baker's Conservative successors), and the consequential increases in the numbers of sixth-formers. Moreover, since under the then existing Public Expenditure Survey rules, fees – unlike the block grants to the institutions – were not cash limited, Treasury was effectively underwriting the additional enrolments by not clawing back the extra cash to which the expansion of student numbers would commit it (for both teaching and student support). This was on the basis that whilst overall expenditure might go up, cost per student would go down, as indeed it did. As we shall shortly see, these rapid increases in student numbers (and the resultant additional call on the public purse) were only brought to an end with the introduction of institutional quotas in 1994–95.[4]

The introduction of maintenance loans

As we have already noted, from 1962, as well as having their tuition fees fully covered by the state, British students had had their living costs met by a system of means-tested maintenance grants, which remained virtually unchanged although their real value had declined. Nevertheless, they became an increasing item of public expenditure as participation in higher education increased. It is not therefore totally surprising that the reduction or removal of grants, together with a system of loans, was one of the '13 Points' (essentially, ideas for reducing costs) that the Secretary of State, Shirley (later, Lady) Williams put to the vice-chancellors in 1969 (Kogan and Hanney, 2000).

Although student loans were not introduced until 1990, according to Lord Lawson (1992), Sir Keith Joseph had talked to him shortly after he became Chancellor in June 1983 about maintenance loans. There was no formal contact until 1985. The idea was that the loans would be interest-free but with repayments linked to inflation. However, whilst Lawson was receptive, the Prime Minister, Margaret Thatcher, was opposed; this is confirmed by Lord Baker (1993) and by Denham and Garnett (2001). When Baker succeeded Joseph as Secretary of State in 1986, he persuaded the PM that the issue should be reopened.

An internal departmental review group was therefore established to look at the costs of student support. It was chaired by the Minister for Higher Education, George Walden. Two years later, the Government published a consultative paper (DES, 1988a) based on the work of the review, and proposing that from 1990–91 a loan facility at nil real interest for £420 (average) in a full year should be introduced (£310 in a student's final year). The existing parental contribution and the maintenance grant would be held steady in cash terms: in effect, grants were being phased out. The loan facility would be increased each year until it was equal to the value of the grant and the parental contribution together.

The reasons given for the proposals were:

- to share the cost of student maintenance more equitably between students themselves, their parents and the taxpayer.
- to increase the resources available to students.
- to reduce, over time, the contribution to students' maintenance which is expected from parents.
- to reduce, over time, direct public expenditure on grants.

- to implement the Government's decision to reduce the students' dependency by removing them from the social security benefits system.
- to increase economic awareness among students, and their self-reliance.

(DES, 1988a, p. 1)

Legislation to give effect to the new system of support was enacted in 1990, the Education (Student Loans) Act. Loans subsequently accounted for an increasing proportion of student support. Students' eligibility for social security benefits like housing benefit and income support during vacations was removed. However, a small amount of additional funding (£25 million) was made available for Access Funds for students facing financial hardship (Woodhall and Richards, 2006). This amount was subsequently doubled.

Although repayments could be deferred where a graduate's income was low, the Government rejected a fully income-contingent repayment scheme along the lines advocated by Nicholas Barr and actually introduced in Australia in 1989 (Chapman, 2006). Barr first proposed such a scheme at a meeting with the Higher Education Minister, Robert (now Lord) Jackson, in July 1988 (Nicholas Barr, personal communication). Barr's first publications on the subject appeared the following year (Barr, 1989a, b and c). As we shall see, income contingency was not accepted for maintenance loans until 1998, and for fee loans not until 2006.

Contractual funding and bidding for numbers

The increase in the undergraduate fee and the introduction of student loans were just two of a number of reforms introduced by the Government at this time, with the declared aim of increasing competition and reducing costs; others included increased selectivity in the funding of research (discussed in Chapter 4) and the abolition of tenure for newly appointed academic staff. The reforms were implemented by two new funding agencies – UFC and PCFC – that were more directly accountable to government than their predecessors, UGC and NAB.

Another important move was to introduce 'contractual' funding and institutional competition for teaching funds. The 1987 White Paper *Higher Education: Meeting the Challenge* (DES, 1987) announced that, instead of grants, the two new agencies would operate a new system of 'contracting' with institutions. The Government's intention was to:

- Encourage institutions to be more enterprising in attracting contracts from other sources, particularly the private sector, and thereby to lessen their present degree of dependence on public funding.
- Sharpen accountability for the use of the public funds which will continue to be required.
- Strengthen the commitment of institutions to the delivery of the

> educational services which it is agreed with the new planning and fund-
> ing body they should provide.
>
> (DES, 1987, paragraph 4.17)

This approach was reflected in the initial guidance letters to the new agencies (DES, 1988a and b).

Although the UFC and PCFC began operations in the autumn of 1988, they did not take over the functions of their predecessors until April 1989. In the UFC's case, the transition should have been eased by the fact that the last Chairman of the UGC, Sir Peter Swinnerton-Dyer, was also the first Chief Executive of the UFC. In accordance with the requirement that funds should only be provided in return for a 'product' – the 'something for something' principle – both councils introduced a system whereby institutions had to bid for grants to cover a fixed number of student places, the aim being to encourage the provision of higher education at a lower cost to the Exchequer. But there were significant differences in their approaches.

The PCFC:

- Aimed to cover only the first year of the new planning period (1991–92).
- Invited bids for up to 5 per cent of existing places.
- Proposed no 'guide price'.

The UFC:

- Attempted to cover the whole of the planning period.
- Expected bids to cover the whole of an institution's teaching.
- Proposed a set of 'offer prices' based on the average unit cost in each subject in 1989–90.

The PCFC's methodology achieved a 6.5 per cent increase in funded places in 1990–91, together with a reduction on funding per student of 2.6 per cent (Turner and Pratt, 1990). The UFC's exercise was a fiasco. The Council was well behind the PCFC, the guide prices only being announced in January 1990, far too late to take effect later that year. Only a small proportion of the bids submitted (13 per cent) was below the guide price. The Council had therefore to abandon its methodology so that in 1991–92, as well as in 1990–91, universities received funding based on their historic allocations but with an imposed 1.5 per cent efficiency gain as their reward (for a fuller account, see Taggart, 2004; see also Johnes, 1992). As we noted in Chapter 3, the existing universities' unwillingness to bid, coming on top of similar 'failures' to expand numbers in the 1980s, helped to 'cook their goose' in the Government's eyes and was one of the factors that contributed to the Government's decision to abolish the binary line.[5]

The introduction of top-up fees

An important development in the regulation of public expenditure on universities was the Government's decision in late 1993 that, with effect from 1994–95, institutions should be set student number limits: Maximum Aggregate Student Numbers or MASNs. Any institution recruiting more than 1 per cent above its quota would incur a financial penalty. The change of policy ('consolidation'), which also involved a 45 per cent cut in the level of the fee, was announced in a statement by the Secretary of State, John Patten, on 30 November (DES, 1993). The Funding Council subsequently explained how the new policy would be applied: as well as maximum and minimum numbers of full-time and sandwich places for each institution, there would be no marginal funding for growth in full-time or sandwich students (HEFCE, 1993b).[6]

As the minister made clear, this was a response to the expansion which had occurred since the late 1980s in the context of the public expenditure crisis which accompanied Britain's departure from the Exchange Rate Mechanism of the European Monetary System in September 1992. Student numbers in fact increased from 937,000 in 1985–86 to 1.72 million in 1995–96, a substantial proportion of the latter having entered before the MASNs took effect. A particular consideration was the cost of maintenance grants, which had not been 'cash limited' under the Baker expansion. In the meantime, the unit of funding for teaching had continued to decline: the Dearing Committee found that public funding per student for higher education had declined from a value of 100 in 1976 and 79 in 1989 to 60 in 1994 (National Committee of Inquiry into Higher Education, 1997).[7]

A senior civil servant involved at the time has confirmed that the expansion policy had succeeded so well that Treasury began to be alarmed almost as soon as it was launched. However, there was also the difficulty of reconciling actual non-cash limited expenditure with plans, the nature of such expenditure being that such discrepancies are almost certain to arise. Eventually, in 1993, Treasury insisted that more vigorous steps were taken to control spending and MASNs were born.

Two years later, in November 1995, the universities received outline information about the funding settlement for 1996–97 (DES, 1995). This meant a real terms reduction in capital and recurrent funding of 7 per cent in a year. It was discussed at the Main Committee of the Committee of Vice-Chancellors and Principals (CVCP) in December. The committee had already, in September 1993, and following a review of funding options, accepted that a student contribution to the cost of teaching was inevitable, alongside increased public funding, preferably through an income-contingent loan scheme. The Budget statement was received with a mixture of horror and incredulity. It was suggested that consideration should be given to a possible charge of a top-up fee, a standard fee payable at all institutions which would include a contribution for scholarships. It should be made clear that such a move was a response to the Budget statement. The fee could be increased in line with future funding cuts. The discussion also referred to a possible withdrawal of cooperation with regulation. It was agreed to return to the matter early in the New Year. In the meantime the committee reaffirmed its commitment to a graduate contribution to fees and maintenance through an income-contingent loan scheme (CVCP Main Committee minutes, 8 December 1995).

At its next meeting, in February 1996, the committee considered a paper setting out options for a collective response. The paper recommended that unless by the end of the year there was movement towards a new system of funding, a special levy should be introduced on all full-time Home and EU undergraduate entrants from 1997–98. The amount of the levy would depend on the scale of the cuts for 1997–98, so that government spending plans would trigger the levy. The committee agreed to consider this with the institutions, with a view to decisions being taken at the September conference. The impost would be called the 'government deficiency levy' (CVCP Main Committee minutes, 2 February 1996). By this time, however, the Government was looking at various ways of taking higher education funding off the agenda, and in particular keeping fees out of the General Election due by the following year. It had already approached Sir Ron Dearing, former Chair of PCFC and HEFCE, and a well known government 'fixer', about conducting an inquiry. This was eventually announced in May 1996 after consultation with the Opposition Front Bench.[8]

It is interesting to speculate why these pressures did not surface sooner. Watson and Bowden (1999) suggested two main reasons. First, there was undoubtedly room for efficiency gains within the system. Second, until the really significant expansion of the late 1980s, the two former sectors consciously behaved differently. The university sector resisted the temptation to grow by enrolling students at the marginal cost of tuition fees. The public sector met the challenge as if growth had no end, with institutions like Ealing (later Thames Valley University, now the University of West London), and Dorset (now Bournemouth University), expanding with the objective of enhancing their status.

The Dearing Committee

The Dearing Committee's terms of reference were couched in very broad terms:

> To make recommendations on how the purposes, shape, structure, size and funding of higher education, including support for students, should develop to meet the needs of the United Kingdom over the next 20 years, recognising that higher education embraces teaching, learning, scholarship and research.
> (National Committee of Inquiry into Higher Education, 1997, p. 3)

However, there was little doubt in most people's minds that the central task was to find a politically acceptable way of getting more private financial support for university teaching. Moreover, there was a very tight timescale, the committee being required to report by the summer of the following year.

The committee – which was composed of a wide range of members but where representatives of higher education and large companies predominated – reported in July 1997, two months after a General Election which had brought 'New' Labour into Government, with Tony Blair as Prime Minister. The report acknowledged and confirmed the wider public benefits of higher education which justified continuing state involvement in funding:

> Society as a whole has a direct interest in ensuring that the United Kingdom has the level of participation in higher education which it needs for sustained economic and social viability, and, therefore, to match those of its competitors. This has been a recurring theme in our report. This means that the state needs to ensure that higher education provision is adequate and receives the level of funds needed to support the necessary levels of participation. Whilst the measurable financial benefits from higher education qualifications accrue largely to individuals, the costs of a shortfall in the numbers of those obtaining such qualifications will fall to the UK as a whole and its citizens.

> Firms and individuals are most likely to engage primarily in training specific to their immediate needs. There is therefore a danger that, if left to employers or individuals, the nature and level of higher education will not best serve the long term needs of the economy as a whole; and there will be under-investment. The state alone is able to ensure that tomorrow's workforce is equipped with the widest range of skills and attributes.

> The state must also ensure that access to higher education is socially just, and that talent is not wasted.
> (National Committee of Inquiry into Higher Education, 1997, p. 288)

But the committee also considered that graduates in employment should make a greater contribution to future costs. It therefore recommended that the Government should shift the balance of funding, in a planned way, away from the block grant towards a system in which funding followed the student, with a target of distributing at least 60 per cent of total public funding to institutions according to student choice by 2003 (National Committee of Inquiry into Higher Education, 1997, p. 297).

At the same time, the committee rejected – at least for the short to medium term – the market-based approach advocated by the Confederation of British Industry. This would have seen qualified applicants issued with cash credits equivalent to current funding, and institutions able to charge fees above the value of the credit where they felt able and wished to do so. Instead, the committee recommended that the Government should introduce arrangements for graduates in work to make a flat-rate contribution which over time would equate to around a quarter of the average cost of tuition. The contribution, of about

£1,000, should be made through an income-contingent mechanism which should also be applied to student maintenance, in place of the mortgage-style loan arrangements introduced in 1990. The proportion of tuition costs met in this way should not be increased without an independent review and an affirmative resolution of both Houses of Parliament. The proceeds of the graduate contributions should be reserved for meeting the needs of higher education.

The abolition of maintenance grants

The Dearing Committee noted the 'almost universal' view among those it consulted that maintenance loans, with their fixed-term mortgage-style repayments, should be replaced by an income-contingent system, where payments were based on a per centage of a graduate's income:

> The main advantage of such schemes ... is that they fix monthly payments at a level charged to be affordable in relation to an individual graduate's income. Instead of all graduates with an outstanding loan of a certain size paying the same monthly amount once their income has reached a threshold, those on the lowest incomes pay the least each month and those on higher incomes pay more. The higher the graduate's income, the sooner he or she will complete their payment. Unlike the current arrangements, income contingent schemes provide reassurance to those entering higher education that they will not face unmanageable repayment burdens, whatever their post-graduation income.
>
> (National Committee of Inquiry into Higher Education, 1997, p. 309)

The committee recommended that such income contingency should apply to both maintenance and fee loans.

In response, the Government accepted the principle that a greater proportion of funding should follow the student. But the committee's proposal for an income-contingent contribution paid after graduation was replaced by a contribution of the same amount from students at the start of their course: a 'top-up' fee. To assuage concerns about the possible disincentive effects on access, and to mollify the National Union of Students, the contribution would be means tested. Students from lower-income families who would previously have been eligible for a maximum maintenance grant would pay no fee at all. As a result, around one in three of all students in England and Wales (in Scotland, over 40 per cent) whose parental income was assessed would receive free tuition, and another third would not have to pay the full amount.

Instead of maintenance grants, additional subsidised maintenance loans were to be provided on an income-contingent basis, with a threshold of £10,000 to ensure that no student, parent or family need be worse off than under the previous arrangements. Hence the expected parental contribution towards fees and maintenance would be no greater in real terms than the current expected contribution to maintenance costs for students. The Government would monitor the impact of the arrangements on participation. Finally, the Government accepted the committee's recommendation that any increase in the proportion of tuition costs met privately should be subject to Parliamentary approval (DFEE, 1998). The necessary changes were enacted in the Teaching and Higher Education Act 1998, and came into force in autumn 1998.

It seems clear that the main reason for the Government's rejection of the Dearing recommendation was the need to keep higher education expenditure within the limits set, in effect, by the previous administration (the new Government having pledged to keep within the previous Government's spending plans). The legislative process was rushed, with changes to fees and funding introduced which would affect students who had already applied to university for entry in 1998, creating difficulties for individuals, and administrative problems for institutions.

As we have seen, the Government rejected the principle of income contingency for fee loans. Whilst accepting it for maintenance loans, it also abolished maintenance grants although a number of special provisions, such as Hardship Funds for specially needy (but generally full-time students), were introduced (Woodhall and Richards, 2006). Although initially not the subject of much attention or protest, over time the abolition of maintenance grants, alongside the introduction of up-front tuition fees, was a significant contributor to the almost universal unpopularity of the post-1998 funding regime.

The fact that within a few years a further review was set in train by the same Government was an early acknowledgment that the changes generated longer-term problems too, not least the fact that the increased level of debt was seen as a particular problem for low-income students. Indeed, it was only a few months after the first students who had paid tuition fees under the changes introduced by the 1998 Act had graduated that the Secretary of State, Estelle Morris (2001), said:

> Four years ago we took the brave and right decision to expand higher education by changing the way we funded student support. However, it was clear during the General Election that student debt was a major issue. I recognise that for many lower-income families the fear of debt is a real worry and could act as a bar to higher education. I want to make sure that our future reform tackles this problem. Our aim is to get more children from less privileged backgrounds into higher education and we hope to better achieve this by changing the combination of family, student and state contributions.

Watson and Bowden's (2005) verdict seems just:

> Essentially, New Labour was too greedy. They took the Dearing recommendation of a student contribution to course costs and ignored what the Report said about living costs, especially for poorer students. Simultaneously, they completed a Conservative project of turning all student grants into loans. This precipitate decision has become the Achilles heel of subsequent New

Labour policy for higher education. Almost every major policy initiative, and certainly every discussion of how the system should be funded overall, has been drawn back into a kind of maelstrom of misunderstanding, of posturing and of bad faith about costs and charges to students, exacerbated by an aggrieved middle class sense of entitlement.

(Watson and Bowden, 2005, p. 2)

The introduction of variable fees in England

In spite of the introduction of MASNs and top-up fees, student numbers continued to increase. The Government had in the meantime committed itself to increasing 18–30-year-old participation in higher education to 50 per cent by 2010 (Blair, 1999). Tuition fees (and the abolition of maintenance grants) were unpopular and among the most frequently raised issues on the doorstep during the 2001 General Election. Accordingly, Prime Minister Tony Blair's speech to the October 2001 Labour Party Conference (Blair, 2001) mentioned that there would be a review of student support. The financial position of the institutions had again worsened and there remained the substantial backlog of under-investment highlighted by Dearing, which had estimated an annual shortfall of £250 million in capital funding (National Committee of Inquiry into Higher Education, 1997, p. 277).[9]

Almost as soon as the ink was dry on the new regime, in fact, there began to be lobbying by the most prestigious universities to be allowed to charge higher fees, for example, the report by Greenaway and Haynes (2000) for the Russell Group. Major Parliamentarians such as Lord Jenkins of Hillhead (also Chancellor of Oxford), influential commentators like the *Financial Times's* Martin Wolf, and leaders of major institutions such as Sir Richard Sykes (Imperial College) and Anthony (now Lord) Giddens (LSE) added their voices to the throng.

UUK published a series of reports on funding options. The final report stated:

Significant damage has been done by many years of underfunded expansion, which since 1989 have seen resources per student fall by 38 per cent, following a decrease of 20 per cent between 1976 and 1989; staff-student ratios decline to an average of 1 to 17 (1 to 23 if funding for research which is included in the average unit of funding is excluded); the academic labour market made uncompetitive by institutions' inability to pay their staff adequately; the quality of the teaching and learning infrastructure diminished by insufficient investment; increasing levels of non-completion experienced particularly by universities offering access to the disadvantaged; and a realisation that without additional funds the cost of legislation on disability and on equal pay for work of equal value will not be met.

(UUK, 2001, p. 1)

The report identified four ways in which (in addition to voluntary contributions from alumni, employers and other benefactors) an estimated gap of £370 million in 2004–5 (or £272 per student in 2001–2 prices) could be plugged: increased public funding through the block grant; additional (but not full-cost) fees; an income-contingent graduate contribution; or institutional endowments through the sale of public assets. It did not express any preference for the strategy that should be adopted.

In January 2003 the Government published a White Paper *The Future of Higher Education* (DFES, 2003). The document began with a sharp critique of the effects of previous policies:

- Higher education must expand to meet rising skill needs.
- The social class gap among those entering university remains too wide.
- Many of our economic competitors invest more in higher education.
- Universities are struggling to recruit and retain the best academics.
- Funding per student fell 36 percent between 1989 and 1997.
- The investment backlog in teaching and research facilities is estimated at £8bn.
- Universities need stronger links with business and [the] economy.

(DFES, 2003, p. 4)

This appears to have been the first explicit recognition by the Government of the significant underfunding of investment in higher education (Tony Bruce, personal communication).

The Government envisaged a three-pronged strategy to meet the sector's financial needs.

First, there would continue to be an increase in public support. Spending on higher education would increase from around £7.5 billion in 2002–3 to almost £10 billion in 2005–6, a real terms increase of over 6 per cent each year. Within this, expenditure on teaching and learning would increase from £3.9 billion to £4.9 billion.

Second, the Government would encourage universities to build up their endowments. However, the only concrete proposal was for the establishment of a 'time limited, matched endowment fund', to which any university could apply. The matched funding would 'incentivise university fund-raising from individuals, companies and other sources such as the disposal of underused assets' (DFES, 2003, p. 82).[10]

Third, the Government would introduce a new Graduate Contribution Scheme. Universities would be allowed to seek a contribution of up to £3,000 per year for each course. Up-front payment of tuition fees would be abolished. Every student would be allowed to defer payment until after they had graduated. Payments would be made through the tax system and be linked to the ability to pay, with the lower threshold, for both fee contribution and maintenance loan repayment, raised to £15,000. Maintenance grants for up to £1,000 a year for students from lower-income families would be reintroduced, and the Government would also pay the first £1,100 of fees for such students.

The White Paper justified the decision to allow fees to vary by institution and course in the following terms:

> It is absolutely clear that students get different returns from different courses. The graph below shows the different earnings premia obtained by women students taking different degree subjects. More recent research found a 44 percentage point difference in average returns between graduates and institutions at the two extremes of the graduate pay scale. We believe that a revised contribution system should recognise these differences properly, and not ask students who can't expect such big prospects in the labour market to subsidise those that can, through a flat fee. This also means that institutions will be able to reap rewards for offering courses that serve students well. This will make student choice a much more powerful force, and help choice drive quality.
>
> (DFES, 2003, pp. 83–84)[11]

The Government did, however, recognise that a wholly unregulated fee scheme posed dangers to access, with some institutions setting fee levels that some students might not be able to afford and which could deter others. Thus institutions wishing to introduce a contribution higher than the current standard fee (by now, £1,100) would first need an Access Agreement approved by a new access regulator (OFFA). This would outline the plans of the university or college for student financial support (bursaries and scholarships) and for outreach activities designed to widen participation; it would also contain milestones that the institution had set itself to monitor progress in improving access.

The legislation to implement the new policy was enacted as the Higher Education Act 2004 and came into effect in 2006. In order to get the legislation through Parliament, the Government was forced to make a number of concessions. Three of the most important were:

- A requirement that institutions charging fees of over £2,700 should provide bursaries worth at least the difference between their fee and £3,000 (i.e., up to a maximum of £300) to students receiving the full state maintenance grant, although in practice the large majority established more generous bursaries. This condition was set so that, together, the maximum grant of £2,700 (increased, under Parliamentary pressure, from the £1,000 a year originally proposed) and this specified minimum bursary covered the fees of these students. Such students could therefore choose not to take out a fee loan, and would only need to borrow money to cover maintenance costs. Presentationally, therefore, students from the lowest income families could be considered to have the costs of their fees covered from non-repayable funds; notwithstanding the fact that this argument conflated grants, that had traditionally been seen as a contribution towards living costs, with a means to fund tuition.

- Acceptance on the part of the Government that the monies raised by institutions from higher fees should be *additional* to the monies provided to support teaching through the block grant. Grants now represented about 60 per cent of institutions' funding for teaching, as compared with nearly three-quarters before 2006 (Nigel Brown, personal communication).
- An assurance that any increase in the maximum fee (beyond annual index-linking) would require a vote in Parliament and agreement that the new regime, and especially the impact on access, should be the subject of an independent review before any proposal to increase the real value of the fee/contribution was made (this was established in November 2009, see below).

It appears to have been accepted quite early on in the 2001 Labour administration – and in spite of its 2001 manifesto pledge *not* to introduce top-up fees – that an increased student (or graduate) contribution to the cost of teaching was unavoidable. However, the actual form of such a contribution was an issue between the Prime Minister and the Chancellor, with the former favouring an increased fee and the latter a graduate tax (where the graduate contribution was not limited to the cost of the course). There was also a prolonged debate about the level of the fee, the *Times Higher* finding under a Freedom of Information request in 2005 that until quite close to the publication of the White Paper the intended maximum was £5,000, as sought by the Russell Group (Baty, 2005).

There can be little doubt that the figure was reduced because of nervousness on the part of the Government Whips, a nervousness that proved to be well founded: even with the concessions, the draft legislation passed its crucial Second Reading in the House of Commons on 27 January 2004 with a majority of just five, even though the Labour Government's Parliamentary majority at that time was 161. Among that majority were more than five MPs representing constituencies in Scotland, a region of the Kingdom to which the provisions of the resulting Higher Education Act (2004) did not apply, the West Lothian issue in earnest.[12]

Once the resulting changes to undergraduate fees and funding had been introduced in 2006 – other than a small peak in admissions in 2005, followed by a slight drop in 2006 – there was little evidence that they had affected participation, a point we shall revert to in Chapter 7. However, the Government was keen to ensure that maintenance grants were available to a significant proportion of undergraduates. In January 2007 the Minister for Higher Education, Bill Rammell announced that from 2008–9 onwards the eligibility thresholds for grants would be changed, the objective being to increase the proportions of students receiving maximum or partial grants to a third each (Rammell, 2007). So from 2008–9 students with residual household incomes of up to £60,000 (as compared with £37,500 in 2007–8) would receive a partial grant, while those with a residual household income of up to £25,000 (as opposed to £17,500 in 2007–8) would receive a full grant. However, it soon became apparent that this extension of eligibility had resulted in a higher proportion of students than intended receiving at least partial grants. The Secretary of State, John Denham, therefore announced in October 2008 that from 2009–10 the upper limit of residual family income for receiving some grant would be reduced to £50,020, with students from families with income of up to £25,000 still getting the maximum grant (Denham, 2008). On this basis, about 40 per cent of undergraduates would receive a full grant, with a further 26 per cent receiving a partial grant (Carasso, 2010).

A full-cost fee regime in England

The independent review conceded by the Government was established on 9 November 2009. It published its report a year later. The review was conducted by a committee chaired by Lord Browne of Madingley, former Chief Executive of British Petroleum. The small committee included two serving vice-chancellors, one of whom had also been Chief Executive of HEFCE. By this time, a new Conservative/Liberal Democrat Coalition Government had succeeded the Labour administration that had established the review, and the country was undergoing an economic crisis with big cuts in public expenditure from May 2009 onwards.

The terms of reference were to:

> analyse the challenges and opportunities facing higher education and their implications for student financing and support. It will examine the balance of contributions to higher education funding by taxpayers, students, graduates and employers. Its primary task is to make recommendations to Government on the future of fees policy and financial support for full- and part-time undergraduate and postgraduate students.
>
> (Independent Review of Higher Education Funding and
> Student Finance, 2010, p. 57)

Like the Dearing Committee before it, the Browne Committee argued that more investment was needed for the sector. But unlike Dearing, the Browne group believed that the student/graduate contribution should be increased so that for all but a small group of 'priority subjects', the tuition fee should be met *wholly* from private sources, albeit with the continuation of publicly subsidised income-contingent loans (which should for the first time be extended to part-time students). The priority subjects might include science and technology, clinical medicine, nursing and other health care degrees, and 'strategically important and vulnerable' language courses, a group now referred to as 'SIVS'. Institutions would continue to receive block grants for teaching only in these cases.

Moreover, other than through consumer resistance, there should be no limit to the fees institutions could charge, although there should be levies on institutions charging fees of over £6,000, which would in effect claw back most of the additional revenue: at £9,000 and above, institutions could retain £7,500 with the rest used to subsidise student support. The overall costs to public expenditure would be contained through centrally regulated minimum entry standards laid down each year by the Government and based on the UCAS Tariff (a system of 'equivalences' between different types of entry qualification). Candidates admitted with lower qualifications would not be eligible for state support, whether directly through grants or indirectly through subsidised loans. The new regime would be controlled by a new Higher Education Council bringing together and integrating the funding and regulatory responsibilities of HEFCE, the QAA, OFFA and the OIA.

The committee claimed three main benefits for these proposals.

First, there would be financial scope for the sector to expand. There should be a 10 per cent increase in the number of places as well as increased support for part-time and low-income students.

Second, quality would be improved:

> Our proposals are designed to create genuine competition for students between HEIs, of a kind that cannot take place under the current system. There will be more investment available for the HEIs that are able to convince students that it is worthwhile. This is in our view a surer way to drive up quality than any attempt at central planning. To safeguard this approach, we recommend that the Higher Education Council enforces baseline standards of quality; and that students receive high quality information to help them choose the HEI and course which best matches [sic] their aspirations.
>
> (Independent Review of Higher Education Funding and Student Finance, 2010, p. 8)

Third, higher education would be put on a better long-term financial basis:

> In our proposals, the system is put on a more sustainable footing by seeking higher contributions from those that can afford to make them, and removing the blanket subsidy for all courses – without losing vital public investment in priority courses. These measures create the potential to allow the numbers of student places to increase by 10 per cent and enhance support for living costs whilst still allowing public spending reductions to be made.
>
> (Independent Review of Higher Education Funding and Student Finance, 2010, p. 8)

Considering student support, the Browne Committee recommended that the loan system for the cost of living should be simplified so as to create one flat-rate entitlement of £3,750. This would mean that anyone applying for a loan would know exactly how much funding they were eligible for, and that no means test would be needed if they were only seeking a loan. Maintenance loans would be repaid on the same terms as fee loans. The maximum grant for living costs for students from low-income backgrounds on top of the loan should be raised to £3,250, with the full grant available up to a household income of £25,000 (very close to the national median income), and a partial grant up to a household income of £50,000 (about double the median income). All students should receive at least as much cash in hand as at present (total of grant and maintenance loan).

The Government welcomed the thrust of the report (DBIS, 2010) but indicated its intention to continue to limit fees. There would be a new 'graduate contribution threshold' of £6,000 a year. 'In exceptional cases', universities could charge up to £9,000 if they met 'much tougher conditions on widening participation and fair access'. Universities and colleges charging above £6,000 would have to meet conditions set by OFFA, demonstrating how they would spend some of the additional income to make progress in widening participation and fair access. These proposals would be set out in annual Access Agreements for which OFFA's approval would be needed if the institutions and their students were to access public funding. The Government agreed that fee loans should be extended to part-time students studying at the rate of at least 25 per cent of a full-time course.

The Government also announced that graduates would not need to make a contribution towards tuition costs until they were earning at least £21,000, up from the previous £15,000. The annual repayment would be set at 9 per cent of income above the £21,000 threshold. All outstanding repayments (which the Government estimated at some 30 per cent of all loans taken out) would be written off after 30 years. To make the system financially sustainable, a real rate of interest would be charged on loan repayments, but with a progressive taper up to a maximum of inflation plus 3 per cent. The net result would be that between 25 and 30 per cent of graduates with the lowest lifetime earnings would pay less than under the existing system.

As regards support, the Government agreed that maintenance loans should be increased for students from families with incomes of up to £60,000. Students from families with incomes up to £25,000 should be entitled to a more generous student maintenance grant of up to £3,250, and those from families with incomes up to £42,000 should be entitled to a partial grant (DBIS, 2010). The 2011 White Paper (DBIS, 2011a) confirmed that students from families with a household income of £25,000 or less would receive a full grant of £3,250 together with access to a maintenance loan of £3,875 (if they were studying away from home outside London). Those with household incomes below £25,000 might also be eligible for help under the new National Scholarship Programme, co-funded by the Government and individual institutions, which would guarantee for 'bright potential students from poor backgrounds' benefits in kind such as a free first year or a foundation year (DBIS, 2010).

Implementing the 2012 reforms

The House of Commons voted in favour of the new fee cap of £9,000 (effective from 2012–13) in December 2010, with significantly less Parliamentary controversy than had preceded the vote six years earlier to introduce variable fees. However, given that during the General Election Campaign earlier that year, one of the partners in the Coalition – the Liberal Democrat party – had made a manifesto pledge to abolish university tuition fees, there was inevitably critical comment in the media. There were also a number of protests around the country, some of which turned violent, including one on 10 November 2010, when some 200 of an estimated 52,000 marchers broke into Conservative Party Headquarters in London.

Most comment at the time focussed on the fee increases and whether the loan repayment terms were more or less equitable than those they superseded. However, in the context of the argument in this book, the critical issue was the switch away from subsidising institutions to subsidising students. This reflected the view, also held by the Browne Committee, that student education was now essentially a private good, as it had been adjusted to be for non-EU students since 1980. Moreover, the increase in the fee cap was only one element of the Government's planned reforms. In June 2011 the Government issued a White Paper *Higher Education. Students at the Heart of the System* (DBIS, 2011a) justifying its package of proposals. Whilst the £9,000 limit would remain, institutions' core student number allocations would be reduced in order to create a margin for redistribution. Those core student numbers would exclude places filled with students whose entry grades were at least AAB in A levels (or equivalent, known as 'AAB+'), an estimated 65,000 entrants. Student places in this category were to be uncapped – creating an element of the system in which it was hoped that provision would adjust to satisfy demand (whether those universities that recruit the majority of their students with AAB+ qualifications will actually expand their undergraduate provision is something we shall consider in Chapter 7).

From the remaining core student numbers, a 'margin' of 20,000 places was to be created, by a proportional reduction across institutions. Those charging fees averaging no more than £7,500 (after any fee waivers) would then be free to bid for an allocation from those 20,000 places. This created an incentive for the provision of additional places at the lower end of the expected range of fees to be charged. This was a clear response to the large number of institutions that had indicated their intention to charge the maximum fee or very close to it; indeed, once the details of this policy had been announced, 24 universities and one college took the opportunity that was offered to revise their Access Agreements, and lower their fees, to enable them to bid for places from the margin (OFFA, 2011).

The details of the new funding methodology were the subject of consultation, the outcomes of which were announced in October 2011 (HEFCE, 2011c and g). The main change from the White Paper was that the SIVS would be exempted from the cut to create the margin. Direct HEFCE funding will continue to be available for these subjects, for small and specialist institutions, and for the additional costs of attracting and retaining students from disadvantaged backgrounds.

The funding allocations for 2012–13 were published in March 2012 (HEFCE, 2012b). Alongside the grant allocations, the Funding Council published the student number control limits for 2012–13. These include estimates of the total number of undergraduates each institution will be likely to recruit and the likely year-on-year change. Some 34 institutions have seen their number limits cut by 10 per cent or more, the overall reduction being 3 per cent. Those hit hardest were those that have lost places under core-and-margin, were unable to successfully bid them back, and are unlikely to be able to increase significantly their numbers of AAB+ students. Many are large metropolitan universities. The medium to longer-term likelihood is that, depending on what happens with student demand, these providers will reduce their fees, downsize or merge with others. Even before the implications of the AAB+ policy were clear, the Government announced (Willetts, 2012b) that the removal of the numbers cap would be extended to ABB+. The structural implications of the new funding regime are considered further in Chapters 7 and 9.

The other countries of the UK

During the period under consideration, responsibility for higher education policy has increasingly been devolved to Scotland, Wales and Northern Ireland. Where policies did not apply across the whole of the UK, those described above applied to England. By the time the Higher Education Act 2004 had been implemented in England in 2006, the differences were already so significant that fees for undergraduate degrees within the UK ranged from £0 to £3,000 – and the variability applied not only to the location of the institution, but also to the home address of the student within the UK (EU, non-UK students attending universities in each UK country were, and are, admitted on the same basis as local students although they are not eligible for maintenance support). The introduction of the maximum fee of £9,000 in England from 2012 has exacerbated these differences, to the extent that students from England could pay fees of £36,000 over a four-year undergraduate course in Scotland, whereas Scottish students on the same course will pay nothing.

It is not only in fees that policies vary; in their account of the changes up to 2006, Woodhall and Richards (2006) argued that the reintroduction of means-tested grants – admittedly on a far more restricted basis than before 1990 – was almost certainly influenced by the fact that both Scotland and Wales had already done so. It is time to look, albeit briefly, at the evolution of the arrangements of funding student education in the Scotland, Wales and Northern Ireland (for a detailed account, see Bruce, 2012).

Scotland

Under the Scotland Act 1998, the funding of higher education institutions in Scotland became the responsibility of the new Scottish Parliament, which in 1999 established an independent inquiry under Mr (later, Sir) Andrew Cubie. The committee recommended that the up-front tuition fees introduced in 1998 should be replaced by compulsory contributions to a Scottish Graduate Endowment, payable after graduation and collected through the tax system on an income-contingent basis. There should also be non-repayable, means-tested bursaries for low-income students. This new regime was introduced in an amended form in 2001–2, with an initial contribution of £2,000, subsequently index linked. The contribution could either be paid on graduation, or a loan could be taken out for the full amount and repaid after the graduate's income reached £10,000 (later increased to £15,000). These tuition contributions only applied to Scottish – and EU – domiciled students at Scottish universities, whilst the means-tested bursaries were limited to Scottish-domiciled students at Scottish institutions (this was subsequently modified so that Scottish-domiciled students outside Scotland could receive such bursaries but at a lower rate). This was the first significant departure from the UK-wide arrangements for funding student education that had applied since significant state funding began after the First World War.

In 2008, the Scottish Parliament abolished the post-graduation levy. (Scottish) graduates earning over £15,000 a year continued to be eligible for means-tested maintenance loans. Non-repayable bursaries continued to be available for low-income students. In 2011, the Scottish Education Secretary announced (BBC News, 2011b) that undergraduate courses in Scottish institutions would continue to be free for Scottish students. Scottish universities and colleges would be able to charge up to £9,000 to students from elsewhere in the UK, replacing the fixed fee that has been charged to such students since 1989. In September 2011, Edinburgh University announced that it would charge non-Scottish students £9,000 a year, making a total of £36,000 for what is usually a four-year course.

In December 2011, the Scottish Government announced that it had allocated additional funds to Scottish institutions to ensure that they 'kept up with England'. The main teaching grant will rise by 10.6 per cent and the research grant by 4.7 per cent. On average, universities will see their main teaching and research grants grow by 14 per cent (Matthews, 2011d).

Wales

In 2000 the Minister for Education and Lifelong Learning appointed an independent committee under Professor Theresa Rees to investigate future funding options. The committee reported the following year. Since the Welsh Assembly did not then have the same powers as the Scottish Parliament, the committee could only recommend the Assembly to use its best endeavours to persuade the UK Government that up-front tuition fees should be abolished and replaced by an end-loaded income-contingent Graduate Endowment Contribution. In the meantime, they recommended a considerable increase in resources for student support, the introduction of means-tested bursaries for Welsh-domiciled students in both higher and further education, and the establishment of a Financial Contingency Fund to act as a 'safety net' for all learners at Welsh institutions, including those domiciled in England or other parts of the UK. As a result, there were significant increases in funding for student support. In 2002 the National Assembly introduced Assembly Learning Grants for low-income students domiciled in Wales, including those studying elsewhere in the UK.

The Higher Education Act 2004 gave the National Assembly the same powers to determine policy on tuition fees as the devolved administration in Scotland (and Northern Ireland). The Assembly invited Professor Rees to lead a further inquiry and her committee's report was published in 2005. Its main recommendation was that universities and colleges should be able to charge 'deferred flexible' fees, from 2007–8, and up to £3,000. A National Bursary Scheme should be established – by 'top slicing' the additional fee income – to provide 'targeted bursaries' for Welsh and non-Welsh-domiciled UK students at Welsh institutions (Independent Study into the Devolution of the Student Support System and Tuition Fee Regime in Wales, 2005). The introduction of an Assembly fee grant meant that Welsh students studying in Wales did not have to pay an increased fee. The fee grant was introduced in 2007 and abolished in 2010.

In 2011, the Welsh Assembly administration decided to reintroduce a fee grant for Welsh-domiciled students. From 2012 Welsh institutions can charge non-Welsh students fees of up to £9,000. Welsh students will have to pay £3,465 a year. However, Welsh students studying elsewhere in the UK are also subsidised so that they pay only £3,465. It should be noted that the previous fee grant applied only to Welsh students studying at home.

In January 2012, the Welsh Assembly administration announced its decision that almost half of the available student places in 2012–13 would be placed in a margin (unlike in England where the margin will be 8 per cent). Half of these places were to be allocated on the basis of research and total income, and half to institutions charging below £7,500. This could have meant individual institutions losing up to 57 per cent of their places unless they reduced their fee (Matthews, 2012b). In the event, five institutions were forced to lower their fee below £7,500 (Matthews, 2012c).

Northern Ireland

Until recently, Northern Ireland has followed closely the fees policy adopted in England, reflecting financial necessity rather than any enthusiasm for market principles. During a period of direct rule, in 2004, the Northern Ireland Office decided to apply the same variable fees and maintenance grant policies as were to be introduced in England in 2006, although subsequently the level of maintenance grant payable to Northern Ireland domiciled students from low-income families was increased. Among the various funds provided to assist poorer students, was a non-repayable maintenance grant for students from lower-income households of £3,145, which was introduced in 2008.

Northern Ireland has faced considerable funding pressures as a result of the new fee arrangements being introduced in England in 2012 but, following a consultation, the Executive rejected the advice of an independent review which had recommended an increase of the fee cap to between £5,000 and £5,750 (DELN I, 2011). It has sought to minimise the resulting funding gap of £40 million by restricting fee concessions to Northern Ireland domiciled students studying in their home country (and other EU students) who will continue to pay fees at their 2011–12 level. It will also mitigate the effect of public expenditure cuts on higher education funding by redeploying resources from other government departments and securing efficiencies in its two universities and elsewhere. Northern Ireland students studying in the rest of the UK will not receive a grant to meet the cost of the higher fees because this would be unaffordable. The Department for Employment and Learning, Northern Ireland (DELNI) will continue to be responsible for the cost of tuition fee loans for these students and it is considering how institutions could be encouraged to reduce the outflow of students from Northern Ireland.[13]

The English fee cap of £9,000 has also been applied to their incoming students from the rest of the UK, with the aim of increasing fee income while avoiding any significant increase in recruitment levels. However, the decision to exclude these students from student number controls may reduce opportunities for home-domiciled students who could find that entry requirements rise as a result.

The funding of undergraduate education – summary

The history of the funding of undergraduate education in the UK between 1979 and 2012 may be summarised thus:

- At the beginning of our period, the funding of teaching was mostly through block grants to institutions. Fees were nominal and paid by the state. This pattern began to change with the introduction of full-cost fees for overseas students in 1980. It culminated in the introduction of such fees for all students in most subjects in England from 2012, with the remaining direct state subsidies being confined to a handful of priority areas. As a result, the HEFCE teaching grant is expected to decline from 64 per cent of teaching funding to institutions in 2011–12 to about 25 per cent by 2014–15.
- In 1980 the fee represented only a small part of the average cost of provision. After 2012 in England it will equal or exceed the average cost in most institutions and subjects.
- Similarly, in 1980 the fee represented a claim only on the resources of overseas students. After 2012 in England it will be a claim on the resources of all students once they graduate and are earning enough.
- In 1980 the home fees were recommended levels which all institutions followed. After 2012 in England there will be genuine competition on price between institutions within the limits set by the Government. There is also likely to be more competition on bursaries and scholarships than there was after 2006.
- In 1980, students' living costs while studying were met by a system of means-tested maintenance grants. By 2012 in England, students' living costs are being met by a combination of maintenance grants and subsidised loans, where the maximum value of the grant is £3,250 and that of the loan is £5,500.

If we now recall the analytical framework introduced in Chapter 2, we can see that the funding of undergraduate education in the United Kingdom, and especially in England, is almost a textbook case of a transition from a 'non-market' towards a market-based system, albeit that both prices and, for a majority of enrolments, student places will continue to be controlled, at least for the time being.

Chapter 6

Quality assurance

> There are few indicators of teaching performance that would enable a systematic external assessment of teaching quality to be made. [If universities knew] the Committee would be glad to be told how they had done it.
> (UGC, 1985, p. 16, quoted in Cave *et al.*, 2000, p. 9)

> We have developed the Key Information Set, which will give prospective students access to high quality information about different courses and institutions, enabling them to make informed choices.
> (DBIS, 2012c, paragraph 1.4)

> Now it's the market, not the commonweal, that calls the shots.
> (Kirp, 2003, p. 3, quoted in Burke and Associates, 2005, p. 9)

Introduction

Between 1979 and 2012 the UK moved away from a non-market system of regulating teaching quality so that by the end of the period the market was beginning to play a much more significant role in quality assurance, the protection of quality. The main developments were:

- The creation of system-wide quality assurance arrangements in the 'old', pre-1992 university sector from 1990.
- The creation of a single quality regime for the newly unified sector after 1992.
- Attempts to link institutional funding to quality judgements, from 1993.
- The introduction and growth of information requirements on universities from 2001, and especially from 2005, so that market information has become a key element in quality assurance.

The underlying theme is one of how successive governments sought to incentivise the raising of quality through regulation, funding and information.

Although not as radical as the divergences over tuition fees, there were after 1992, and especially after 2001, growing differences in the way in which quality assurance developed in Scotland and Wales. These will also be described. The chapter ends with some reflections on how the structure and governance of quality assurance changed over the period.

The creation of system-wide quality assurance arrangements in the university sector before 1992

In 1988, the Committee of Vice-Chancellors and Principals (CVCP) agreed to establish a unit to monitor and review universities' quality assurance arrangements. The Academic Audit Unit began work two years later but had only a brief existence before being incorporated into the new Higher Education Quality Council (HEQC) in 1992. To appreciate the significance of the vice-chancellors' decision, we need first to provide a brief sketch of the quality assurance arrangements then appertaining in the two sectors.

From their inception, the polytechnics and colleges were subject to a dual system of quality regulation. CNAA, an independent chartered body established in 1964, actually awarded the qualifications to which their degree programmes led. At diploma level, a similar function was performed by the Business and Technology Education Council (BTEC, now EdExcel). Some institutions also offered courses leading to External University of London degrees. In addition, Her Majesty's Inspectorate (HMI) inspected their provision. On top of this, programmes aiming to confer exemptions or advanced standing upon those seeking to qualify for the practice of a particular profession were subject to accreditation by the relevant professional body. It is true that over time CNAA moved away from the scrutiny of individual courses to the periodic review of institutions, with responsibility for validation and approval of new courses being delegated to those institutions that were felt to have earned it ('accreditation': see Harris, 1990). But CNAA never delegated the awarding function, and even to the end it retained the right to approve institutions' external examiners.

By contrast, the universities each had their own degree-awarding powers. They employed external examiners to protect comparability and fairness in assessment. But there was no external assurance regime, although where they sought exemptions for their students from professional exams they were also subject to professional body accreditation; this in effect extended to programmes of Initial Teacher Training, where HMI were 'invited' into the providing institution (the same formula being used in the initial academic audits). With these limited exceptions, the universities were effectively sovereign, their quality and standards not being subject to any external scrutiny or oversight.

In September 1983 the Secretary of State, Sir Keith Joseph, wrote to the UGC saying that it was particularly important that the universities undertook a realistic assessment of the means by which standards were to be maintained and enhanced, and asking what prospects there were for more radical changes directed to the maintenance or improvement of quality in the context of a more efficient use of resources in universities (CVCP Main Committee, 28–29 September 1983, Paper 83/91, MSS 399/1/1/43). In response, and after some discussion, the CVCP established an Academic Standards Group under Professor Philip Reynolds, Vice-Chancellor of Lancaster, to study and report on institutions' methods and procedures for maintaining and monitoring academic quality and standards (CVCP, 1986, p. 10). This was welcomed by the Secretary of State (Main Committee Minutes, 16 December 1983, MSS 399/1/1/43).

Between 1984 and 1986 the Reynolds group produced codes of practice on external examining, postgraduate training and research, and institutional appeals procedures. There were also papers on external involvement in academic standards and institutions' internal procedures (CVCP, 1986). A year later, the Group reported that the majority of universities' practices generally followed, 'albeit more informally', the Reynolds guidance. In nearly all institutions some changes had been made (CVCP, 1987). A second report in 1988 indicated that although all universities 'had embraced the standards in general', there were a number of specific areas where the guidance was not being followed in all places. These included the need for external examiners' reports to be in writing and be seen by the vice-chancellor, the separation of examination from supervision for postgraduate students, the need for centrally planned and monitored course monitoring, the desirability of seeking students' views on courses on a regular basis, and the benefits of the systematic monitoring of student performance (CVCP, 1988).

By this time, discussion in the committee was moving towards putting the collective oversight of universities' control of quality and standards on a more permanent basis. An office note for the January 1988 Main Committee (VC/88/5) (MSS 399/1/1/47) referred to a speech by the Secretary of State, Kenneth Baker, to the recent North of England Education Conference, in which he had asked whether the universities accepted an obligation to give an account of their stewardship to their customers and the taxpaying public. The note sought preliminary views on whether the committee should assume a stronger role in reviewing and reporting on academic standards and quality. It observed that the committee's role so far had been that of offering guidance and advice to universities on academic matters, and more recently of seeking general information about how far practice conformed to such advice. In the light of developments affecting higher education as a whole, and the increasing pressure for public accountability, there might be a case for CVCP setting up some form of permanent national academic review body for the university system. Such a body, composed of senior academic members, could promote the maintenance and improvement of academic standards and quality by undertaking regular reviews of aspects of universities' academic activities (courses, exams, teaching), giving advice to the committee and individual universities, and issuing public reports from time to time.

Supporting the paper, the Chairman (Sir Mark Richmond, Vice-Chancellor of Manchester) said that there now seemed to be a case for a further central initiative. The General Purposes Committee (GPC) recommended that agreement should be given to this in principle, and that detailed proposals should be brought forward. The Main Committee agreed that a special group should be appointed, to report back via the GPC; it was also agreed that the group should have some external members (CVCP Main Committee Minutes, 15 January 1988). Accordingly, Dame Sheila Browne (Principal of Newnham College, Cambridge, previously Senior Chief Inspector), Patrick Coldstream (Director of the recently created Council for Industry and Higher Education), and Kenneth Kitchen (Registrar of Manchester) joined several vice-chancellors under the chairmanship of Michael (later Sir Michael) Thompson, Vice-Chancellor of Birmingham.

The majority of this Group favoured a stronger central role, not least because otherwise the UGC/UFC – and in due course possibly a single funding body armed with CNAA/HMI experience – might move in; a minority view was that this 'would only lead to league tables and the like'. The group recommended to the GPC that whilst universities should certainly be more transparent in the ways in which they set and maintained academic standards, the CVCP should *not* set up a central unit. However, perhaps more aware of the wider position, the GPC, at its meeting on 10 June 1988, decided to overrule the Thompson Group, and recommend to the Main Committee that they should agree in principle to the establishment of a central review body, with further consideration being given to its terms of reference and functions in relation to universities and the committee (Paper VC/88/68, Main Committee, 1 July 1988) (MSS 399/1/1/47).

At the Main Committee, the Chairman advised that the CVCP should accept the GPC's recommendation. The Principal of King's College, London, Stewart (later, Lord) Sutherland, who had been a member of the Thompson Group, drew attention to its emphasis on the need to review practices and procedures in relation to academic standards. He also referred to the general view of the group that the committee as a whole should be in a position to know and to say whether it was satisfied with the procedures followed by the universities in membership. The Committee agreed to the GPC's recommendation and an announcement to that effect was made after the following, September, meeting (CVCP Main Committee Minutes 1 July 1988; CVCP Press Release dated 29 September 1988) (MSS 399/1/1/47). What was called the AcademicAudit Unit was established in 1990. It audited 29 universities before its absorption into HEQC (see next section). Professor Sutherland was the Chair of the Steering Committee for the new unit and played a key part in building support for it within the Committee.

It is clear that the vice-chancellors saw the Reynolds Group as a 'task and finish' exercise, and that without external pressures they would not have gone further. These pressures were not only from government. There was a growing feeling from early in the decade that as the system expanded and competition increased, there needed to be greater accountability for quality, and that this could not just be left to individual institutions. For example, the SRHE/Leverhulme Report in 1983 stated:

There is certainly a case for some convergence of practice … along with some universities [the polytechnics and colleges of higher education] may in the future find themselves under pressure to compromise academic quality in attempting to maintain student numbers or earn income from other sources. Some coordination of arrangements is desirable to try to ensure, for example, that academic standards for similar activities do not diverge too widely between institutions, that students are not misled about the nature of courses they select, that they are assessed fairly and in an equivalent manner throughout higher education, that the requirements of professional bodies are not oppressive for individual students or institutions, that criteria for student credit transfer are efficient and fair, and that funding bodies are well informed about the academic merits of different activities.

(SRHE, 1983, pp. 14–15)[1]

Another important influence was the Lindop report (DES, 1985b), with its critical comments about the variability of universities' validation of college courses, something confirmed when HEQC began its audits of collaborative provision in 1994. The Thompson Group had before them a number of recently published academic articles about variations in standards between different departments and subjects, from both sides of the binary line. But it is also clear that the vice-chancellors were well aware of the risk that if they themselves did not take action, someone else might do so: the office note mentioned previously referred to the post-Lindop role of CNAA as being to promote and disseminate good practice and to maintain and enhance the quality of courses, primarily in the public sector, but also in the higher education system as a whole. It also mentioned a recently published article in the *Higher Education Quarterly* in which Pauline (later Baroness) Perry, Director of the Polytechnic of the South Bank but previously a Senior Inspector, had argued that HMI need not threaten university autonomy.

We should nevertheless not underestimate the amount of 'trauma' involved in the decision to accept some collective responsibility for institutions' standards. This indeed was one of the key differences, in the author's view, between the leaders of the pre- and post-92 universities. Although they complained, sometimes with good reason, about the CNAA, the Committee of Directors of Polytechnics (CDP), PCAS (the public sector admissions agency, subsequently merged with the universities' admissions agency UCCA to form UCAS) and PCFC, the polytechnic directors recognised that such agencies had been a vehicle for collective action that had developed their institutions and raised their status to the point where, as we saw in Chapter 3, incorporation and university title were by the mid-1980s almost inevitable. In contrast, the vice-chancellors cherished their autonomy and were always instinctively opposed to collective action even when, as with CVCP and, later, HEQC, it was under their control. This does, incidentally, make it even harder to understand the sector's increasingly supine attitude towards growing government involvement in quality assurance since 1997, culminating in the White Paper proposals for an enhanced role for HEFCE (see below).

The creation of a unified quality regime

The AAU had hardly commenced operations before it faced a major threat to its existence. As described in Chapter 3, the Government issued a White Paper *Higher Education: A New Framework* (DES, 1991) in May 1991 announcing its intention to abolish the binary line and allow the polytechnics and certain other colleges to obtain a university title; the CNAA would be abolished. Paragraphs 58–59 of the document stated:

> The prime responsibility for maintaining and enhancing the quality of teaching and learning rests with each individual institution. At the same time, there is a need for proper accountability for the substantial public funds invested in higher education. As part of this, students and employers need improved information about quality if the full benefit of increased competition is to be obtained.

> As demand for higher education expands further, and as competition among institutions increases, as a result of the changes outlined in the preceding chapters, the Government considers that new arrangements for quality assurance in higher education will be required.

The White Paper proposed another 'dual' system:

- A quality audit unit to 'check that relevant systems and structures within an institution support its key teaching mission'. This would be owned by the institutions but the Government would take reserve powers to establish it if the institutions did not.
- A quality assessment unit in each Higher Education Funding Council to 'assess the quality of what is actually provided'. These assessments of quality 'should continue to inform the funding decisions of the new Funding Councils'. This aspect of their role is considered in the next section.

> (DES, 1991, p. 24)

In the event, the quality assurance arrangements for the newly unified sector were not quite as set out in the White Paper. The representative bodies, led by CDP, argued that to gain the maximum benefit from CNAA experience, the institutionally owned quality audit unit should have a broader remit than simply reviewing institutions' quality arrangements. There also needed to be a research/ dissemination of best practice function along the lines of the CNAA's successful Quality Support Group (this became in due course the new Council's Quality

Enhancement Group). The new organisation should also continue the CNAA's work in promoting credit accumulation and transfer and, with CVCP, accrediting recognised providers of Access Courses. The author drafted the necessary documents as CDP Chief Executive.

The Department accepted these proposals and the name of the new organisation was broadened to reflect this: the Higher Education Quality Council. HEQC also soon took on the job of advising ministers on applications from institutions for degree-awarding powers and university title. This was all on the basis that the institutions collectively had a responsibility to ensure adequate systems of quality assurance across the sector. HEQC began operations in autumn 1992 and the first HEQC audits were carried out the following year. The author was HEQC's Chief Executive from July 1993 until its demise (for a fuller account of these developments, see Brown, 2004).

Subsequent changes

There were four major changes in the national quality assurance arrangements between 1992 and 2012.

First, after much discussion between the Department, the funding councils and the representative bodies, HEQC was dissolved and its responsibilities passed to a new agency, the Quality Assurance Agency for Higher Education (QAA) in August 1997. The assessment activities of the funding councils (though not the responsibilities) also moved to the new agency, which operates them under a contract with the Funding Council. The rationale was that quality assurance would be more effective if it was carried out by one body rather than two organisations that were perceived to be competing with one another. The representative bodies (CVCP and SCOP) were the legal owners of the new agency, but institutional representatives were in a minority on its board (the funding councils also nominated four directors with the balance being held by six independents).

Second, after an announcement in March 2001 by the Secretary of State, David Blunkett, of a 40 per cent reduction in quality assurance, Teaching Quality Assessment, by now known as Subject Review, came to an end other than on an exceptional basis: for a transitional period audit teams would follow 'disciplinary audit trails' up to a maximum of 10 per cent of an institution's provision (for a fuller account of these developments, see again Brown, 2004). The disciplinary audit trails were eventually laid to rest following a review by the cross-sector Quality Assurance Framework Review Group in 2005, of which the author was a member (HEFCE, 2005).

Third, following a critical report on the national quality assurance regime by the House of Commons Innovation, Universities, Science and Skills Committee (IUSSC) in 2009, a number of changes were made to institutional review. The number of areas scrutinised by reviewers was expanded from two to four; the judgement categories were increased from three to four; students were to become full members of review teams (following successful experience in

Scotland); to make the process more flexible and responsive, there would be a rolling programme of reviews rather than a fixed cycle; and a distinction would be made between a core coverage of activities based on common criteria, and one or more 'thematic elements' to be determined centrally. Although never officially acknowledged, the main purpose of the changes was to respond to the Committee's charge that the review process was not sufficiently focussed on academic standards (for the details of the changes and the background to them, see Brown, 2010a).

Finally, the 2011 White Paper *Higher Education: Students at the Heart of the System* (DBIS, 2011a) announced the Government's intention that while all providers should be covered by a single quality framework, options should be explored in which the frequency, and perhaps even the need, for full scheduled institutional review might depend on 'an objective assessment of a basket of data, monitored continuously and at arms length', the aim being to achieve 'very substantial deregulatory change for institutions that can demonstrate low risk'. This was termed a 'risk-based approach to quality assurance'. In May 2012 HEFCE published a consultative document (HEFCE, 2012c) proposing that institutions with two 'successful' institutional reviews should receive less frequent and possibly less intensive reviews ('Route B'); 'successful' would mean that they had made 'timely improvements', where the review judgement had been that the provision concerned required improvement or did not meet expectations. The frequency of such reviews might be as much as ten years. Other institutions would continue to receive full regular reviews ('Route A') until they had reached the Route B threshold. However, out-of-cycle reviews could be triggered by student concerns 'at departmental or institutional level'. There would also be annual reviews of 'key data and information', which could prompt an earlier than anticipated investigation where there were 'warning signs or indications of long-term trends' that suggested that quality or standards might be at risk. These reviews would be conducted by an internal HEFCE group, together with a new external review panel: come back, CNAA, all is forgiven!

As a result of all these developments, the national quality assurance framework now has four main strands:

- Institutional review.
- The new UK Quality Code for Higher Education, which sets out the expectations all providers of UK higher education are expected to meet. The new code has three sections: on standards, quality and information. It incorporates the existing Code of Practice, covering all aspects of quality management; the Framework for Higher Education Qualifications, containing descriptors of the academic expectations associated with each level of award; Subject Benchmark Statements outlining what can be expected in terms of the abilities and skills needed to develop competence and understanding in (currently) 93 subjects or fields of practice at Honours and Masters levels; and guidelines for 'programme specifications', setting out the intended

aims and outcomes of each programme of study. The existing code, the
Framework, the benchmark statements and the guidelines for programme
specifications were previously known as the 'academic infrastructure'; all
stem from HEQC's work on graduate standards in the mid-1990s which
was endorsed and adopted by the Deary Committee (see Brown, 2004).

- A Causes for Concern procedure enabling the QAA to investigate serious
  complaints about quality or standards from any source.
- Enhanced information for students (see below).[2]

Linking funding and quality

As already indicated, one of the Government's purposes in introducing Teaching Quality Assessment was to link institutional funding to quality. Institutions
that provided better teaching were to be both rewarded directly, through greater
funded student numbers, and indirectly, through an enhanced reputation with
students. This had in fact been one of the themes or requirements of the Department's initial Guidance Letters to the new Funding Councils in 1988 (DES,
1988b and c) although, as we saw in Chapter 5, they had gone about it in very
different ways.

As described there, the PCFC's new funding methodology for teaching involved
institutions receiving the equivalent of 95 per cent of their previous year's funding and then bidding for funded places equivalent to the value of the remaining
5 per cent. Institutions' bids were considered on the basis not only of price, but
also of quality. The necessary decisions were made with the advice of official subject groups broadly representative of the sector, but also involving HMI: HMI
judgements covered teacher performance, student learning and the educational
environment (HMI, 1989). In effect, institutions had to meet a threshold quality judgement for their bids to be successful: a high quality judgement ('Q')
meant a higher discount on their bid price (and therefore potentially more funded
places) than a lower-quality one ('q'). This approach was adopted after CNAA,
against the advice of its Chief Executive, declined to furnish such comparative
information. By contrast, rather than weighting bids according to quality, the
UFC's approach was to regard quality as just one factor in the allocation process:
'Although the UFC wanted universities to bid against each other to create a market situation for teaching allocations [it] needed to ensure that cheapness did not
lead to a loss of quality'(Taggart, 2004, p. 71).

In accordance with the White Paper and the 1992 Guidance Letter to the new
Council (DES, 1992), and informed by PCFC practice, the 1993 HEFCE Circular outlining the purposes and features of assessment included 'to inform funding and reward excellence' (HEFCE, 1993a, p. 4). Accordingly, the provision
assessed would be categorised as 'Excellent', 'Satisfactory' or 'Unsatisfactory'.
On the basis of a self-assessment, institutions would decide what to claim and
peer assessors would visit a large sample, including all those that had established
a 'prima facie' claim to excellence, or where there were potential grounds for

concern. In this way, 553 of the 972 completed self-assessments were the subject of a visit (HEFCE, 1995a). In 1995, following a review, the Council moved to a different framework whereby institutions received scores of between 0 and 4 on each of six aspects of provision).[3]

In practice, as Wagner (1993) pointed out at the time, the funding councils' scope for linking funding to assessment outcomes was limited. The Council funded teaching in eleven 'programme areas' but carried out its assessments in subject groups that formed only part of each area. Moreover, most of the judgements were expected to fall in the Satisfactory category. In any case, the whole exercise was overtaken by the ending of the late-1980s expansion and the introduction of quotas (MASNs) from 1994, which meant no more additional funded places for anyone (see Chapter 5). So the only use that was made of assessment scores for funding in England was in connection with the Fund for the Development of Teaching and Learning in 1995, where the lead department in a bidding consortium had to have an Excellent rating; this was not repeated when the successor programme, the Teaching Quality Enhancement Fund, was established in 1999. In Scotland, institutions receiving an Excellent rating in a subject area received an additional 5 per cent of funded student places in the successful department. In Wales, institutions received either additional funded places or financial support for institutional projects.

However, this was not the end of government attempts to link funding to quality.

In July 1996, HEFCE issued a consultative paper about the method for funding teaching from 1998–99 (HEFCE, 1996a). Amongst the aims of the proposed new method was 'to promote quality in teaching and learning'. For this purpose, 'quality' was envisaged as one of the criteria to be taken into account in assessing institutions' bids for additional funded student places. The paper outlined various ways in which this could be done. In response, the CVCP argued that, with the discussions then going on about a single quality agency, this could be premature (CVCP, 1996). The proposal was dropped.

As noted in Chapter 3, the 2003 White Paper *The Future of Higher Education* (DFES, 2003, p. 7) proposed the establishment of 'Centres of Excellence to reward good teaching and promote best practice'. The invitation to institutions to bid for funding (HEFCE, 2004a) suggested a wide range of sources of evidence of excellence, including 'specifically commended aspects in QAA subject reports with evidence of follow-up and dissemination'. The sum of £315 million was spent on 69 CETLs between 2005 and 2010. However, a recently published independent evaluation of the scheme found that the results were mixed:

> We would ... question whether the competitive and selective bidding approach used ..., and which included a significant amount of capital funding, was the most effective way to enhance and reward excellence in teaching and learning across the sector.

We do not believe the CETL programme ... has led to material changes in non-participating HEIs and across the sector as a whole.

(SQW Ltd, 2011, pp. 52–53)[4]

In March 2010, HEFCE consulted institutions about possible further changes to the method for funding teaching. One of the issues raised was whether, in the context of a more targeted and less formulaic approach, 'quality provision' should receive specific reward (HEFCE, 2010a, paragraph 60). The review was over-taken by the change of government later in the year with a very different approach to institutional funding.

However, as also described in Chapter 5, the 2011 White Paper *Higher Educa-tion: Students at the Heart of the System* (DBIS, 2011a) proposed that, to reduce tuition fees and increase competition, some 20,000 places – about 8 per cent of the total number of new Home/EU entrants in any one year – should be subject to bids from institutions intending to charge £7,500 or less in 2012. This would 'reward universities and colleges who [sic] combine good quality with value for money' (DBIS, 2011a, Executive Summary, paragraph 8).

In the subsequent consultative paper, the Funding Council accepted that there was:

> no formulaic way to measure the qualities [sic] of higher education provision. The panel will therefore make a holistic assessment of quality, based on infor-mation that the institution provides, rather than making a decision based on a single measure or metric. We will encourage proposals that draw on sector-wide indicators of quality and are therefore comparable between institutions, for example, audits/reviews by the Quality Assurance Agency for Higher Education; benchmarked National Student Survey results; or HESA per-formance indicators such as non-continuation and completion rates. Other objective indicators may also be used, where appropriate and available.
>
> (HEFCE, 2011c, p. 31)

This was confirmed in the subsequent invitation to institutions to bid for places (HEFCE, 2011g, Annex B). It is not clear what part quality considerations played in the Council's judgements; in any case, none of these indicators refers to the actual quality of what is offered, especially as the Funding Council was seeking evidence at course level.[5]

The strengthening of information requirements – I

At the time, the most remarked-upon outcome of David Blunkett's March 2001 announcement was the anticipated slimming down of audit and assessment. But in a somewhat longer perspective, the most important outcome was the introduc-tion of greater requirements on institutions to publish information on quality and standards.

In view of the framework outlined in Chapter 2, the importance of adequate consumer information for a functioning market in any product or service hardly needs emphasising. Nor, especially given the amount of scholarly literature devoted to it, does the increasing commercial production of institutional rankings or 'league tables': in her recent, comprehensive survey, Hazelkorn (2011) claimed she had read or consulted nearly a thousand books, articles or presentations on the subject. These semi-official productions are accompanied by websites like *ratemyprofessor.com* and the reviews posted on the internet; as an example, the author's own former university, Southampton Solent, is the subject of more than 55,000 electronic reviews at the time of writing.

A decisive push in the direction of greater information about quality and standards was given by the consultative document on the post-2001 quality assurance regime, which was published by HEFCE in July 2001 on behalf of itself, the Northern Ireland Department for Employment and Learning, the representative bodies, and the QAA. In contrast to previous official statements, which emphasised quality enhancement, this stated that meeting public information needs was now the 'first principle' of the new arrangements (HEFCE, 2001a, paragraph 9). A task group would be established under the leadership of Ronald (later Sir Ronald) Cooke, Vice-Chancellor of York, to identify the categories of data, information and judgements that should be made available. This was in effect a quid pro quo for the scaling back of assessment/subject review.

The Cooke Committee published an interim report in November 2001 and a final report in March 2002, quick work even by Dearing standards. The Committee set out the following purposes and principles for collecting and publishing information about programme quality:

a. To secure the availability within each HEI of relevant information which the HEI uses actively and continuously to sustain and improve the quality and standards of learning and teaching on the programmes it offers.
b. To enable students, employers and other stakeholders to match their needs and objectives with the provision on offer, so that they can take decisions on the basis of informed judgements.
c. To secure accountability for the use of public funds by demonstrating where quality and standards are high, and by identifying cases where improvement is needed as a basis for rapid follow-up.

(HEFCE, 2001c, pp. 5–6)

In spite of a consultant's report (SQW Ltd, 1999) finding little evidence of demand for more quality related information, either from students or from anyone else, the Committee proposed what seemed at the time to be a fairly extensive information set. The quantitative data was to include student entry qualifications; performance indicators and benchmarks on progression and successful completion for full-time first degree students; class of first degree by subject area; and performance indicators and benchmarks on first destination/employment outcomes for full-time first degree students. The qualitative data should include summaries of external examiners' reports for each programme; a voluntary commentary by the institution on the findings of external examiners' reports; feedback from recent graduates collected through a national survey (see below); feedback from current students collected through the institution's own surveys on a more consistent basis than previously; a summary statement of the institution's learning and teaching strategies; summary statements of the results of, and the actions taken in response to, periodic programme and department reviews, at intervals of not more than six years; and summaries of the institution's links with relevant employers, how the institution identified employer needs and opinions, and how they expected to use these to develop the 'relevance and richness' of learning programmes (HEFCE, 2002b). This information was subsequently incorporated into an official website, first HERO/TQI now Unistats.

Two main issues arose in the Committee's discussions.

The first was the treatment of external examiners' reports. The Cooke Committee proposed that external examiners should be asked to prepare summaries of their reports and that these should be published 'as a new form of public information'. The full reports for the institution would continue to be confidential. This had been welcomed by students and employer representatives but strongly opposed by the institutions, which feared that it could compromise the quality of reporting and perhaps create an adversarial situation.

The second issue was how to obtain and publish graduates' views about the quality of the teaching they had experienced. The Committee had recommended that the long-established First Destinations Survey (concerning the early careers of recent graduates) should be used to collect graduates' views about the quality and standards of their learning experience. However, it was subsequently agreed that it would be more practicable to have a separate survey of students in their final year, the National Student Survey, or NSS. This was based on the Australian Course Experience Questionnaire that has operated since 1991 (Ramsden, 1991). The NSS was first conducted in 2005 and the results incorporated into the official website.[6]

In 2005–6, the Quality Assurance Framework Review Group looked at the information requirements of the post-2001 quality framework. The author was again a member. The committee's terms of reference precluded any questioning of the rationale for the framework, the discussion was more about how the information set could be made more 'fit for purpose'. In its report, the committee recommended that the qualitative data should be removed from the site (HEFCE, 2006c). This was on the basis that it did not appear to be useful to potential students, was used inconsistently between providers, and was costly and burdensome to produce. However, the committee also recommended that institutions should give consideration to publishing some qualitative information on their websites.

Once again, external examiners' reports were a subject of much discussion. The committee found that students were not making much use of this information but that getting and publishing it involved institutions in a quite disproportionate amount of effort. The committee were also influenced by the findings of a QAA review that found that little use was being made by institutions of the qualitative information. The committee therefore recommended that summaries of external examiner reports should no longer be published, but that the full reports should be shared with student representatives 'as a matter of course'.

It should be noted that in the consultation on the Cooke Report, universities and colleges expressed considerable reservations about the information that the Committee was proposing should be published by institutions (see HEFCE, 2002b, Annex B). This was partly on grounds of potential infringement of institutional autonomy, but also because of doubts about the likely benefits to students, on the one hand, and concerns about the resourcing demands on institutions, on the other. In spite of periodic concerns about over-regulation and value for money (Brown, 2007a), no indication of the benefits or estimates of the costs of producing and publishing this information has ever been offered (Brown et al., 2007).

The strengthening of information requirements – 2

The 2009 White Paper *Higher Ambitions: The Future of Universities in a Knowledge Economy* (DBIS, 2009) stated that:

> as the most important clients of higher education, students' own assessments of the service they receive at university should be central to our judgement of the success of our higher education system. Their choices and expectations should play an important part in shaping the courses universities provide and in encouraging universities to adapt and improve their service. But these choices must themselves be well-informed by objective information about what different courses involve, and their implications for future career prospects.
>
> (DBIS, 2009, p. 70)

The Government would therefore ensure that:

> students are better informed about what their higher education choices will involve in terms of course content, mode and place of learning, their own study responsibilities, and subsequent career progression.
>
> (DBIS, 2009, p. 70)

Following the White Paper, HEFCE commissioned two surveys of student information needs.

The first, by Oakleigh Consulting and Staffordshire University, considered what information students needed to support their decisions about higher education. Paragraph 54 of the Executive Summary stated:

The research found that only a limited set of information is regarded as a priority by most prospective students. Only around half of the respondents had tried to find this information. This indicates that many prospective students do not look for information even when they think it would be very useful to them. This evidence does not suggest t here is an appetite for, or likely to be much use made of, any new large-scale information system.

(HEFCE, 2010d, p. 13, present author's emphases)

Instead of expanding the information set, the consultants recommended that efforts should be made to raise the profile of the information sources currently available to show prospective students, careers advisers and teachers what they offered and how they could be used.

The second report, by the Centre for Higher Education Studies at the Institute of Education, University of London, was about enhancing and developing the National Student Survey. In recommendation 4, the consultants noted the finding of the first report that there was little evidence of students using the NSS results to inform their choices. This was just as well because:

The design of the NSS means that there are limitations on its use for comparative purposes (recommendation 5). In particular, its validity in comparing results from different subject areas is very restricted, as is its use in drawing conclusions about different aspects of the student experience. One issue to be borne in mind is that, in most cases, the differences between whole institutions are so small as to be statistically and practically insignificant.

(HEFCE, 2010c, p. 4)

The consultants (who included the former Chair of HEFCE's Teaching Quality Assessment Committee and the recently retired Chief Executive of the Higher Education Academy) confirmed that the NSS results could be used to track the development of responses over time, to report absolute scores at local and regional levels, to compare results with agreed internal benchmarks, to compare the responses of different student groups, to make comparisons (with appropriate vigilance and knowledge of statistical variance) between programmes in the same subject area at different institutions, and to help stimulate change and dialogue about teaching and learning. But they could not be used 'responsibly' to:

Compare subject areas, e.g. Art and Design vs. Engineering, within an institution – unless adjustments are made for typical subject area differences nationally.

Compare scores on different aspects of the student experience (between different scales, e.g. assessment vs. teaching) in an unsophisticated way.

Compare whole institutions without taking account of sources of variation such as subject mix and student characteristics.

Construct league tables of programmes or institutions that do not allow for the fact that the majority of results are not materially different.

(HEFCE, 2010e, p. 48)

The consultants recommended that these features of the survey should be declared more clearly both when the survey was administered and when its results were reported. The NSS had, however, been of some value for quality enhancement and this aspect should be more widely exploited; this incidentally coincides with the author's earlier assessment of the value of Teaching Quality Assessment/ Subject Review (Brown, 2004). The report concluded that the core NSS should remain as it was for the present, with its continuing usefulness and relevance kept under review.[7,8]

The strengthening of information requirements – 3

In July 2010, HEFCE published a statement of the 'principles and objectives' of the new quality assurance regime to apply from 2011. This confirmed, as the first principle and object of quality assurance:

[To] provide authoritative, publicly accessible information on academic quality and standards in higher education.

(HEFCE, 2010b)

Later the same year, the Funding Council published a consultative document proposing that, from 2012–13, institutions should be required to publish additional course-level information. This should include learning, teaching and assessment methods and (where relevant) professional accreditation. Subject-level data should include NSS results and employment and salary data. Institution-level data should include bursaries, accommodation costs, and information about the students union. Institutions should publish on their websites information about the support provided at institutional level to enhance students' employability ('employability statements'). This would be in addition to the information already published on the Unistats website covering entry qualifications/salary points, students continuing/completing/leaving without awards, First Destinations, links to QAA reports, etc. This was described as a 'key information set', what has since become known as the KIS (HEFCE, 2010f).

A further report in June 2011 stated that:

Information that the HE sector provides for the public is increasingly significant and is a key concern for the present Government, which has asked us to work on this as a priority. Public information should be robust, easy to find, and easy to compare between higher education institutions, wherever in the country they are. Access to robust, reliable information is particularly important for prospective students, who are making decisions about where to apply amid greater demand for places and the expectation that they will pay more for their education.

(HEFCE, 2011b, p. 7)

The report listed no fewer than 17 items of information that should be available for each undergraduate course. These should include the proportion of time spent in various learning and teaching activities (by year/stage of study, with a link to further detail); the mix of summative assessment methods used (by year/ stage of study); the destinations of graduates six months after graduation; of those employed, the proportion in managerial/professional jobs six months after graduation; and salary data (upper quartile, median, lower quartile) six months after graduation from the course concerned and for all courses in the subject across all institutions, six and 40 months after graduation (HEFCE, 2011b, pp. 12–15).

The report noted that there were areas where providing this information might be difficult, especially joint honours courses, part-time and collaborative provision. Where full data were available, the KIS would cover 40 per cent of the student body; after allowing for aggregation, the proportion where some information was available was likely to increase to 90 per cent. The report also acknowledged institutional concerns about the value of DLHE (Destinations of Leavers from Higher Education) data. The report outlined a wider set of information – beyond the KIS and existing Unistats material – which should be made available by institutions. This included information about institutional context (this is where the employability statements would sit), other information about courses/ awards, and details of quality procedures (HEFCE, 2011b, pp. 31–33). This has become known as the Wider Information Set (WIS). Yet again, no information was included about the benefits and costs.[9]

To reflect and reinforce these new information requirements, from 2012 institutional review will involve QAA auditors making judgements about the quality of the public information provided by institutions, including especially that produced for actual and prospective students (previously, auditors had only commented on accuracy and completeness (QAA, 2011a). The grades to be used will be 'commended', 'meets UK expectations', 'requires improvement to meet UK expectations' or 'does not meet UK expectations'. The expectations will be set out in the new UK Quality Code (QAA, 2011b). It remains to be seen how exactly this will be done.

The strengthening of information requirements – 4

The 2011 White Paper *Higher Education. Putting Students at the Heart of the System* (DBIS, 2011a) emphasised even more strongly than the previous one the importance the Government attached to information:

Our reforms aim to make the English higher education system more responsive to students and employers. This depends on access to high quality information about different courses and institutions ... The issue, for the most part, is not the existence or collection of the data, but how it can be made available and linked in ways that make sense to potential students, their families, schools, employers and others with an interest

(DBIS, 2011a, paragraphs 2.8–2.9)

So the Government was asking the main organisations holding student data to make detailed data available publicly, including on employment and earnings outcomes, so that it could be analysed and presented by private – the Government clearly could not quite bring itself to use the word 'commercial' – organisations in a variety of formats to meet the needs of students, their parents and other advisers. The consumer organisation *Which?* and the independent 'not for profit' organisation *bestcourse4me* were amongst those said to be interested in doing this, and indeed *Which?* has now gone ahead (see Chapter 9).

But there were also proposals for yet more information to be published:

- UCAS and institutions should make available, course by course, new data showing the type and subject of the actual qualifications held by previously successful applicants.
- Institutions should publish anonymised information for students and prospective students about the teaching qualifications, fellowships and expertise of their teaching staff at all levels (this is the only reference to academic or other staff in the entire document).
- Institutions should publish information showing how teaching revenue is spent, along the lines of local councils describing what council tax was being used for.
- Institutions should publish summary reports of their student evaluation surveys on their websites (by 2013–14).
- Consideration should be given to extending the National Student Survey to taught postgraduate students and whether to encourage institutions to provide a standard set of information similar to the KIS for each of their taught postgraduate courses (DBIS, 2011a, paragraphs 2.11–2.21).

This section of the White Paper concluded:

Wider availability and better use of information for potential students is fundamental to the new system. Students will increasingly use the instant communication tools of the twenty first century such as Twitter and Facebook to share their views on their student experience with their friends, families and the wider world. It will be correspondingly harder for institutions to trade on their past reputations while offering a poor teaching experience in the present. Better informed students will take their custom to the places offering good value for money. In this way, excellent teaching will be placed back at the heart of every student's university experience.

(DBIS, 2011a, paragraph 2.24)

The next chapter of the White Paper contained a number of proposals to enhance students' ability to influence provision and seek redress if their needs were not being met:

- The publication of student charters setting out the 'mutual expectations' of universities and students (initially voluntary but could be made mandatory).
- A student-led awards scheme for excellent teaching.
- Earlier involvement of the Office of the Independent Adjudicator (OIA) in handling student complaints (information from the Office could also be one of the 'triggers' for special institutional reviews, as could student concerns).

In addition, the OIA was asked to consult on various ways of 'tightening up' institutions' treatment of student complaints (DBIS, 2011a, paragraph 3.26).

The result of all this is that the UK will be providing more information about quality than any other comparable system. We have moved a long way from the notion of universities as expert providers of specialised services. The vision now is of a market in which consumers with the right information will (and should) determine what is provided.[10]

Scotland and Wales

After 1992, and the establishment of separate funding councils, Scotland and Wales each began to adopt a different approach to assessment from that adopted in England.

To begin with, Scotland adopted a three-point scale like England but then quickly – to head off 'grade inflation' – moved to a four-point one: 'Excellent', 'Highly Satisfactory', 'Satisfactory', 'Unsatisfactory'. Unlike England, this was a basis for funding decisions (until 1998), as we have already seen. After 2001, however, quality assurance in Scotland began to move much more in the direction of quality enhancement. In December 2001 a SHEFC circular proposed a new process – Enhancement Led Institutional Review (ELIR) – with five main elements:

- Institutional audits as in England but without disciplinary audit trails and with greater emphasis on quality enhancement and effective student feedback.
- Only an internal subject review process would apply, except where institutions had insufficient experience of higher education quality assurance, or where there was evidence from other sources suggesting serious concerns about quality in specific subject areas.

- Public information would not include the compulsory publication of external examiners' reports or summaries.
- A strengthening of the 'student voice', with students as full members of review teams.
- A separate quality enhancement process with specific engagements within sector-wide 'themes', with the overall aim of identifying and disseminating good practice.

(SHEFC, 2001)

The new approach was promulgated in 2003 (QAA, 2003). Further, minor changes were made for the second cycle from 2008 (SHEFC, 2008). The current enhancement theme is *Graduates for the 21st Century: Integrating the Enhancement Themes*. Scotland has decided to continue to operate a fixed four-year review cycle from 2012. The terminology used in reviewers' judgements will change from 'confidence' to 'effectiveness', but the current three-point scale will remain: 'institutional systems are effective', 'have limited effectiveness' or are 'not effective'. There is no sign of a 'risk-based' approach.

As the author has pointed out previously (Brown, 2004), ELIR bore a striking resemblance to the July 1995 HEQC proposals for the reform of audit and assessment, which were summarily rejected by both the funding councils and the representative bodies. So it is perhaps not entirely surprising that the independent external evaluation of ELIR was highly complimentary:

The approach to quality that we review here is ambitious, distinctive and, so far, successful. It was conceived as a reaction to quality assurance processes that seemed to be intrusive; emphasise compliance; concentrate on the current state of play, rather than on making things better; and represent poor value for money ...

QEF brought right to the fore the simple and powerful idea that the purpose of quality systems in higher education is to improve student experiences and, consequently, their learning ...

Not surprisingly, we have found evidence of the persistence of behaviours redolent of the displaced quality assurance regime. We have also noticed, though, that when it comes to enhancement-led institutional review (ELIR), institutions are increasingly willing to lay out areas of imperfect practice and publicly consider ways in which they could improve on them in coming years. Perhaps the shift from the concealing behaviours associated with the previous quality assurance regimes operating in UK HE in the 1990s towards – and let it be clear that this is a direction of travel – disclosure of areas for improvement is the biggest cultural shift in thinking and the most distinctive feature of Scotland's fresh thinking about quality.

(SHEFC, 2007, pp. 5–6)[11]

Wales also moved in an enhancement direction with, again, a greater emphasis on the central agency and the institutions working in partnership, something made easier in both countries by the relative scale of provision. From the outset, the Welsh Funding Council sought to involve institutions in the design of the process. Attempts were even made to get away from a single summative judgement about the quality of provision but the Funding Council retained the excellent/satisfactory/unsatisfactory descriptors so as to keep in step with England.

In 2003 HEFCW, following consultation with the institutions, set out the core principles, requirements and key features of quality assurance from 2003–4 (HEFCW, 2003). Wales was operating on a different timescale to England because of the much smaller number of institutions. The approach adopted was similar to that in England but with two important differences. There would be no disciplinary audit trails (partly because of the scale of Welsh provision), and there would be no publication of summaries of external examiners' reports (or of summaries of internal annual and periodic monitoring reports). There was a strong emphasis on the use of student evaluations in quality assurance.

The 2003 institutional review cycle came to an end in 2009. At the beginning of that year, and again after consultation, the Funding Council announced its intentions for the next, current cycle (HEFCW, 2009). These included a number of changes, some of which were subsequently taken up in the new method for institutional review in England after 2011. The main ones were:

- Increased emphasis on enhancement.
- A greater focus on the learner experience.
- Students to be full members of review teams.
- Reviews to be a rolling process rather than a fixed cycle.
- A more risk-based approach. Institutions not gaining a 'confidence' judgement in their previous review would be reviewed at no more than four-yearly intervals. Those gaining a 'confidence' would be reviewed at no more than six-yearly intervals.
- The previous single judgement about quality and standards would be divided into separate judgements about quality and standards.

Review teams would also be asked to consider the extent to which the institution was aware of the European and international dimension.

However, in 2011, and taking advantage of the fact that a rolling process enables changes to be made at any time, the Funding Council consulted institutions on amendments designed to bring the Welsh review method closer to that adopted for England and Northern Ireland from 2011 (HEFCW, 2011a). The main changes proposed would bring the numbers and categories of judgements and the grading of recommendations into line with those in England and Northern Ireland (which has always followed England). This would facilitate comparability and avoid Welsh universities and colleges being at a disadvantage compared with institutions elsewhere in the Kingdom.

Conclusion: quality assurance and the market

In 2009, the author suggested that in Britain quality assurance had moved through a three-stage, evolutionary process (Brown, 2009b).

In the first stage – the 'secret garden' – quality assurance is seen chiefly as an internal, institutional affair. The emphasis is on the inputs to quality. The qualifications of academic staff and students are the key quality safeguards, reinforced by some external networking within the academic community, for example, external examiners. Quality is raised by improving the 'quality' (or qualifications) of staff, students and other inputs. There is very little information about quality processes or outcomes even within institutions, let alone externally. Quality assurance processes are usually informal and not written down or codified. Professional body accreditation is an important but partial exception, but even there academics are very often the key personnel. Quality judgements are threshold judgements, often only implicit. There is a very limited state role: quality and quality assurance are seen as the universities' business, and academics are trusted to know that business. This was essentially the position in the pre-1992 universities, at least up to the late 1980s. It was in the context of limited competition for students and income between institutions, as well as a much smaller system in which it was possible in many subjects for all or most of the practitioners to know one another, their work and their students.

In the second stage – 'collective security' – quality assurance is shared between individual institutions and institutions collectively through arrangements supervised and underpinned by the state (Kells, 1992). The state is now more interested in quality assurance, or at least in seeing that it takes place. Externality and peer review are the key quality safeguards, underpinned by greater public exposure of quality assurance outcomes. Emphasis has shifted from inputs to the existence and efficacy of quality assurance processes, which are now formalised and codified. There is growing interest in outcomes, with pressure for institutions to be more explicit about the aims and objectives of programmes and the levels and meanings of academic standards. External quality agencies identify and disseminate best practice as well as criticising bad. Quality is raised through improved academic practice (enhancement). There is more information available than previously but the key information for quality purposes remains what institutions receive through their own internal procedures, and from periodic external reviews, which enables them to improve their systems and practices. Quality judgements may be threshold or graded but threshold judgements remain dominant. There is less trust in professional judgements and procedures than in the first stage. This was how the CNAA operated in its later years, and HEQC was the final, misunderstood and unsuccessful attempt to replicate it across the sector.

In the third stage – 'markets rule, OK?' – quality assurance is shared between institutions, individually and collectively, the state and the market (Clark, 1983). Market competition is seen as the key safeguard of quality. Hence the importance of liberalising market entry, raising the proportion of teaching funding that goes via the student, and increasing the volume of information for consumers. The information as far as possible concerns outcomes, replacing the earlier interest in inputs and processes though these remain important (most of the indicators in the league tables are inputs). Where possible, graded quality judgements facilitate consumer choice, enabling each student to determine their 'best buy'.

Whereas previously the definition of quality and judgements about the achievement of quality were both left to the academic community, individually and collectively, in a market the key judgements are those of consumers or those who claim to be working on their behalf, e.g., commercial publishers (professionals are mistrusted). Judgements shift from being 'authority-based' (merit judged by 'the authorities') to 'market-based' (Marks, 2007, p. 173). The state's job is to facilitate and extend the market and to ensure that the only barriers to market competition are where there is a clear and overriding public interest in having them. Also unlike the first two phases, economic elements – price and ability to pay – enter into consumer calculations. This is the model espoused by the current Government but elements of it began to appear even before the unification of the sector in 1992 (see also Westerheijden, 2007).

It is important to bear in mind the fact that, like Trow's famous model of the move from elite to mass HE systems (Trow, 1974), the three stages are not sequential but coexist as a series of layers. So even by the end of the period we are describing, much quality assurance remains of the traditional kind based on trust in the qualifications and/or the peer review processes of the wider academic community. Nevertheless, the balance is clearly shifting away from the academic community to the market.

This is also reflected in the changing balance of power within the political community responsible for determining and overseeing the quality regime. We have already noted the fact that prior to 1990 the existing universities were subject to no external supervision, whilst the major public institutions had negotiated a substantial measure of autonomy within an increasingly enhancement-focussed CNAA regime. In both cases, the sector-wide arrangements were independent of government (HMI were by this time government – as opposed to Crown – agents but retained and prized their professional independence). Between 1993 and 1997 HEQC shared power with the funding councils' assessment units: in effect, a government-sponsored assessment regime ran alongside a sector-owned assurance one. But academic standards were universally regarded as 'off limits' to the Government and its agencies.

To be fair to the Government, ministers always made it plain that if there were to be a single quality agency it could not be wholly self-regulatory. In any case, under its first Chief Executive, QAA policies and actions were very much in line with the thinking of the new government (and the Dearing Committee) that the agency should be more detached from the institutions, and this was reflected in the agency's constitution where, as already noted, the largest element on the board consisted of independents, the institutional nominees were in a minority, and the representative bodies were not even allowed to send observers to board meetings.

Since the events of 2001, however, the Funding Council has been increasingly in the driving seat, seemingly with the connivance of the representative bodies, so that the QAA's role has been reduced almost to that of technical adviser. Hence the definitive statement about the post-2011 quality assurance regime published in July 2010 by the Funding Council on behalf of UUK, GuildHE, HEFCE and the Department for Employment and Learning in Northern Ireland (HEFCE, 2010b) was described as being made 'with the advice and guidance of the QAA'. Similarly, it is the Funding Council that is consulting on the criteria and means for selective institutional reviews under the risk-based approach. As noted in Chapter 3, the Government also intends that HEFCE will take over from QAA the role of advising ministers on applications for degree-awarding powers and university title, what has previously been seen as a key 'gatekeeping' function. We are a long way here from an independent body with its own charter, or even a sector-owned body sharing power with the Funding Council (Brown, submitted for review).

Chapter 7

The impact of marketisation
Efficiency, diversity and equity

> This analysis points to the importance of autonomy, competition and suitable funding if there is to be responsiveness and high quality in universities. In contrast to the position in much of continental Europe ... universities in the UK have had a long tradition of both autonomy and competition. The UK reforms have enhanced competition. The introduction of tuition fees ... has led to more adequate funding and more direct influence by universities over the level of that funding.
>
> (Clark, 2009, p. 15)

This chapter summarises what we know from the existing literature about the impact of the marketisation of higher education across the globe and considers how far what has happened in the UK since 1979 is consistent with this picture, referring to efficiency, institutional diversity and widening participation. Chapter 8 looks at the effects on quality and on the universities' ability to control the 'academic agenda'. An overall assessment of the impact of marketisation in the UK to date is at the end of that chapter.

Marketisation for and against

The literature on the marketisation of higher education is extensive and becoming even more so almost by the minute (e.g., Thornton, 2012). What follows in this section is taken principally from the author's recent (2011a and b) international surveys, updated as necessary.

Williams's (1995, p. 179) formulation of the assumptions on which the marketisation of higher education is based remains as valid as any:

> That efficiency is increased when governments buy academic services from producers, or subsidise students to buy them, rather than supplying them directly, or indirectly through subsidy of institutions

> That as enrolments rise, the private sector must relieve governments of some of the cost burden if acceptable quality is to be obtained

> That many of the benefits of higher education accrue to private individuals, so criteria of both efficiency and equity are served if students or their families make some contribution toward the cost of obtaining the benefits.

The two main benefits of market-based policies are greater efficiency and greater responsiveness. Market competition increases the efficiency with which resources are used because institutions would otherwise be unable to survive or be competitive. It makes the publicly allocated resources go further whilst stimulating institutions to increase their funding from private sources. Market competition also makes universities and colleges more attentive to the needs, interests and views of external stakeholders, especially students and prospective students and their families, but also employers, public bodies and funding agencies. It may also make them more innovative and entrepreneurial. Finally, market competition may keep in check some activities that are of interest to the faculty but that may have no wider utility or value, though it may by the same token limit the amount of innovation that can arise from academics investigating things simply out of curiosity (Brown, 2011a).

But there are also drawbacks. These arise chiefly from the difficulty – in reality, the impossibility – of obtaining and timely and suitable information about product quality. It is conventional in the economics literature to view market failures due to information in terms of 'information asymmetry', where access to information about quality varies significantly, for example, between suppliers and consumers. However, the problem in higher education is not so much that information is distributed unequally but that *no one* has or can have the information that would enable them to make the same judgements about quality and suitability that they might make about a physical product or a less complex service (Brown, 2007c). Higher education is what Weimer and Vining (1992, pp. 75–76) termed a 'post-experience' good, the outcomes of which may not be apparent (if at all) for many years, and which may not be traceable to any particular educational experience (see also Lovelock, 1983; Hamlin, 1994; and many others).

What therefore happens is that students and their advisers and research funders seek, and institutions try to provide, indirect or symbolic indicators of quality (McPherson and Winston, 1993). The indicators chosen often refer to prestige, reputation or status (Brewer *et al.*, 2002; van Vught, 2008). This reinforces higher education's traditional function of allocating status through the granting of credentials (Collins, 2002). This is a function that has become of even greater importance as the number of top level positions in society fails to increase as much as the number of those qualified to occupy them, in what Robert Frank has termed the 'winner-takes-all' society (Frank and Cook, 1997).

The inevitable consequence – given the market and political power exercised by the leading institutions in most countries – is the creation or, more likely, the intensification of stratification, both of the institutions and of the socio-economic constituencies they serve (for a partial exception to this view, see Shavit *et al.*, 2007). The other main 'external' consequence is a reduction in institutional diversity as institutions pursue prestige, the process often referred to as 'academic drift'

(Pratt and Burgess, 1974) or 'mission creep' (Lane, 2005). Important factors in both enhanced stratification and reduced diversity are the power exercised by the faculty in the longer-established institutions, and the greater esteem accorded to research in systems where universities conduct research as well as teach (Calhoun, 2006; for a good general discussion of the problem, see Dill, 2007).

Market competition also has an impact on the internal functioning of institutions, contributing to an increase in the proportion of resources devoted to management and administration and an increased differentiation of activities, structures and personnel. It may also diminish collegiality and reduce the ability of the academic community to control or influence the 'academic agenda': what is to be taught and enquired into. A major factor here is the ever- increasing growth of knowledge and the concomitant increase in specialisation which in itself weakens collegiality even without any external factors.

The impact of market competition on quality is strongly contested. Market competition may improve quality as institutions respond to students and research funders by improving quality of service. But competition may also damage quality by commodifying knowledge, creating or reinforcing student 'instrumentality', and lowering standards through grade inflation, and acceptance of plagiarism and other forms of cheating. It may also lead to a diversion of resources away from learning and teaching to activities like marketing, enrolment, student aid and administration (and in the US, athletics).

Finally, marketisation may change higher education's relationship with society. Because they produce valued public goods, universities typically enjoy a high degree of autonomy. For the same reasons, institutions often benefit from tax breaks, charitable status, etc. But if universities increasingly behave like ordinary commercial entities the continuation of these concessions may be called into question as Geiger (2004) and others have warned.

How far does what we know of the impact of the marketisation of UK higher education since 1979 conform to this broad picture?

The impact of marketisation in the United Kingdom

We need first to remind ourselves that although the provision of higher education in the UK – and England in particular – has moved further in a market direction than almost any other comparable country, it will still fall short of being a genuine economic market of the kind sketched in Chapter 2:

- Entry to the market (especially access to degree-awarding powers and university title) remains restricted.
- Prices (i.e., tuition fees) will still be controlled, and limited to a maximum of £9,000, which will not be increased in line with inflation in 2013–14 (Willetts, 2012a).
- The overall number of funded places available will remain subject to financial limits.

- Loans for fees and maintenance are still subsidised, whilst a significant number of students are receiving maintenance grants, bursaries, fee remission and other forms of financial support.
- University research remains heavily subsidised.

Nevertheless, the UK has clearly moved in a market direction since 1979:

- Market entry barriers have been lowered and formal distinctions between institutions removed or reduced.
- From this year (2012) there will be price competition in the full-time undergraduate market for the first time. Fees will vary within a range up to £9,000, with at least 8 per cent of places reserved for institutions charging £7,500 or less; half of these places have been allocated to FE colleges as we saw in Chapter 3. Fee waivers will also vary. There will also be competition on support packages (bursaries and scholarships).
- The fee is intended to cover the cost of teaching for most subjects. Provided they earn enough, graduates in employment will be meeting these costs from their own pockets. The average fee of £8,354 in 2012 (OFFA, 2011) is higher than that of nearly every 'public' university in nearly every comparable system.[1]
- Controls have been lifted on a quarter of places and this proportion will be increased in 2013. A significant minority of institutions will in effect have no limits on their student recruitment.
- As we saw in Chapter 6, there will be substantial amounts of information for students and prospective students.
- Research is subject to intense quasi-market competition through selective funding by both the funding councils and the research councils (as we noted in Chapter 4, funding by other public and private bodies tends to follow these allocations).
- Finally, other areas of university activity not covered here (e.g., postgraduate teaching and research, applied research and technology transfer) are already subject to market or quasi-market disciplines.

One indicator of this movement towards the market is the proportion of institutional revenues now gained from private sources: students and former students, companies, charities, individual donors. According to the OECD (2011a, Table B3.1) in 2008 only Korea and Japan among member countries had a higher proportion of private funding than the UK; this proportion will of course increase even further after 2012.

Efficiency

The UK has the second strongest higher education system in the world and our country's future economic strength will more than ever depend on the growth and competitiveness driven by our world-leading universities. The strength of the UK higher education system has been underpinned by its flexibility and responsiveness within a fast changing global environment, leading to innovation across all activities and ensuring effectiveness in operation and delivery. Indeed, UK higher education has been highly successful to date in sustaining its global standing with significantly less investment (both public and private) than our competitor countries.

(UUK, 2011, p. 12)

Whatever else may be said, market competition has undoubtedly made British universities and colleges more efficient, as well as more entrepreneurial, especially in international terms.

Over the period 1979 to 2011 the overall student population increased by 320 per cent. There was also much greater diversity in the student population, with increasing proportions of women (up from 41.8 per cent of full-time undergraduates in 1979–80 to 54.4 per cent in 2009–10), students from ethnic minorities (the proportion of UK-domiciled undergraduates from Black and Ethnic Minority backgrounds rose from 10.7 per cent in 1990 to 18.1 per cent in 2009–10), and students declaring a disability (7.6 per cent in 2009–10) (ECU, 2011). These increases reflected successive increases in Home/EU participation rates, from just over 12.4 per cent in 1979–80 to 47 per cent in 2010–11.[2]

Overall public expenditure on higher education rose substantially, from £3.5 billion in 1979–80 to £22.9 billion in 2011–12 (£5.8 billion in 1979 prices), an increase of 165 per cent. However, total expenditure as a share of GDP remains below the OECD average: 1.2 per cent, compared to 1.5 per cent; in the share of *public* expenditure in GDP, the UK is below every other major OECD country apart from Japan (OECD, 2011a, Table B2.3). This disparity between student numbers and expenditure has naturally had an impact on spending per student. We noted in Chapter 5 the Dearing Committee's estimate that public funding per student fell from the equivalent of 100 in 1976 to 79 in 1989 and 60 in 1994. There was a further fall to 1998–99, when top-up fees were introduced, but a substantial recovery up to 2009–10 when there was a further fall; but even the 2009–10 figure was well below the 1989–90 level. Unfortunately, for technical reasons, neither HEFCE nor the Department for Business, Innovation and Skills (DBIS) is continuing with these calculations.

Largely reflecting this picture since the 1980s, student-staff ratios rose sharply, from 10.3 (FTE students to full-time staff) in 1985–86 to an average of 17.1 since 1996–97 (Universities Statistical Record and HESA). This squeeze on institutional incomes has meant a shortfall of expenditure on infrastructure: new buildings and equipment, adaptation and maintenance. Such expenditure requires steady annual surpluses because most capital spending comes ultimately from revenue, given the declining value of government grants (only Oxford and Cambridge have substantial levels of endowments, and even these are small in comparison with those of the leading US institutions).[3]

In spite of these reductions in relative funding, graduation rates remain respectable. Of our major international competitors, only Australia (48.5 per cent) has a higher graduation rate than the UK (47.8 per cent); the OECD average is 38.6 per cent. This can be taken as one indicator of the continuing success of the system. Others include:

- The absorption of a high proportion of those qualified to attend university and wishing to do so, though we should note that in recent years there has been a steady rise in the proportion of applicants failing to receive offers, with 29.7 per cent of applicants unplaced in 2011, compared to 22.3 per cent in 2004 (UCAS, 2011).
- Continuing high levels of student satisfaction. The latest (2011) National Student Survey results showed 83 per cent overall satisfaction among those surveyed (HEFCE, 2011e). This is in line with the results for previous years since the survey was first carried out in 2005. Within this, satisfaction levels varied from 84 per cent for 'teaching on my course' to 68 per cent for 'assessment and feedback'. This has consistently been the lowest-scoring category. There has, however, been a steady rise in student complaints to the OIA: in 2011, OIA received 1,605 complaints, an increase of 20 per cent on the previous year, and the sixth successive year of increases. However, this represents dissatisfaction among only 0.07 per cent of eligible students (OIA, 2012).
- Continuing high levels of first employment. In 2009–10, according to HESA data, 75.4 of all UK-domiciled graduates were in work or work and further study; 7.3 per cent were assumed to be unemployed; most of the rest were in further study.
- Continuing positive rates of economic return. According to the study carried out for DBIS in 2011 (London Economics, 2011), the marginal earnings return associated with an undergraduate degree stands at approximately 27.4 per cent compared with the possession of two or more A-levels. This is in line with other recent estimates (e.g., PriceWaterhouseCoopers and UUK, 2007). These returns also compare favourably with those in most other OECD countries (OECD, 2011a, Table A9.3).[4]
- The UK has the second highest share of internationally mobile students, after the US. Moreover, students studying abroad on programmes leading to British university awards – over 500,000 in 2010–11 – are now equivalent in number to about a sixth of all UK students (HESA). By contrast – and in spite of speculation that higher fees would drive many of them abroad – the numbers of UK-domiciled students going abroad remains small.[5]
- Similarly, the UK continues to rank second only to the US on various measures of research performance (DBIS, 2012c; see also Evidence Ltd, 2008). However, as we shall see later, our research reputation rests very heavily on a limited number of highly cited individuals.

- UK higher education continues to be attractive to multinational companies (Council for Industry and Higher Education, 2006).
- UK universities and colleges have strong links with business and the public sector. According to the latest (May 2012) HE-BCI survey (HEFCE, 2012d), in 2009–10 UK higher education institutions earned over £3 billion from collaborative and contract research, consultancy, facilities and equipment-related services, continuing education, regeneration and development programmes, and intellectual property (£2.27 billion in 2003–4).[6]

Finally, it is often pointed out that the UK is the only country, other than the US, to have more than one university in the top echelons of the various international institutional rankings. When one adjusts for population the picture is even better, as Hotson (2011) has pointed out. The UK has considerably more top-rated universities per head of population, and if one factors in the respective levels of investment, the UK wins comfortably:

> The UK has somehow managed to maintain top-ranked universities for only about a fifth of the US price.
>
> (Hotson, 2011, p. 20)[7]

Even more important, however, Hotson shows how UK universities are distributed fairly uniformly across the various tiers, indicating a strength in depth that neither the US, nor any other comparable country has. It is this strength in depth which, as we shall see, is most at risk from the further round of marketisation introduced by the present Government.

It seems clear that UK higher education in 2012 is in nearly every respect much more efficient, service-oriented and entrepreneurial than it was in 1979, and this must at least in part be due to the market-driven policies of successive governments. Whether this has been achieved without significant detriments is something that will now be considered.

Diversity and stratification

> [A] diverse range of autonomous, well-managed institutions with a commitment to excellence in the achievement of their distinctive missions.
>
> (National Committee of Inquiry into Higher Education, 1997,
> paragraph 1.5)

> Despite all the talk about selectivity and 'world-class' universities the reputational range of British universities has almost certainly narrowed in the last ten years. What we continue to have, instead, is an untidy and rather volatile hierarchy of institutions distinguished not by different functions but by patterns of condescension.
>
> (Scott, 2005, p. 70)

> Stratification, the logical outcome of excellence or its absence, now serves as an explicit instrument of public policy rather than reflecting an implicit social perception.
>
> (Neave, 2005, p. 18)

There is general (though not universal) agreement amongst scholars that one of the properties of a healthy higher education system is institutional diversity (for a dissenting voice, see Huisman *et al.*, 2000). To quote from one of the classic statements:

> the search for excellence can be aided by specialisation which allows not only a concentration of attention and effort, but also a higher status of some endeavours, of some endeavours that is, than they would have if they were subordinated to others in the same institution.
>
> (Birnbaum, 1983, p. 5)

This is on the basis that in a modern mass system there is a wide range of learning needs, which is best met through a wide array of institutions. A subsidiary argument is that diversity is a handmaiden to innovation: diversity permits experimentation because any failure is limited to one institution or group of institutions. There has also been a view, again a pretty general one, that historically the UK system has exhibited a considerable amount of such diversity, with institutions varying enormously in age, tradition, mission and orientation, size and range of provision. Finally, there is a view that market competition is good for diversity, as each institution 'plays to its strengths', and finds its own particular 'niche'.

However, the literature on diversity also suggests that higher education contains many of the features that can lead organisations to become more similar in structure, culture, and output ('isomorphism'). The main conditions are: poorly understood organisational technologies, ambiguous organisational goals, and an environment that creates symbolic uncertainty. These lead organisations to model themselves on others that they regard as more legitimate or successful. Other pressures for homogenisation are strong entry barriers (which may of course be justified on grounds of quality or consumer protection), and a powerful cadre of professional staff who move between organisations and who do not necessarily obtain their status from their organisational position (DiMaggio and Powell, 1983). In higher education this is reinforced by the various institutional rankings or 'league tables' (Dill and Soo, 2005; Brown, 2006a; Centre for Higher Education Research and Information *et al.*, 2008; Hazelkorn, 2011). What we have therefore is competition by emulation (Rhoades, 2007; see also Riesman, 1958; Clark, 1983; Trow, 1984, and many others).

The period under review has seen a number of cases of such competition through emulation in Britain. They include:

- In 1992 all but one of the former polytechnics entered the Research Assessment Exercise. The only one that did not – the University of Central England at Birmingham, now Birmingham City University – was castigated for foregoing the £363,000 that it would have gained had it participated. The university participated in the next exercise in 1996.
- The quick and comprehensive rejection of the Dearing Committee proposal in 1997 (Recommendation 34) that institutions should be compensated for not entering departments in the RAE, what a colleague once termed, by analogy with the EU Common Agricultural Policy, 'academic set-aside'.
- The similar rejection, in 2003, and at institutional insistence, of the option in the Roberts Review of the Research Assessment Exercise (RAE) for consideration to be given to a different assessment method for institutions still developing their research (see Chapter 4).
- The fact that, seven years on, nearly all of the universities that acquired their titles under the 2004 legislation in 2005–6 have sought and obtained research degree-awarding powers, even though this is no longer needed for a university title and having such students almost certainly costs them tens of thousands of pounds each year.

However, perhaps the best and clearest evidence of competition through emulation comes from institutions' responses to the opportunities given them by successive governments to undercut others' charges.

In 1998, no one availed themselves of the opportunity to charge less than the £1,000 top-up fee. In 2006, only four institutions decided to charge less than £3,000, and by 2010 they were all charging the maximum. In 2011, a third of institutions initially decided to charge the maximum £9,000 for all courses from 2012, with a further third charging the maximum fee for some, and it took strenuous action by the Government to force some of them down. There could hardly be a better example of how higher education – or at least full-time undergraduate education – is a positional market (Hirsch, 1976) where what counts with many institutions, students and employers is status and relative position, and where price is a synonym for quality rather than a reflection of it.

It should next be acknowledged that there are some good reasons for restraining diversity. Some years ago, Watson (1998, p. 76) used the phrase 'a controlled reputational range' to describe and justify the quality assurance mechanisms – formal and informal – through which variations in quality in Britain had historically been limited, such as external examining. These indeed represent one of the strengths of the British system, and also contrast it most notably with America where in some states (e.g., California) there are not even any restrictions on the use of university title, and where in any one city there are, almost certainly, greater variations in quality than are to be found in the whole of the UK. There have also been some constraints on variations in resourcing. The Funding Council's methodology for allocating block grants for teaching has allocated the same level of support to teaching wherever it is delivered, and also aimed to harmonise institutions' resources for teaching (HEFCE, 2007). Similarly, the fact that RAE funding is allocated selectively does not alter the fact that the criteria for allocating the moneys are common ones (Scott, 2005).

In Chapter 3 we noted that the differences between the polytechnics and the old universities were never as great in Britain as in most European countries with a binary system. Scott (2009) even went so far as to say that the differences were administrative and legal rather than educational. He has also reminded us (1995, 2005) that even though the UK is now a mass system, it remains largely dominated by elite values (see also Brennan, 2004). Moreover, as he and other writers (e.g., Watson and Bowden, 2002) have pointed out, there has been some degree of convergence since 1992. Most of the former polytechnics have developed research and postgraduate provision, whilst many of the pre-1992 universities have developed part-time, modular and applied courses.

Unfortunately, we lack a really rigorous, conceptually-based analysis of changes in institutional diversity in Britain in the period covered by this book. However, Chapter 3 described the removal of the formal distinctions between institutions and the substantial reduction in the number of specialist institutions – the colleges of education, the London medical schools, and the art and design institutions. In his recent survey for HEPI, Ramsden, B. (2012) pointed to further ways in which the system has become more convergent. There are now fewer institutions which specialise exclusively or largely in full-time, part-time, postgraduate or undergraduate study: only one institution now has no postgraduate students, compared with five in 1994–95. Over the past 12 years, many more institutions have enrolled significant numbers of students from outside the UK: it is now the norm for institutions to enrol more than 15 per cent of their students from outside the UK. A diminishing number of institutions require the highest entry qualifications. A majority of institutions are now recruiting over 90 per cent of their entrants from state schools (Ramsden, B., 2012).[8]

Ramsden nevertheless describes these changes since the mid-1990s as 'marginal':

> There are still a large number of institutions that have differing characteristics and do different things. Moreover, to the extent that there has been convergence, to a large extent the changes that have been observed represent a response by institutions to the changes and constraints of the external environment, most particularly changes in student demands and needs.
>
> (Ramsden, B., 2012, pp. 4–5)

He concludes:

> As far as the balance between teaching and research is concerned, perhaps surprisingly in view of the apparent national policy towards greater concentration, this investigation has concluded that there has not really been much convergence of mission over time; although there has been a marginal

increase in diversity amongst the most highly research active institutions, as research concentration has been promoted.

(Ramsden, B., 2012, p. 5)[9]

It may be helpful at this point to refer to the distinction made some time ago by Teichler (2006) between 'horizontal' and 'vertical' differentiation (see also Brennan, 2007). In horizontal differentiation, institutions discharge different functions in meeting various societal needs: liberal or general education versus professional preparation; undergraduate versus postgraduate; education versus research; national versus regional, etc. The criteria by which they are evaluated are primarily related to their function(s). In vertical differentiation, institutions are distinguished by status or reputation, i.e., esteem. They are judged by a common set of criteria which often emanate from within the academic community and are echoed in the mass media. What seems to have happened in Britain since 1979 is that there has been a small reduction in horizontal or functional diversity but a larger shift in vertical or status diversity. This is fully consistent with what we know about the likely impact of market-based policies in higher education.

It is fair to say that over the period covered by the book, government policies on horizontal diversity – the institutional 'division of labour' – have varied. For example, David Blunkett's February 2000 Woolwich speech (Blunkett, 2000) was criticised for laying down a 'universal agenda' for all institutions to follow (Watson and Bowden, 2001). Under his successor, Charles Clarke, the boot moved to the other foot as attempts were made to incentivise different institutional missions, as we saw in Chapter 3. However, the fact that virtually the same language was used in the 2009 White Paper as in the 2003 one indicates that this policy enjoyed only limited success.

There were various reasons. The resources devoted to some of the different missions were neither sufficiently substantial nor sufficiently 'new': the widening participation moneys, for example, were virtually all 'old', i.e., non-additional to already planned expenditure, as well as greatly inferior to the sums for research (they were mostly taken off the teaching grant). Institutional autonomy and competition also played its part. But undoubtedly the main reason was that the parity of esteem pass had already been sold, if indeed it had ever had a chance, with the introduction of research selectivity, which gained its power by meshing in with the interests, values and preferences of many academic staff and managers. As in the US, so in Britain, research has become what Massy once called the 'coin of the realm':

The best way to get one's ticket punched for institutions and professors alike.

(Massy, 2003, p. 19)[10]

Historically, there was always a status hierarchy in British higher education, not only between the different sectors (universities, polytechnics and technical colleges, colleges of education; later universities, polytechnics and HE colleges) but also within the old university sector, where it broadly corresponded with longevity as a degree-granting body. Nevertheless, at least within the university sector, it was not as pronounced or apparent as it would later become:

> But until the 1980s, in what had been the larger part of the system (the universities), equality in formal terms, at least, was assumed in terms of roughly equal funding per commensurate unit, the expectation that all teachers would be researchers for about a third of their time, and the common standards putatively ensured by the external examiner system. This was reinforced by the funds provided through the UGC which was the part of the dual funding mechanism supposed to ensure that there were well equipped and funded laboratories in all universities. Research Council funding was the other part of dual support.
>
> (Kogan and Hanney, 2000, p. 93)

Research selectivity has been used not just to concentrate research funding but to restructure the system by determining institutional missions and status. This concentration, together with institutional longevity and an inescapable lack of success in finding robust criteria to underpin any significant measure of selectivity in teaching funding (see Chapter 6 and below), helps to explain the major differences in institutional resourcing, the extent of which even now are not fully appreciated or understood.

Some years ago, Watson and Bowden drew attention to the resourcing disparities between institutions, and the high correlation between overall levels of resourcing and each institution's position in the *Times League Table* (Watson and Bowden, 1999). Income from all sources per FTE student was seen as a quantitative measure of the institutional resources that a student would experience. In 2006, Brown, N., and Ramsden found that, taking together teaching and research income per weighted full-time equivalent student, and allowing for subject mix, the best-funded institution (Imperial College) in 2004–5 enjoyed an income of up to two-and-a-half times the mean sectoral figure, whilst the least well-funded institution had an income of under half the mean (Edge Hill University). These figures have recently been updated, though without allowing for subject mix or London weighting, for the institutions covered in the recent (May 2012) *Guardian University League Tables 2013*. In 2010–11, gross income per FTE student ranged from £65,840 (Cambridge) to £7,050 (Edge Hill again). The sector mean average was £14,710.[11]

It is virtually certain that these disparities will increase even further after 2012. To begin with, the Government has confirmed the previous policies of research concentration and even reinforced them, as we saw in Chapter 4.[12] Those institutions that get the lion's share of the available research funding will also be those that are able to charge the full £9,000 fee and thus put even greater economic and reputational distance between themselves and their competitors; they are also the institutions that charge the highest fees to overseas and postgraduate students. The new funding regime for teaching described in Chapter 5 will reinforce this; it may also lead to further concentration and hierarchy within the select group. Even before it is implemented, the AAB+ threshold is doing for teaching what research selectivity and the 'spin' put on RAE judgements by successive governments have over time done for research, in creating an elite group of institutions comfortably distanced from their domestic rivals and increasingly referred to, even by people who should know better, as 'top' universities.

To quote the independent Higher Education Policy Institute analysis of the 2011 White Paper:

> The logic of the twin measures [the AAB+ threshold and the introduction of core and margin funding] is to create two sets of institutions, a new binary divide. One group will charge fees over some Government limit (currently £7,500) and be free to recruit students without any Government quota. Their students will be eligible for a range of bursaries and scholarships, and there will be increased resources for teaching. The other group of providers will charge below a fee level set by the Government, in effect a maximum fee. Each institution would be allocated a quota of student places which would cover part-time as well as full-time students that it could not exceed. There would be fewer resources for teaching and less generous bursaries and scholarships than awarded by the other group of institutions.
>
> (Thompson and Bekhradnia, 2011, paragraph 217)

In fact, the new funding regime is more likely to produce a three-tier system, with the elite institutions able to charge £9,000 to as many students as they can be bothered to recruit, a bottom tier of FE colleges, private providers and one or two universities charging £6,000 or less, and a middle group, the 'squeezed middle', unable to compete with the elite on resources or reputation but unable to compete with the new entrants on price, flexibility or convenience. As Marginson has often pointed out (e.g., 2004), the market in undergraduate education is a positional market towards the top and an economic market towards the bottom.

But whatever form the increased stratification takes, it is clear that the Government's reforms will produce a system that is more vertically than horizontally diverse. Given the broad correspondence between institutional selectivity and the social make-up of institutions, this takes us inevitably to the issue of equity.

Equity

> Fair access is a fundamental principle of our reforms. It is vital that all those with the ability should have access to higher education. We have introduced a new National Scholarship Programme, which will begin in the 2012–13 academic year, and will provide financial benefit to some of the least well-off young people and adults as they enter higher education. And we are taking

action to strengthen the Office for Fair Access to ensure it can provide support and challenge to institutions on fair access.

(DBIS, 2012c, paragraph 1.6)

The picture that emerges is of a socially differentiated higher education sector, with the elite institutions tending to be dominated by middle-class, white and male students, many of whom are from the private schools sector. These students benefit from the intrinsic and positional benefits of going to a 'good' university, and the elite continues to reproduce itself, with the status of a university increasingly defined by the profile of its student intake.

(Leathwood, 2004, p. 38)

It is well established that the expansion of the system since 1979 has led to virtually no reduction in the disparities in participation between students from different socio-economic backgrounds (e.g., Bekhradnia, 2003; Reay, 2005). However, there has recently been some (small) narrowing of the gap. A HEFCE analysis for the OFFA a couple of years ago (Harris, 2010, Annex C) looked at young participation trends by area distinguished by parental education, i.e., areas were classified by the proportions of children with one or more graduate parents (a good indicator of the propensity to enter higher education). This found that between 1994–95 (the first year in which there were statistics for the unified sector) and 2009–10, the participation of young students from the most advantaged 20 per cent of neighbourhoods rose from 49 to 56 per cent, whilst that of young students from the most disadvantaged 40 per cent of areas rose from 13 to 20 per cent. For the sector as a whole, the ratio of the participation of more to less advantaged areas averaged 2.6 between 2006–7 and 2009–10; this compared with a ratio of well over 3 at the start of the period.

These results were then disaggregated by looking at entry tariff, with the sector being divided into high, medium and low groups depending on the UCAS tariff points required for entry: these broadly corresponded to the institutional mission groups described in Chapter 3. It was found that most of the institutions in the low-tariff group had a ratio below 2, with some having a ratio of 1 or even less. In contrast, the high-tariff institutions always had a ratio of 3, three-quarters of them had a ratio of 5 or more, and some even went up to 15, i.e., these were institutions where the most advantaged young people were 15 times more likely to enter than the most disadvantaged. In addition, whilst in the sector as a whole, and in the low- and medium-tariff groups, the relative proportions of entrants from the most disadvantaged areas had increased, for the high-tariff institutions the participation rate at the end of the period was no higher than it had been in the mid-1990s. In contrast, young people from the most advantaged areas were *more* likely to participate in high-tariff institutions than they were in the mid-1990s (compared with no change for young people from the most disadvantaged areas).

This analysis and others (e.g., Watson, 2006a) suggests that the differential participation problem in England has two components: a general problem of aggregate numbers of students from disadvantaged areas participating in higher education ('widening participation'), and a specific problem of students from disadvantaged areas participating in highly selective institutions ('fair access'). What difference will more market-based policies be likely to make to this picture?[13]

It is suggested that three sets of considerations may be relevant to the discussion: economic factors, capacity issues and institutional stratification.

Economic factors

Callender (2003) summarised a large number of US studies showing links between various aspects of participation and economic factors. A number of UK studies (e.g., Callender and Jackson, 2005, 2008; Pennell and West, 2005; Davies *et al.*, 2008) have drawn attention to the rising cost of higher education, and the associated debt, as influencing the decisions of students from low-income families, either about whether to participate in higher education at all, or about what and where to study, including whether to study from home. Callender (2009a, 2010) has also drawn attention to the risk that, as has happened in the US, institutions will switch their student support packages (bursaries and scholarships) from being primarily need-based to a mixture of need- and merit-based; this in turn will perpetuate, if not exacerbate, existing divisions across the sector. We should also note the use of fee waivers to reduce the fee to get the institution below the threshold for margin bidding (with government encouragement, see below) when a number of writers (e.g., Sweeting, 2011) have suggested that students would rather have the assistance in the form of cash (bursaries and scholarships). Finally, there are indications from research conducted by the NUS (2012) and within universities (Carasso 2010) that students prefer financial packages that are clear and transparent – so that, for example, course fees include the cost of any compulsory field trips.

However, there has so far been little evidence that economic factors of this kind have significantly affected participation (Harrison, 2011). Neither the introduction of maintenance loans in 1990, nor the introduction of top-up fees in 1998 appears to have affected participation. The introduction of variable fees in 2006 actually coincided with the *increase* in entrants from disadvantaged areas that has already been noted. Dorling (2012) shows how this increase was due to improvements in GCSE performance at around age 16, and that this in turn could be predicted from increases in average funding in secondary education. In other words, spending levels matter, but in the schools rather than in higher education. This is of course one of the main reasons for the success of the private schools, with fee levels up to three times the per pupil spend in state schools and tax breaks for those claiming to be charities; ironically, several studies (e.g., Bekhradnia, 2003) show that this advantage is not sustained once students enter university.[14]

As with rising costs to the individual student, it appears that so far the amounts and terms of institutional bursaries and scholarships have not been significant factors in student choices: the main problem with such awards has been the number and complexity of them (Adnett, 2006; Carasso, 2010). Harrison (2011) notes an estimate that after 2006 350 separate schemes came into existence, focussing on income, academic merit, geographical location, school type, disability, ethnicity, etc.

However, all this may be about to change. A recent survey of 500 applicants for 2012 entry by OpinionPanel (Steenhart and Newton, 2012) suggests that nearly a quarter were changing their approach because of higher tuition fees, with the proportion of those charging being far higher for those from low-income backgrounds with lower predicted grades. These applicants were much more likely to look for universities with lower fees, universities with good financial support packages, or universities closer to home; in contrast, fee levels were unlikely to deter students with good predicted grades, whatever their background. It is also known from the March 2012 UCAS Statistics that whilst applications for 2012 entry to full-time first degree courses from 18-year-olds have fallen by only 1 per cent since 2011 after allowing for demographic factors, students from age groups of 19 and older were between 15 and 20 per cent less likely to apply in 2012 than in 2011 (UCAS, 2012). There also signs that higher fees are beginning to be a deterrent for students thinking of going on to a Masters course, especially those from the poorest socio-economic groups (Wales, 2012). Widening participation has long been recognised as a problem at postgraduate level (Wakeling, 2010).

Turning to institutional aid, 'merit aid' is increasingly used by American universities and colleges to boost student entry scores and thus prestige (see, for example, Heller, 2007). A recent report by the National Center for Education Statistics (Lederman, 2011) found that between 1995–96 and 2007–8 the percentage of students receiving merit aid rose from 6 to 14; over the same period, the percentage receiving need-based aid rose from 32 to 37; the shift was most pronounced at four-year and private institutions. Since in America, as in Britain, educational attainment correlates broadly with social class, this means that institutions are investing more of their resources in wealthier students. Here, the uncapping of places for undergraduates entering with grades of AAB+ has created an incentive for institutions to introduce merit-based scholarships into their student support packages from 2012.

For courses where the standard entry requirement is (generally, only slightly) lower than AAB, a number of universities are offering scholarships to 'overqualified' entrants who have achieved AAB+; in some cases there is an additional condition that the applicant must have made the awarding university their first choice, so they are committed to studying there if they meet the terms of their conditional offer, and do not have the option, in that year, of going to a university that requires higher grades. Thus the decision to uncap places for better qualified students may be creating a market for the most highly qualified freshers among universities rather than, as the Government hoped, encouraging the most selective institutions to expand the number of places on offer.

System or institutional capacity

Another theory is that differential participation may be affected by (a) the overall size of the system and/or (b) the (un)willingness of highly selective institutions to expand.

On the first, the Coalition Government has followed the previous Labour Government in cutting numbers of funded places: in January 2012 the Government announced a further cut in funded Home/EU student numbers for 2012–13 (DBIS, 2012a). This cut of 5,000 places is on top of the 10,000 additional places funded in 2011–12, which will not be repeated in 2012–13. It has led to a statement of despair by the well-known advocate of wider participation, Sir Peter Lampl (Williams, Z., 2012). We noted earlier the recent increase in qualified applicants not receiving offers. This proportion will have grown since, and will continue to grow, especially if, as seems all too probable, the Government responds to the increased costs of the system to the taxpayer by further reducing the number of places (see Chapter 9).

On the second, as we noted in Chapter 5, one of the Coalition Government's motives in removing the controls on the number of well-qualified entrants is to enable more selective institutions to expand. However, this may well not happen. Both American and British experience suggest that as systems expand, the most prestigious institutions do not increase their capacity pari passu; indeed they cannot do so to any large extent without risking a loss of status. Astin and Oseguera (2004) argued that many of the more prestigious American private institutions have little incentive to expand, whilst the public ones are constrained by levels of state appropriations (a position that is even more critical now than it was eight years ago). This comes on top of, and reinforces, the selectivity practised by the highly ranked institutions that inevitably discriminates against less well-educated (or well-prepared) students, who tend to come from poorer backgrounds (Wellman, 2008; Blumenstyk, 2011).[15]

In Britain, we noted in Chapter 5 how in the 1980s and early 1990s most of the existing universities chose to protect the unit of resource rather than expand in line with government policies (see also Thompson and Bekhradnia, 2011). We can be fairly certain that this selectivity will continue and that in Britain, whilst a few of the most selective institutions will seek to take advantage of the new funding regime to expand their numbers, most will not. There may even be an element of cynicism in current government thinking about widening participation in that it is the more selective and less participation-focussed institutions that are being allowed to expand their numbers.

Institutional stratification

Just as capitalist markets generate inequality of wealth in the economy, market coordination in American higher education has tended to exaggerate

> financial inequality across colleges and universities and encourage social ine-
> quality in student access to educational opportunities.
>
> (Geiger, 2004, p. 180)

How far is increased institutional stratification likely to be a barrier to wider
participation? Work at London Metropolitan University in the early part of the
decade (Archer, 2003) suggested that the very fact that the former polytechnics
are generally less prestigious may in itself be a significant disincentive to participation, incidentally giving the lie to the claim of proponents of league tables that
they are of particular benefit to students from less-favoured backgrounds (see also
Leathwood and O'Connell, 2003). Similarly, Reay *et al.* (2005) found that some
working-class students were put off applying to some of the post-1992 universities that advertise heavily, on the grounds that 'good universities shouldn't need
to advertise'.

   In a 2010 study, Reay *et al.* explored how different institutional cultures or
'habituses' affect working-class students' experiences of fitting in or standing out
in higher education. They found a clear 'institutional effect' but also that some
of the institutions in the survey did not always have the personnel or resources to
give students a personally focussed learning experience. They concluded:

> Working-class students, for the most part, end up in universities seen to
> be 'second class' both by themselves and others. And as Bourdieu (1999,
> p. 423) asserts, 'after an extended school career, which often entails consid-
> erable sacrifice, the most culturally disadvantaged run the risk of ending up
> with a devalued degree'. The success stories of the very few working-class
> students who make it into UK elite universities, whilst welcomed, have little
> impact on the broader picture of continuing classed and racialised inequali-
> ties (Blanden and Machin, 2007).
>
> (Reay *et al.*, 2010, p. 121)

If, as seems all too probable, the resourcing and status differentials between institutions increase still further as a result of the Government's reforms, this must
become even more of a factor in student choice in Britain, as it already is in the
United States (Brown, 2011e). It is also necessary to bear in mind the fact that
the current policy changes are not taking place in a vacuum. To the extent that
our entire system of education is moving in a market direction, this must be to the
advantage of students and prospective students with the necessary social capital
and networks to navigate the system, almost certainly at the expense of those who
do not. This is already a factor in the schools, as Le Grand pointed out many years
ago (Le Grand, 1987).

   It seems clear from all the evidence that (a) the main reason for the general widening participation problem is the insufficient number of those from disadvantaged
backgrounds with the necessary qualifications for university entry (Bekhradnia,
2003; Raffe *et al.*, 2006; Greenbank, 2007; Gorard, 2008; NAO, 2008; Vignoles,

2008; Chowdry *et al.*, 2011); (b) the main reason for this is the very variable performance of the schools (Forsyth and Furlong, 2000; Vignoles, 2008); and (c) this in turn reflects wider policies affecting schooling and society generally, and especially segregation by area and social class (Gorard *et al.*, 2006).

Whereas across all OECD countries, on average, 57 per cent of the performance differences between schools can be attributed to the social character of the intake, in the UK the social intake accounts for over 70 per cent of the performance differences (Centre for Learning and Life Chances in Knowledge Economies and Societies, 2011; see also Thrupp, 1999, and Jenkins *et al.*, 2006). The OECD (2008) argued that there was a clear relationship between variability in school performance and the fairness of progression to higher education: countries providing fairer access to higher education – such as Finland, Ireland and Spain – were also those with the most equal between-school performances in PISA 2000. This has led the Organisation, in its recent Economic Survey of the UK (OECD, 2011b), to recommend that the Government should experiment with proscribing the use of residence criteria in admission to local government maintained schools in some areas. This would be an important step towards the objective of trying to ensure that state-funded schools are as similar in character, intake and process as possible, so that a child's background, or where they live, makes little difference to the kind of school they attend or the kind of education they receive.

Leathwood has suggested that, as well as being a problem in itself, the increased stratification of higher education increases the pressure on middle-class parents to choose private or selective schooling for their children:

> Fear of failure or falling back, and 'defence against uncertainty' (Walkerdine *et al.*, 2001: 167) remain powerful motivators of middle-class success. The extended hierarchy of universities and the widening gap between the elite and the rest, therefore directly contributes to the sustenance of class divisions within the school sector, just as the divisions within schooling maintain the class divide in higher education.
>
> (Leathwood, 2004, p. 41)

Similarly, Roberts:

> A significant difference from times past is that nowadays positional competition continues into, throughout and beyond higher education. There are no earlier, secure destinations. This used to be admission to a good secondary school (independent or grammar), or into a university which guaranteed secure progress into the narrow band of what are now called 'traditional' graduate occupations. Today, middle-class parents believe that *which* secondary school can make a crucial difference to the grades that their children will achieve in the 16-plus and 18-plus examinations, which will decide whether they will become serious competitors for the best graduate jobs.
>
> (Roberts, 2010, pp. 223–224)

In other words, the stratification of higher education contributes to and rein-forces the stratification of the school system, and vice versa. This will be even more true as greater competition is introduced into the school system through larger numbers of academies and 'free schools': academies now form the major-ity of state secondary schools in England (Shepherd, 2012a). Yet it is quite clear from international evidence that those countries with comprehensive, integrated school systems – such as Finland, Canada and Japan – outperform those – such as Britain, America and Australia – that focus on differentiation and competition (OECD, 2008; Alegre and Ferrer, 2010; Glatter, 2010). Finally, we should note that Cheng and Gorard (2010) have identified several types of segregation, all of which increase with increases in the number of secondary schools.

Before leaving this issue, it should also be observed that the post-2012 funding regime places a premium on AAB+ students at the possible cost of students with lesser grades who might nevertheless have the potential to benefit from attending a more selective institution but who may not have the chance they might have had previously through the use of 'contextual' data. To quote Scott (2012):

> To rely on A-level grades alone is, in effect, further to privilege the already privileged, to give disproportionate rewards to those whose way in life has been smooth. The correlation between school performance and social advan-tage is too plain to deny. For years universities have attempted, feebly per-haps, to level the playing field by making differential offers. Now, on the fiat of David Willetts, they are no longer so free to do so.

Callender (2011) noted that because of the strong links between high A-level grades and socio-economic advantage, under-represented students are the least likely to benefit from the lifting of the limits on AAB places. Disadvantaged stu-dents are also less likely to have the qualifications to access the reduced number of 'core' places. She also points out that the Government itself has acknowledged that the squeeze on places at these institutions 'will impact disproportionately on opportunities for widening participation students', many of whom will apply to these universities. It should also be noted that the terms of the new National Schol-arship Programme (NSP) require institutions to establish mechanisms through which they can offer support to students from low-income backgrounds through means other than cash bursaries. Under this scheme, each institution charging fees of more than £6,000 has an allocation of scholarships – to be co-funded by HEFCE and the university or college – for undergraduates who are eligible for the maximum maintenance grant. At least £2,000 of the £3,000 annual award must be in the form of indirect benefits – such as fee waivers, a free 'foundation year' or discounted accommodation – obliging institutions to operate these 'discounts' and, in practice, resulting in such offers being built into many financial support packages beyond those operating under the NSP. While it may be argued that such initiatives reduce the amount that students may need to borrow, they also reduce the total value of subsidised student loans, and thus the call on the public purse.

Equity: conclusion

> [R]ather than providing low cost HE for everyone, the free market mecha-
> nism results in a highly segmented system where the most advantaged can
> afford to attend the high priced prestigious institutions and the least advan-
> taged can only attend the lower-priced lower-status institutions. Despite
> pressures for the HE system to be more inclusive, a free market approach
> exacerbates the inequalities that consumers bring to the market.
>
> (Hemsley-Brown, 2011, p. 122; see also Ranson, 1993)

It seems clear that, whatever may have happened in the past, the intensification
of market-based policies in the compulsory sector, alongside huge spending cuts
to education generally, will widen the existing class-based differentials between
schools, and thus reduce even further the supply of students from disadvantaged
backgrounds with both the qualifications and the desire to enter higher education. At the same time, the increasing stratification of higher education will present a further barrier and disincentive to many such students. We seem bound to
continue with the situation where the more selective institutions mainly draw
their student body from private schools and middle-class households, while the
less selective ones recruit more heavily from state schools, FE colleges, minority ethnic communities and working-class households (Harrison, 2011; see also
Greenbank, 2007). Whatever the Government may claim, this is not a recipe for
increased social mobility.

Chapter 8

The impact of marketisation
Quality

In this chapter we review what the available evidence suggests about the impact of market-based reforms on quality, distinguishing between student education and research. We also discuss more briefly the effect of marketisation on the academy's ability to control the 'academic agenda', what is to be taught and researched and how. This in turn has implications both for quality and for universities' broader relationship with society.

Educational quality

> Our proposals are designed to create genuine competition for students between HEIs, of a kind which cannot take place under the current system. There will be more investment available for the HEIs that are able to convince students that it is worthwhile. This is in our view a surer way to drive up quality than any attempt at central planning. To safeguard this approach, we recommend that the [proposed] Higher Education Council enforces baseline standards of quality; and that students receive high quality information to help them choose the HEI and courses which best matches [sic] their aspirations.
>
> (Independent Review of Higher Education Funding and Student Finance, 2010, p. 8)

As we have seen, it has been the view of successive governments that market competition improves quality as institutions 'raise their game' to attract students. Against that, a number of writers (e.g., Smith *et al.*, 1993; Yorke and Alderman, 1999; Naylor, 2007; Alderman, 2008, 2009, 2010; Gibbs, 2012) have claimed that academic standards may be falling and that increased competition, reinforced by institutional league tables, is one of the main reasons. A 2004 survey of 400 academics by *Times Higher Education* (Baty, 2004a) found that five out of six agreed that 'the squeeze on the resources of higher education institutions is having a general adverse effect on academic standards'. Seventy-one per cent agreed that their 'institution had admitted students who are not capable of benefitting from higher level study', 48 per cent reported that they had 'felt obliged to pass a student whose performance did not really merit a pass', 42 per cent said that 'decisions to fail students' work had been overruled at higher levels in the institution', and almost one in five admitted to turning a 'blind eye' to student plagiarism. A further survey in 2008 (Gill, 2008b) had 500 responses. Whilst there was only a bare majority for the view that reports of 'dumbing down' were not incorrect or overstated, more than 80 per cent felt that resourcing constraints were affecting academic standards, about 77 per cent saw plagiarism by students as a growing problem, more than 70 per cent agreed that the need to maintain acceptable retention rates had led to lower failure rates on courses at their institution, and almost 70 per cent disagreed that rising numbers of 'good' degrees was evidence of improving standards.

In *Higher Education and the Market* the author identified from the literature a number of reasons for suggesting, prima facie, that the quality of education – students consistently achieving worthwhile educational outcomes – might have declined as a result of a combination of marketisation and reduced levels of spending per student. These included: a reduction in the amount of learning due to a reduction of the 'size' of the curriculum, a shorter academic year, less contact with academic staff, heavier staff workloads, larger teaching groups, higher student-staff ratios, more students working in term-time, etc.; lower rates of progression, retention and graduation; increasing reports of students less well prepared for degree level study; greater pressure on pass rates and grade inflation, especially at the more prestigious institutions; more plagiarism and other forms of cheating; declining levels of trust between students and staff seen not only in increasing student complaints, but also in misbehaviour in the form of violence, harassment, public humiliation and rudeness, as well as accusations of unfairness and lack of professionalism; increasing resort to temporary and part-time lecturers and tutors, including graduate students; a growing tendency for programmes and awards to be valued for their 'exchange' value, particularly in the labour market, rather than for their 'use' value, to the student ('commodification'); students adopting a more 'instrumental' approach to their studies, focussing their work on what will gain them good marks; and a diversion of resources away from teaching and learning towards activities like marketing that have only a remote relationship to educational quality (Brown, 2011a).

Time on task

HEPI has conducted a series of surveys of the academic experience of students at English universities (Bekhradnia, 2006, 2007, 2009, 2012). The author was a member of the steering committee for the project. The most striking finding has been the enormous variations in scheduled hours of teaching (contact hours), private study time and total learning load not only between subjects, but also, within subjects, between institutions. The HEPI conclusions were endorsed in a 2009 report for HEFCE by the Centre for Higher Education Research and Information (2009); this showed that besides having the shortest degree courses in

Europe, UK students also study for a shorter period each week (about 30 hours a week compared with 42 hours in France, for example). In 2006 the *Times Higher* reported that students at Sussex were campaigning for a minimum of eight hours a week contact time with lecturers (THE, 2006). The *Higher* in 2008 reported an hour's reduction for social science students at Manchester, subsequently admitted by the Vice-Chancellor (Attwood, 2008b, c). Harding (2009) reported a substantial reduction in contact hours in the Arts Faculty at Edinburgh since 1980.[1]

Term-time employment

A survey of students at four universities (Metcalf, 2003) found that term-time working was affecting the quality of education. It was particularly damaging for students whose father did not have a degree and for female students, especially ones from ethnic minorities.[2] A survey for UUK (Centre for Higher Education Research and Information and London South Bank University, 2005) found that even an average amount of term-time employment could significantly affect the chances of a student obtaining a good degree; students with lower academic attainments were much more likely to be working longer than the average. Using data from 1,000 students in six universities, Callender (2009b) quantified the impact of students' paid work on their actual marks and degree results, whilst controlling for their academic attainment on entry and other factors including their hours of work. Irrespective of the university attended, term-time working had had a detrimental effect on both final year marks and degree results: the more hours students worked, the greater the negative effect. Students working the average number of hours a week (15) were a third less likely to get a good degree than an identical non-working student. Moreover, some of the most adversely affected students were amongst the poorest and least qualified. A 2010 study (Barker, 2010) found that some trainee teachers on PGCE courses were working for more than 21 hours a week on top of their courses, many to stem their debts; nearly a third were working for between 11 and 20 hours a week.

Retention

The National Audit Office (NAO) has investigated retention twice in the past decade (NAO, 2002, 2007). On each occasion it found that in spite of increases in participation rates, projected UK completions continued to show up well in international comparisons. The 2002 report found that 85.5 per cent of students were projected to complete their degree at the institution at which they had started their course, obtain another award or transfer to another institution. This compared with 84 per cent in 1997–98, the earliest year for which comparable figures exist. The 2007 report found a figure of 86.6 per cent. The latest Higher Education Statistics Agency (HESA) figure (for 2009–10) is 86.7 per cent. It is true that many institutions have put a lot of effort into retention in the past decade or so, partly in response to government prodding. However, these figures, whilst reassuring at least in comparative terms, in themselves tell us little about academic standards, especially as low levels of retention can significantly affect institutions' finances (Baty, 2004b).

Grade inflation

Yorke (2009) showed how the proportion of good degrees (Firsts and Upper Seconds) rose between 1994 and 2007 in all subject areas. In the earlier period (1994 to 2002) the increases were most apparent in the Russell Group institutions; in the later period (2002 to 2007) the increases were more evenly spread. However, it should not necessarily be inferred that the cause was grade inflation: the modularisation of curricula, the greater emphasis on learning outcomes (so that students have a clearer idea of what is expected of them), encouragement of examiners to use the full range of marks, and the shift towards assessed coursework and away from unseen exams could all have contributed (see also Hunt, 2008, and Yorke, 2008). This upward trend has continued so that, according to HESA data, 65 per cent of full-time UK students obtained 'good' degrees in 2010–11, compared with 62 per cent in 2006–7.[3]

Student preparation for university study

Grade inflation is not confined to higher education. The Chief Regulator of Ofqual, the government agency that oversees the standards of school exams, was recently reported as saying that A-levels and GCSEs had suffered 'persistent grade inflation' for 'at least a decade' (Stewart, 2012b; see also Shepherd, 2012b). The same report quoted the President of Pearson, the owner of EdExcel, the largest school exam board, as saying that exam boards should be 'worried about' the discrepancy between 10 years of rising A-level and GCSE results and England's failure to achieve better scores on international benchmarks. Two months previously, the man who ran EdExcel was reported as saying that he resigned after being expected by Ofqual to manipulate GCSE results downwards to prevent grade inflation (Stewart, 2012a). The Government has responded by announcing a reform of A-levels in which the universities will play a larger part (Stratton, 2012).

There have been numerous reports of university entrants being inadequately prepared for higher education, a common theme being that sixth-formers are being 'spoon-fed' and that teachers are 'teaching to the test' so that students find the demands of independent study difficult even after a year (Ovens, in preparation). For example, in September 2011 the Institute of Physics found that more than half of the physics and engineering academics surveyed said their first-year undergraduates were 'not very' or 'not at all' well prepared to cope with the maths content of their degrees (Allen, 2011). In the same year, a report by the Advisory Committee on Maths stated that maths A-level and other post-16 qualifications were not stretching pupils enough for many higher education courses (Shepherd,

2011). The nature of the problem can be seen from the fact that the previous year the same committee had warned that making maths A-level harder would mean fewer students studying the subject (Mansell, 2010a). These concerns are not confined to the sciences: in 2008 the *Times Higher* reported a Cambridge University study which found widespread worries about British students' English language skills (Gill, 2008c).

Several years ago the Government introduced an A* grade to distinguish outstanding performance at A-level. A number of universities (e.g., Imperial College) have instituted entrance exams. Increasing numbers of students are resorting to private tuition agencies to help bridge the gap between A-levels and university (Vasagar, 2010). In 2010, counselling services at Oxford and Cambridge reported 'year on year' rises in the number of youngsters seeking help because they lacked the necessary resilience when faced with challenges in their studies (Mansell, 2010b).

Plagiarism

It is generally agreed that advances in technology have facilitated plagiarism and other forms of cheating and misconduct by students. However, the author is not aware of any recent work on the extent of this across the UK, or on any trends. A survey of 100 institutions a few years ago for the Higher Education Academy and the Joint Information Systems Committee (Tennant and Duggan, 2008) found 9,229 cases in one year and 143 student expulsions. There were variations by type of institution (with less selective universities having higher rates) and level of course (with a higher rate at postgraduate level). The great majority of offences were 'first-time' ones. There was no data by subject, but others have suggested (Jack, 2008) that plagiarism is commonest in business studies, computing and accountancy, perhaps because a larger amount of text is available on-line. As regards other forms of cheating, the *Times Higher* in 2008 carried two reports of academic staff encouraging students to give their departments' positive NSS ratings (Attwood, 2008a; Newman, 2008). In 2010 *The Guardian* reported that eight universities were being investigated by HEFCE for putting undue pressure on students to boost their NSS ratings (Kenber and Taylor, 2010). Cheating seems to be common in university admissions in both the US (Marcus, 2008) and the UK (Stewart, 2011).[4]

Student expectations and behaviour

A number of writers (e.g., Bone and McNay, 2006; Lee, 2006; Tahir, 2007; Attwood, 2009) have drawn attention to possible links between a decline in trust between staff and students and poorer student behaviour (see also Jones and Philp, 2011). Leon (2001) reported students adopting a more 'instrumental' attitude to their studies, narrowing the focus of their studies to what will win them marks (see also Broadfoot, 1998; Shepherd, 2008). This was also one of the main findings of the *Times Higher's* 2008 staff survey. In a two-year study, Soin *et al.* (submitted for review) found lecturers increasingly reluctant to write anything critical about students in references; this fear had spread to discussing contentious issues in class, or even putting critical comments on exam scripts. As we noted earlier, complaints have increased, albeit from a low base (Jones, 2006). Students are putting greater pressure on staff about marks but also demanding to see staff whenever it suits them. Much of this arises from the growing view – not least on the part of the Government – of higher education as a commodity and of the student as consumer. Finally, Palfreyman (2010) has warned that the risk of legal action by students unhappy with their marks could even increase if higher education is 'commodified' with 'mechanistic and formulaic' teaching methods. This seems to be an increasing risk.

Commodification and consumerisation

Several writers (e.g., Naidoo and Jamieson, 2005; Cooper, 2007) have identified a growing trend for higher education to be valued for its 'exchange' value (especially in the labour market) rather than its 'use' value (to the student); for a similar argument on the possible commodification of research, see Boden and Epstein, 2006. A number of writers (Barrett, 1996; Scott, 1999; Barnett, 2000; Rolfe, 2002; Morley, 2003; Potts, 2005; White, 2007; Hearn, 2008; Furedi, 2009; Molesworth *et al.*, 2009; Alderman, 2010; Cuthbert, 2010; Molesworth *et al.*, 2011; Naidoo *et al.*, 2011; Williams, J., 2012) argue that standards may be at risk from the reconstitution of the student identity – not least through commercial league tables and exercises like the National Student Survey – from that of 'apprentice academic' to that of 'novice consumer', so that students increasingly see themselves as customers with needs rather than as clients or partners in an educational project. To quote Williams (2011, J., p. 181):

> the consumption model, in shifting the focus so successfully away from learning processes and onto educational outcomes, denies students the transformational potential of higher level study in exchange for satisfactory experience and a suitable product (degree attainment).

(See also Furedi, 2012.) The fact that this student-as-consumer culture is even stronger in the US (Marcus, 2006; Oxford, 2008) is hardly reassuring in this context.

The impact of competition

There have been several reported instances – so far, modest in number but individually important – where competitive pressures appear to have led to management interference with academic judgements. Some of these were reported to the House of Commons Innovation, Universities, Science and Skills

Committee (IUSSC) during its inquiry into students and universities in 2008–9. They included:

- The resignation of Professor Paul Buckland at Bournemouth University in 2007 in protest at the decision of the university authorities that 13 students whom he and an exam board had failed should nevertheless be deemed to have passed. He subsequently won his claim for compensation for unfair dismissal.
- The attempt at Manchester Metropolitan University (MMU) to discipline a lecturer, Walter Cairns, who had protested at management attempts to force him to lower his standards of assessment because of the damage that high failure rates could do to the university's finances. When he subsequently complained to the Select Committee about his treatment, he was removed from the Academic Board at the Vice-Chancellor's insistence (the Vice-Chancellor thereby risked incurring the charge of contempt of Parliament and had to make an apology).
- Another MMU lecturer, Susan Evans, was reported by the *Times Higher* in March 2009 as alleging that marks were often bumped up at the university without consulting tutors, and that in 2004 this had meant nine economics students graduating who should not have done (Gill, 2009).
- *The Times* on 2 July 2008 (p.5) reported the leaking to the BBC of an internal MMU memorandum asking lecturers in maths and computing to bear in mind 'the understandable desire' to increase the number of Firsts and Upper Seconds so as to help the institution to compete more effectively. Lest it be thought that apparent manipulation of academic standards was a post-1992 monopoly, we should also note the Vice-Chancellor of York's memo to all the university's external examiners in 2000 saying that a university of such calibre should be awarding more 'good degrees' (Baty, 2000).
- The case at Kingston University where it was alleged that an external examiner had been pressured into altering her report so that it reflected less badly on a department that had in her view admitted sub-standard students and then assessed them too favourably. This was investigated by the QAA, which publicly gave the university a clean bill of health (QAA, 2009).
- In 2011 the *Times Higher* reported a head of school at a Russell Group university e-mailing colleagues urging them to be 'VERY generous' when assessing student applications for PhDs, and warning them that they 'simply cannot afford to be too choosy' (Jump, 2011).
- Most recently, there was a report of a Dean at Teesside encouraging staff to improve completion rates by resubmitting work, giving 'generous' deadline extensions and passing assignments before they had been seen by external examiners (Matthews, 2012f).

Unfortunately, we lack any serious study of the impact of market competition since 1979 on the quality of student learning and achievement. Even by recent standards of policy making, it is surely extraordinary that in spite of all the attention and resources devoted to quality assurance since at least 1992, and even allowing for the undoubted difficulties of definition, we should have so limited a picture of what has actually happened to quality – the quality of the student experience, the standards of student achievement. Equally depressing has been the failure of any national body to take responsibility and ownership of the problem. Too often, when presented with evidence of these detriments, the sector's response has been tardy and defensive.

Of a number of cases within the author's direct knowledge, three stand out. The first was when HEQC first audited institutions' overseas partnerships. Three universities received consistently damning reports. When the author as HEQC Chief Executive suggested to one or two senior vice-chancellors in 1996–97 that CVCP might invite the institutions to temporarily withdraw from membership of CVCP he received a reaction that can best be described as polite ridicule. The second was the vice-chancellors' reaction to the first of the HEPI student experience reports in 2006: instead of acknowledging that they had failed to collect this quite basic information and agreeing to interrogate it, the HEPI Director was hauled over the coals and in effect 'told off' for embarrassing the sector. The third was the IUSSC inquiry in 2009–10, which the Funding Council and the vice-chancellors together first tried to prevent, then water down the terms of reference, and then ignore, at least publicly, the resultant report.

However, even if there was clear evidence that quality had declined, one would still need to know how far it was due to the introduction of market competition, as opposed to other factors such as changes in resourcing levels, developments in the school curriculum, wider changes in society, etc. We also need to take into account the enormous expansion of the system and the admission of students from a much wider set of backgrounds and with a much wider range of abilities than previously.

Quality and resourcing

One attempt that was made to examine the effects of cost pressures on the quality of student education was the report prepared for HEFCE in December 2008, sometimes called the Crossick Report after the chair of the group that produced it (Geoffrey Crossick, then Warden of Goldsmiths College, subsequently Vice-Chancellor of the University of London). This highlighted five areas where cost pressures were clearly impacting on the fitness for purpose and sustainability of the student learning experience:

- The relationship of staff to students
- The curriculum and assessment
- The student population and its needs and expectations
- Infrastructure for teaching and learning
- Student support services.

(HEFCE, 2008, paragraph 1.10)

The report went on to comment:

> These areas are all inter-related, but the first of them, the relationship between staff and students, has a particular significance because it is at the heart of the distinctive UK higher education experience. It is influenced by a number of relevant issues including staff-student ratios (SSRs); contact hours; group sizes and loads of learning; other activities of academic staff; the needs and expectations of students; and the learning environment and services available to support student learning.
>
> The evidence, from a range of sources, shows that cost pressures in all these areas have grown in the last few years as the task for higher education institutions (HEIs) has become larger and more complex. They have made remarkable gains in efficiency and productivity, and the pressures are being contained by a variety of means. Some of these 'coping strategies' are effective ways of delivering higher education at lower unit costs in a more massified system, but others are incompatible with attaining a world-class experience and delivery of government agendas such as widening access and employer engagement (which impose additional costs).
>
> (HEFCE, 2008, paragraph 1.11–1.12)

Regrettably, there is very little hard UK evidence about the relationship, if any, between funding and quality. The odd QAA institutional review report may refer to problems, but one will look almost in vain for any systematic views; one exception was a 2006 report which stated that students were getting poor academic and personal support because of the 'strain' that tutorial systems were under (QAA, 2006). This may not be an accident. Peter Williams, Chief Executive of the QAA from 2002 to 2010, and previously head of its audit group, confirmed to the author (personal communication) that, for different reasons, neither HEFCE nor UUK was ever keen for the Agency to get into this territory. This will almost certainly change as competition and institutional resourcing differentials increase as a result of the Government's reform programme (for the full argument, see Brown, 2011d).[5]

One important exception was a 2010 survey for the Higher Education Academy, in which Gibbs argued that the key was less the availability of resources and more whether the resources are committed to things that make for student success, such as staff development and teaching and learning centres (things not usually picked up by external quality assurance processes). However, he also noted that low student-staff ratios might be helpful for educational gain, provided they are appropriately exploited throughout the institution. Similarly, Gibbs cited several studies showing how class sizes affect student achievement, as does the amount of contact between lecturers and students (Gibbs, 2010, p. 19). Both these process variables are of course resource-related.

There is more American work on this issue. In a 2006 study of 416 public institutions, Blose *et al.* found a clear correlation between graduation rates and expenditure per student. In a 2007 article, Bound and Turner showed how reduced resources per student in the American states had affected degree attainment in the public institutions. These effects arose from a combination of larger student cohorts and lower state appropriations, precisely the combination we have been facing in the UK since the 1980s. A later article by two of the same authors (Bound *et al.*, 2010) similarly explained how the overall reduction in completion rates in US higher education was mainly due to growing performance differences between more and less selective institutions, which in turn are linked to widening resourcing differentials: in 2006, average spending on education and related spending per FTE student ranged from nearly $37,000 at a private research university to under $10,000 at a public Associate's institution (Wellman, 2008). As we have seen, the UK already has resourcing differentials of this magnitude and these will increase still further after 2012.

Use of temporary and part-time teaching staff

There are also some American studies (Bettinger and Terry Long, 2006; Ehrenberg and Zhang, 2006; Glenn, 2008; Schmidt, 2008) which suggest that changes in the composition of the teaching force – specifically the reduction in the proportion of tenure track faculty and the increasing use of part-time instructors ('adjuncts') – may be having a negative impact on completion. Both are of course the result of declining institutional revenues. Comparable UK studies are scarce. Surveying the use of graduate teaching assistants (GTAs) in a research-led department at the University of Sheffield, Muzaka (2009) noted concerns about subject knowledge and teaching skills only partly offset by good interpersonal skills and recent experience as an undergraduate. The only other UK study the author has been able to find is a recent survey of GTAs in Scotland (Dickie *et al.*, 2012). This points to the danger to universities if undergraduates see that teaching is given a low priority and delivered by an insufficiently trained, inappropriately remunerated and poorly motivated workforce of assistants: research students teaching other postgraduates could be an area of special concern. Both studies call for more training for GTAs. The HEPI academic experience surveys suggest that students at older universities are more likely to be receiving their small group tuition from non-academics (i.e., graduate students) or 'pre-academics' (post-doctoral students at the start of their career); they are also more likely to be taught in larger groups. An NUS survey in 2008 (Attwood, 2008b) found that students did not rate researchers or postgraduates highly as teachers. As regards the resort to temporary and part-time staff, in spite of concerns about increasing use of temporary or short-term staff, the HESA Staff Record actually shows a declining proportion of fixed-term staff since 1995–96 and an increase in the proportion of staff on open-ended and permanent contracts.

Changes in the curriculum

We also lack a proper picture of changes in the curriculum including in the subjects offered for study by the universities. Ramsden, B. (2012, p. 4) notes that there has been a decline in science and technology subjects, alongside a significant increase in creative and performing arts, media studies and politics. However:

> In general, the major changes in subject provision by HE institutions have matched the changes in demand as evidenced by applicant choices – although Mathematics is a notable exception to this, having seen an increase in demand and a reduction in supply.

The latter may of course reflect the problems with maths A-level to which we have just referred.

A number of writers (e.g., Rolfe, 2003) have suggested that, as a result of higher charges and a greater emphasis on the economic benefits of higher education, students are switching to more 'vocational subjects', whilst institutions are increasing the vocational content or relevance of their courses. However, in the fourth of the reports that UUK commissioned on the impact of variable fees in 2009 (Brown, N., and Ramsden, 2009, paragraph 107) the authors concluded:

> There is no evidence either that the introduction of the new full-time undergraduate fees has had any impact on student subject choices. There have been significant changes in subject balance of acceptances onto first degree programmes over the last five years, with significant declines in computer science, business and management and, most recently, subjects allied to medicine. There have been increases in other subject areas. These changes would appear to reflect longer term cyclical changes in the perceptions of individuals about subject choice and career prospects rather than any issue about tuition fees.

This is yet another phenomenon that everyone believes may be occurring, but no one has thought worth seriously investigating.

Dysfunctional expenditure

Increased expenditure on things that help to attract students but which have little or no educational value – such as student residences, cafeteria and recreational activities, what one commentator has called 'gilding their palaces of exclusivity' (Carey, 2011) – has long been noted as a significant feature of modern US higher education. Hearn (2008, p. 209) refers to Luettger's (2008, p. 22) estimate that the amount of money spent on marketing and communications by colleges and universities in the US had risen by over 50 per cent since 2000. This may be why many American students pay far more in tuition than their colleges spend on educating them, something we shall increasingly see here as tuition fees take off after 2012.[6] Much of this expenditure is of course in response to what students, as consumers, need or say they need. In the UK, a number of writers (e.g., Rolfe, 2003) have drawn attention to increased expenditure on marketing and branding as universities seek to maintain and improve their position in the market, even though much of this is ineffective. There has so far been less comment about dysfunctional expenditure on the US pattern, but this can surely be only a matter of time.

Research quality

The UK is the most productive country for research in the G8, producing more publications and citations per pound of public funding than any other major country.
(DBIS, 2011a, Executive Summary, paragraph 21)

The RAE has undoubtedly brought benefits but it has also caused collateral damage. It has damaged staff careers and it has distracted universities from their teaching, community and economic development roles. Higher education should encourage excellence in all these areas, not just in research.
(House of Commons Science and Technology Committee, 2002, Conclusion, paragraph 5, quoted in Bence and Oppenheim, 2005, p. 23)

Nothing less than the positional status of every institution was at stake.
(Marginson, 1997, p. 74, quoted in Hicks, 2008, p. 12)[7]

Long-term evaluation will be needed regarding the quality of research and research education, the national and institutional epistemic ecologies, and the research institutional structures resulting from the changes that have occurred in the United Kingdom. Much of the UK story seems to support Geuna's argument (1999) that the challenges of a new era are opening up an unbridgeable gap between universities; only a few elite research universities will fully adapt to the new demands and also manage to retain some of the assumed defining features of universities; many will be marginalised and little influenced by international changes in the production of knowledge.
(Henkel and Kogan, 2010, p. 380)

Geuna (2001, p. 620) has set out very well the assumptions that underpin a performance-related system of research funding:

- That it is possible to evaluate the quality of the research output accurately.
- That it is possible to identify the most promising research avenues.
- That cost reductions can be achieved without any decrease in the quality of output.

- That due to the existence of scale and scope economies, the concentration of scientific capabilities increases the research output of the system.
- That the administrative costs of assessment and evaluation, for both government and universities, linked to the implementation of a competitive system, are small compared with the cost savings (see also Vincent-Lancrin, 2006).[8]

We noted in Chapter 4 the quite widely held view that the introduction of selectivity, and in particular the RAE, led to better use of research resources, to a reduction or restraint on costs, and to the elimination or reduction of 'poor' research. This was a consequence of the stimulus that selectivity gave to institutions to manage research more tightly. As Geuna and Martin (2003, p. 296), reviewing the widespread adoption of competitive research regimes more widely – some in direct emulation of the RAE – remarked:

> Its main virtue lies in the assumption that it is inherently meritocratic, rewarding success and improving quality ... It gives a mechanism to link research to policy, a way to shift priorities across fields, and a rational method of moving resources from less well-performing areas to areas where they can be used to greater effect. Assessments also give leading departments a 'marketing' tool to attract top researchers and students.

Other benefits include a higher priority being given to research than might otherwise have been the case, and more support being given to researchers, especially in less 'research intensive' institutions.

But it also seems clear – and again there are international studies of the RAE and similar mechanisms that confirm this (e.g., Geuna, 2001; Geuna and Martin, 2003; Himanen *et al.*, 2009) – that these benefits may diminish over time, not least because institutions learn to 'play the game' (Clarke, 2005; Crespi and Geuna, 2006; Lucas, 2006). Hence the need to keep raising the bar higher with each successive RAE (see also Hicks, 2009). In addition, doubts have been raised about the benefits of scale in relation to research. Johnston has produced a series of analyses contesting the assumption that 'big is necessarily beautiful' at department/unit level (e.g., Johnston *et al.*,1993; see also Evidence Ltd, 2011). There is some American work which comes to the same conclusion (Jackman and Siverson, 1996). Evidence Ltd (2003) found that the statistical correlation between size and performance was mainly attributable to the fact that large units rarely have poor research.

At institutional level, Whiteley's (2009) statistical analysis of the 2008 RAE suggested that research performance declines once an institution gets too big (over 10,000 faculty). These are on top of the wider disadvantages of concentration already noted in our discussion of institutional diversity (see also Horta *et al.*, 2008). Watson and Bowden (2002, referring to Ramsden and Brown, 2002) and Evidence Ltd (2005) pointed out that universities with medical schools have been particular beneficiaries of selectivity, receiving not only large amounts of government funding, but also substantial funding from charities such as the Well-come Trust. There is also the problem of geographical concentration and the risk that certain regions (especially the East Midlands and Wales) will lose important areas of research and suffer a reduction in research performance (Evidence Ltd, 2003; Adams and Smith, 2004).

There are further detriments and distortions to research selectivity, including:

- The treatment of all subjects within a 'one-size-fits-all' framework in spite of very different forms of knowledge production across the academy (Griffiths, 2004).
- The unavoidably backward-looking nature of the assessments, which may favour established researchers, research fields and research methods, at the expense of newer and more innovative researchers and ways of doing things.
- A narrowing in the topics chosen for research and in the perspectives and techniques applied.
- A bias in favour of 'pure' and theoretical research at the expense of 'applied' and practice-based research that may be of greater benefit not only to external users but even to the academy itself.
- A bias in favour of research with relatively shorter time horizons.
- A bias in favour of traditional discipline-based research and against inter- and multi-disciplinary research, 'Mode 1' knowledge production rather than 'Mode 2' to use the now familiar terms.[9]
- The risk that the measures become more important than the research itself (Lucas, 2006).

Moving away from the detriments to research, there have also been many costs to teaching and learning. To begin with, many studies (e.g., McNay, 1997a and b) have commented on the separation or distancing of research from teaching. Selectivity has meant researchers spending less time teaching, and more teaching being done by part-time staff and postgraduates (JM Consulting, 2000). Ironically – in view of the claims often made by such institutions about the advantages to students from learning in a 'research environment' – this is more likely to be the case in 'research intensive' institutions (Bekhradnia, 2006, 2007, 2009, 2012). Hence the scope for exploiting the synergies that can arise when research and teaching are conducted together is reduced; it is also reduced because, as well as relegating pedagogical research, selectivity has downgraded research processes and outcomes that might be of particular value to students as well as other 'end-users' (Locke, 2004).

Research selectivity has also meant teaching having a lower priority than research when it comes to rewards, appointments, and promotions, even in primarily teaching institutions (Jenkins, 1995; Court, 1999; Barnett, 2000; Rowland, 2000; Coate et al., 2001; HEA and the Genetics Education Networking for Innovation and Excellence (GENIE) CETL, 2009). This has even been admitted by the former Vice-Chancellor of Cambridge:

The fact is that rankings, prestige and investments are strongly weighted towards our research endeavours. This carries over in some measure to the training of postgraduate students, but makes it ever harder for research-intensive universities to give serious attention to the education of undergraduates. The standing of individual academics, in their disciplines and universities, depends more and more on research accomplishments and less and less on their contributions as teachers. Investment from the public and private sectors reflects and reinforces this asymmetry.

(Richard, 2006, p. 1)[10]

The one serious study of innovation in UK higher education known to the author (Hannan and Silver, 2000) found that the demands of disciplinary research, and especially the RAE, were a major impediment to pedagogical innovation, especially for less senior lecturing staff. Similarly, the demands of the RAE were a major challenge to quality assurance, although again there does not appear to be any recent work on this:

The greatest threat is undoubtedly the prospect of another UFC research selectivity exercise. The overriding urgency with which universities and departments seek to maximise their research outputs (and inputs) is currently the main obstacle to innovation in quality assurance, and, indeed, the systematic improvement of teaching. Not only is time short, but resources in general are painfully inadequate to support innovations in teaching. Whether this is internal or external I refuse to say!

(SWOT analysis of quality assurance by a distinguished academic auditor, CVCP 1992)

Research selectivity has produced a bizarre situation where a large part of the academic workforce has to do some teaching in order to be able to do what they really want to do (research, mainly in the older institutions), whilst another segment (mainly in the newer institutions) has to undertake some form of research to safeguard their positions as teachers. It is strongly arguable that what is really needed is for all academic staff in a department or group to undertake between them the full range of academic tasks, not only teaching and research, but also quality assurance, some administration, serving on committees, admissions, links with schools, etc., all of which should be equally valued. Finally, selectivity has also damaged other forms of scholarship, such as the production of textbooks, one of the classic ways in which academic research feeds into (and from) the student curriculum (see also Henkel, 2000).

As regards research quality, the strong comparative performance of UK academic research has already been noted (see also Wellings and Winzer, 2011). Adams and Gurney (2010) show how, relative to the world average, the citation impact of the UK research base dramatically improved in the late 1980s (see also Adams et al., 2000; Evidence Ltd., 2002 and 2008; King, 2004; DBIS, 2012c).

Adams and Gurney noted that whether this improvement was a result of the RAE or simply a 'correlative outcome' of the policy and management environment in which the RAE has operated is not clear, though it would be 'reasonable to conclude' that it was a consequence of the introduction of the RAE (2010, paragraph 28).

However, the reviews by Williams, B. (1987) and by McNay (1997a and b, 2003, 2007, 2009, 2010, 2011a and b) present a more mixed picture. Managers tend to be more positive in their views than academic staff, with autonomy and freedom to choose what and how to research being a major issue. There can certainly be little doubt that, as a result of the combination of increased evaluation and selective funding, the control of research has moved away from the individual researcher in many institutions: the model of the lone researcher has long been replaced by managed environments (research into higher education may be an exception). Using OECD data, Himanen *et al.* (2009) compared the research performance of five developed systems – Australia, Finland, the Netherlands, Norway and the UK – between 1987 and 2005. They found that when staff are given more autonomy, they do more research and are more productive. Trying to control research at the input stage by resource allocation conditions, as with the RAE and similar exercises, is actually counterproductive.[11]

There is also work that suggests that research quality may be uneven across our system.

Adams (2006) suggested that the overall quality of UK research performance was heavily influenced by a small group of very highly cited performers. More than half the UK's output between 1995 and 2004 was uncited, or had a citation count less than the world average: two-thirds of the UK's papers were in these categories. Typically, a third of papers in the physical sciences and engineering were uncited. As Roberts (2006, p. 17), commenting on this analysis, wrote: 'This translates into there being expensive-to-run laboratories and large cohorts of academics engaged in "handle-turning" research with little academic impact.'

This unevenness applies both at institutional level and within mission groups. Also using citation analysis, Chester and Bekhradnia (2009) showed how the research standing of the Russell Group is heavily dependent on the performance (and, ultimately, the resources) of Oxford and Cambridge. For papers published between 2002 and 2006, 7.9 per cent of articles and reviews published by Oxford and Cambridge were 'highly cited' (i.e., they were cited at least four times as much as the relevant world average); the figure for the Russell Group as a whole was 5.7 per cent, compared to a sector average of 5.2 per cent. In other words, the Russell Group performed only half a per cent better than the sector as a whole: when the other 'golden triangle' institutions (Imperial College, University College London and the London School of Economics) were excluded, the Russell Group actually performed *below* the sector average.

Adams and Gurney (2010) confirmed this analysis. Although the post-1980s improvement in citation impact was associated, at least until 2005, with a rising share of publications authored or co-authored by Russell Group academics, the overall performance not just of the Russell Group but of the entire UK research base was driven 'to a significant extent' by the impact of papers from a small number of institutions. This justified more selective funding for 'the rare peaks of internationally outstanding excellence [but] there is no case for a general and universal policy to concentrate on historical characteristics' (Adams and Gurney, 2010, paragraph 54).

The authors based this conclusion on two considerations: first, the fact that 'the curve of relative excellence' extended across the full range of impact categories for all institutional groups (Adams and Gurney, 2010, paragraph 40 and Figure 2). Second, the fact that over 20 per cent of the UK's research output – and even 15 per cent of golden triangle research – was uncited raised questions about value for money:

> It seems that a significant amount of the research done even in golden triangle institutions might be considered not very good at all, and that the money provided for such research could be better – or at least as well – spent elsewhere. At the very least this suggests that care should be exercised in pursuing a general policy of increased concentration as distinct from selectivity based on merit.
>
> (Adams and Gurney, 2010, paragraph 41)

This was written in the aftermath of the Government's decision, in December 2009, described in Chapter 4, to change the weightings initially adopted after the 2008 RAE so as to provide for greater relative reward for high scores. It makes the present Government's decision to increase selectivity still further even more questionable.

As well as being uneven across institutions (and groups of institutions), quality is also patchy across disciplines, being stronger in clinical sciences, health and environmental sciences than in the physical sciences and engineering (King, 2004; DBIS, 2012c). Finally, there is the issue of the quality, and especially the validity, of the RAE judgements themselves on which the whole edifice rests, which many have questioned (e.g., Sharp, 2004; Johnston, 2008; McNay, 2009, 2011b).[12]

As good a judgement as any on selectivity and quality is that of Thomas (2007, p. 42):

> The conclusion must be that the main increase in the quality of UK research has been in a small amount of top quality output. It is perfectly rational to explain this as a result of increased selectivity. The more infrastructure, resources and staff are concentrated in fewer locations, the more likely that, in general, the output will be high quality, especially in science. There is no evidence that the process that is used to concentrate these resources increases quality; the explanation is the concentration itself.

As Vice-Chancellor of Bristol, previously Dean of the Medical School at South-ampton, and subsequently President of UUK, Thomas is in as good a position as anyone to make such a statement.

What makes all this even more piquant is the fact that the immediate financial consequences of each RAE for individual universities and colleges are relatively minimal: a HEPI analysis of institutional gains and losses between 2001–2 and 2005–6 found that only one institution saw its revenues affected by more than 3.7 per cent after the 2001 RAE: the median impact was less than 0.6 per cent (Sastry and Bekhradnia, 2006). Yet institutions have put enormous effort and money into preparing for, participating in, and adjusting to the consequences of each exercise, including the costs of hiring expensive research 'stars' who will add only marginal financial benefit unless they can generate massive indirect cost recovery on research grants. Thomas indeed (2007, p. 44) considered this 'dam-aging investment behaviour' to be one of the main reasons for the sector's poor financial performance over the years. In fact, the RAE has long had more symbolic than financial importance. As a signifier of status for institutions, departments and individuals, it has become a 'fact totem' (de Santos, 2010) just like, though con-siderably earlier than, the National Student Survey and the AAB+ threshold. The policy question that arises, therefore, is whether the advantages of some degree of research selectivity might not have been achieved with fewer costs, detriments and distortions, especially to academic activities other than RAE-able research. This is an issue we shall revert to when we consider the lessons from the period in Chapter 9.[13]

The control of the academic agenda

> The high protecting power of all knowledge and science, of fact and princi-ple, of inquiry and discovery, of experiment and speculation.
>
> (Newman, 1959, quoted in Naylor, 2007, p. 1)

> It shifts the determination of what is taught in universities away from pro-fessorial power towards student demand power, and what is researched from autonomous disciplinary interests towards the service of industry, gov-ernment, and the practising professions ... There is a decline of donnish dominion.
>
> (Halsey, 1995, p. 12)

As noted in Chapter 2, in many developed countries universities enjoy both legal and operational autonomy in return for providing a wide range of valued public and private goods. In America, the main threats to the universities' control of the academic agenda – the ability of the academic community to determine what is taught and researched – have come from commercial sponsorship of university research, epitomised by the University of California, Berkeley's arrangement with Novartis, whereby the latter obtained first call on the outcomes of the university's biotechnology research (Kezar, 2004; Krimsky, 2005; Washburn, 2005; Greenberg, 2007; and many others). In Britain, in contrast, the main threat to academic control of research has come from a series of state initiatives since the early 1990s to promote what successive governments of all parties have deemed to be in the national economic interest.

Moriarty (2011) gives a useful list of these. Referring to American experience since the 1980 Bayh-Dole legislation, he argues that, by focussing on research impact, near-market deliverables and the privatisation of research results, these policies are not only at odds with the principles of openness, objectivity and independence that traditionally underpin academic research and scholarship, but are also likely to be *economically* damaging by reducing, rather than enhancing, the return on state investment in research (see also Royal Society, 2003; Willmott, 2003; Peters and Olssen, 2005; Boulton and Lucas, 2008; Moriarty, 2008; Henkel and Kogan, 2010; Macdonald, 2011; Smith, 2012). This is highly relevant to our discussion of value in Chapter 9.

The 2009 report by Scientists for Global Responsibility, based on a close study of commercial involvement in university research in five major industrial sectors (pharmaceuticals, tobacco, military/defence, oil and gas, and biotechnology) points to very similar detriments to those identified in the American literature. These include: the introduction of (not always conscious) bias ('sponsorship bias'); an increasing orientation to sponsors' commercial needs, rather than to broader public interest or curiosity-driven goals; as a consequence, the marginalisation of work with potential social or environmental benefits; lack of openness, due to the use of commercial confidentiality agreements and other IPR considerations; conflicts of interest; and a greater focus on IPR, including patents, in academic work, so that knowledge is increasingly being commodified for short-term economic benefit. There has also been suppression of findings. There are also wider risks to academic standards, collegiality and the integrity of the academy. Perhaps of greatest importance is the threat which academics' engagement in commercially funded or sponsored research is likely to pose to the universities' standing with the public (see also Parkinson, 2011).

America also furnishes cases of the dangers that can arise from private donations (e.g., Hundley, 2011). Here, however, one does not need to go so far to find examples. The scandal of Saif Al-Islam's £1.5 million donation to the London School of Economics, which led to its distinguished Director's resignation, as well as considerable damage to the institution, is all too recent. This can also be seen as a failure of governance (Vasagar, 2012); in fact, it is a good illustration of the author's thesis (Brown, 2011f and g) that present university governance arrangements will not be strong enough to cope with increased market competition and greater commercial involvement in higher education.[14]

Conclusion: the impact of market-based policies on UK higher education

It appears that, in broad terms, what has been happening in the UK as a result of the market-based policies described in this book is consistent with the picture painted by the general academic literature on the subject:

- Market-based policies have almost certainly made UK higher education much more efficient, entrepreneurial and responsive to external stakeholders.
- There has been a small reduction in horizontal institutional diversity but a significant increase in vertical institutional differentiation, which the Coalition Government's reforms will further increase. Research selectivity has played a crucial part in this.
- While it is not certain that increased competition has narrowed socio-economic and other forms of participation hitherto, it likely will from 2012, again as a direct result of the Government's reforms.
- Increased competition coupled with significantly reduced expenditure per student over the period has led to a reduction in the quality of education experienced by most students, although we lack the evidence to demonstrate this.
- Whether or not it has raised research quality, selectivity has undoubtedly damaged other academic activities, not only teaching and quality assurance but also non-RAE forms of scholarly inquiry and knowledge exchange. These costs and detriments almost certainly outweigh the benefits to research quality.
- Whilst Government policies on economic impact represent the main threat to academic control of the 'academic agenda', the same detriments that have been attributed to commercial sponsorship of academic research in the US have also begun to appear here.

In effect, market-based policies have partly compensated for – and even been a (deliberate?) distraction from – a failure to consistently invest an appropriate proportion of national wealth in higher education. This has been at considerable cost in terms of quality, cohesion and, probably, equity. In Chapter 9 we shall consider whether and how it might be possible to obtain some gains from the adoption of market-based policies, whilst avoiding or minimising the detriments.

Chapter 9

Lessons from marketisation

There is a place for the market, but the market must be kept in its place.
(Okun, 1975, p. 19, quoted in Kirp, 2005, p. 127)

What the faculty and staff of both public and private institutions have learned is that in the end there is really no market advantage accorded to institutions that provide extra-quality education. What matters in this market is not quality but rather competitive advantage.
(Zemsky, 2005, p. 287)

Graduates from the elite universities seem to have a triple advantage: the reputation of the university, social capital networks, and personal or identity capital.
(Kupfer, 2011, p. 204)

This final chapter considers what lessons may be taken from this account of the marketisation of UK, and especially English, higher education since 1979.

First, it should be acknowledged, yet again, that even after the present Government's reforms, higher education in England will still lack many of the features of a true economic market. Marginson (submitted for review) indeed argues that it never can, partly because of higher education's intrinsic features (the fact that most knowledge is a pure public good and the prevalence of positional competition) and partly because of political constraints.

Second, and not only because of the further wave of marketisation that is now occurring in England, it is necessary to repeat that any conclusions have of necessity to be somewhat provisional, especially as there are some important areas, notably the quality of student education, where there has been very little worthwhile analysis. It has nevertheless been possible to offer some reasonably firm judgements about the impacts of market-based policies to date.

There has clearly been a considerable increase in the efficiency with which institutional resources are used. A huge expansion in student numbers was achieved with a much smaller increase in expenditure, and with respectable graduation and employment rates being maintained. Other crude indicators, such as economic returns, student satisfaction and attractiveness to internationally mobile students, remain favourable, although the UK Border Agency's recently introduced restrictions on entry visas (Acton, 2011) may damage the latter, at least in the short term. Similarly, research selectivity has improved the productivity of research and researchers. There has also been a significant increase in the quantity and value of 'third-stream' activities like applied research, technology transfer, consultancy, and continuing education and training. Britain still has a respected, even envied, university system, with several aspects, such as research selectivity, widely emulated (Aghion *et al.*, 2008; Ederer *et al.*, 2008; St Aubyn *et al.*, 2009; Usher and Medow, 2010; Agasisti, 2011).

What we do not know, however, is how far these gains were offset by reductions in quality or equity. While most of the measurable indicators are respectable, especially in European terms, there is a good deal of qualitative material, reviewed in the previous chapter, that is troubling, and this is even before the current reforms have worked themselves through (see below). Similarly, there are some clear warning signals about the damage to access that can arise in particular from increased institutional stratification, as noted in Chapter 7. This goes to what is surely the nub of the matter, how to obtain reasonable value, both now and in the future and for every group of stakeholders, from the societal investment in higher education, what Belfield and Levin (2005, p. 551) usefully called the 'the maximisation of educational results for any given resource constraint'.

Markets and value

Proponents of market-based policies argue that the market is the best means of allocating resources and is therefore the best guarantee of value for money. What we have seen of the application of such policies to higher education, both in Britain and in other developed systems (Brown, 2011a and b), should surely give us pause. In particular, we should be very aware of the dangers, not only for quality and equity but also, and ironically, for the use of resources, that arise from the challenge of market-based policies to what is surely the best protection for all stakeholders, namely, the existence of an integrated, accessible and functionally diverse system of universities and colleges capable of delivering an appropriate volume and mix of public and private goods.

In Chapter 7 we referred to the view that a mass system needs a variety of institutions offering a variety of subjects and modes of study. It seems clear that in Britain there has over time been some diminution in the diversity of institutional types, as well – given the dominance of research over teaching in many institutions and departments – as in the diversity of institutional priorities. We also noted Ramsden's (2012) comment that in one respect at least the system does appear to be becoming more diverse, if not divergent, namely in the increasing resourcing and status gaps between the most research-intensive and other institutions.

This was symbolised by the March 2012 announcement that four members of the 1994 Group of universities (Durham, Exeter, Queen Mary and York) would be joining the Russell Group (Russell Group, 2012). In commenting on Exeter's decision to leave the 1994 Group, the Vice-Chancellor, Sir Steve Smith, is reported to have said that the 'sector is changing' and that 'the AAB thing [had] changed the debate'. He added that 'Durham and ourselves were up there and then York was a little bit lower, but not much' (Morgan, 2012c). There could be no clearer indication of the positional values that are now driving the leaders of our universities (Sir Steve was until recently President of Universities UK (UUK), in which capacity he represented the universities in their dealings with government in the 2010–12 reform period).

In November 2010, *Times Higher Education* reported the Secretary of State, Vince Cable, as saying that one of the reasons for raising the fee cap was to prevent 'Oxford, Cambridge, the London School of Economics, University College London and a few others' from going private: 'If we had not opened up the system, they would have had a very strong incentive to do so' (Gill, 2010). The raising of the cap, along with the ending of numbers controls on AAB students, on top of the renewed concentration of research funding, shows how the aspirations of a handful of would-be 'world-class' institutions may be distorting our higher education policies. Bearing in mind the fact that whilst private in legal status, they receive (and will continue to receive) large amounts of public funding (both directly and via their students), we need to consider whether the benefits of such preferential treatment outweigh the costs and detriments to the system and the country as a whole.

Because of their market power, elite institutions in most systems often receive high levels of both public and private funding. In principle, and excepting differences in local costs, the only justification for such treatment can be higher levels of quality (and even then there is always an argument about whether marginal resources should be used to reward 'excellence' or bring every provider closer to a common standard).

The two core activities of most universities are research and teaching. As we saw in Chapter 7, the evidence that the concentration of research resources has led to better research is mixed. There is even less justification for the concentration of resources for teaching.

There is a considerable amount of American work on this issue. In their meta-survey of how colleges affect students, Pascarella and Terenzini concluded:

> Institutional quality, as reflected in various measures of admissions selectivity, has a significant and positive direct effect on student persistence, educational aspirations, and degree completion, even after statistical adjustments for the characteristics of entering students and other institutional traits. But the effect of selectivity is small and intertwined with the kinds of experiences students have at college.
>
> (Pascarella and Terenzini, 2005, p. 594)

In their 2004 article drawing on the National Study of Student Learning and the National Survey of Student Engagement (NSSE), Kuh and Pascarella stated:

> Our results clearly show that institutional selectivity is a weak indicator of student exposure to good practices in undergraduate education. This conclusion holds regardless of whether the data represent the performance of the institution or individual students.
>
> (Kuh and Pascarella, 2004, p. 56)

Similarly:

> On average, across all good practice variables we considered, more than 95% of the between-institution differences [in measures of academic expectations] and almost 99% of the total differences were unexplained by the academic selectivity of a college or university. Put another way, attending a selective institution in no way guarantees that one will encounter educationally purposeful academic and out-of-class experiences that are linked to a developmentally influential undergraduate experience.
>
> (Pascarella *et al.*, 2006, p. 279)

A more recent study (Ro *et al.*, submitted for review) confirms that within-institution characteristics – how the university organises itself for student learning, what sort of environment if provides, etc. – are far more important for student educational gains than the structural-demographic criteria usually applied (see also Pascarella, 2001).

There is no comparable UK work. However, the TLRP (2008) Project *What Is Learned at University? The Social and Organisational Mediation of University Learning* found that reputational differences between institutions did not always correspond to differences in what was learned:

> The project has identified many commonalities to the experiences and outcomes of university study, almost irrespective of where and what one studies. And where differences exist they do not automatically match reputational hierarchies ... The dominant hierarchical conception of diversity in UK higher education in policy discourse provides only a very limited reflection of the diversities that exist, and neglects the commonalities that can be found.
>
> (TLRP, 2008, p. 2)[1]

Similarly, a still-continuing study of social science degrees at four very different British universities found a significantly higher incidence of good teaching at the two lower-status institutions (Ashwin *et al.*, 2011).

But if the case for of giving elite institutions preferential treatment on grounds of quality is not proven, the costs and detriments are clear:

- partly because of the pricing behaviour of the elite (mostly, private) universities and colleges, American higher education costs far more than it should. According to OECD figures, and excluding R&D, in 2008 the US spent $26,908 on educational services per tertiary student; the OECD average was $9,349 (figures adjusted for purchasing power) (OECD, 2011a, Table B1.1a). This inflation in costs would almost certainly have happened in England if ministers had acceded to Russell Group demands that the fee cap be not merely raised but abolished altogether.[2]
- if the overall quantity of resources for higher education is constrained, it is almost certain that the leading institutions are receiving income that could and should have gone to institutions that are playing a more socially useful role, and making a better job of it. The AAB+ rule effectively transfers resources away from the less prestigious institutions to the more prestigious ones, exacerbating the already substantial resourcing gaps between them that we registered in Chapter 7.
- there are the costs of the emulatory behaviour of the institutions that are trying to become 'world-class', about which Altbach has frequently warned us (e.g., 2004). This wastage is likely to be seen on a global scale as more and more institutions in more and more countries aspire to elite status with the support or connivance of their governments.
- there is the damage that singling out certain institutions does to the notion of a higher education 'system' as such, when one of the our great strengths has been David Watson's (1998) 'controlled reputational range'. It is strongly arguable that what we need is not more 'world-class' universities but a 'world-class' higher education system.[3]
- there are the social implications. It is not only in Britain that there is an unhealthy nexus between the leading private schools and the elite universities, with highly damaging effects on social mobility that are well established (e.g., Milburn, 2012; see also Williams, G., and Filippakou, 2010).

The present Government has followed its New Labour predecessor in favouring institutions that have already benefitted from years of special treatment. Renewed marketisation will strengthen these institutions still further, in both resources and esteem. Students at these institutions will continue to have far more spent on them and their education than students at other institutions. They will get better paid and more numerous staff, better libraries and laboratories, better residences and recreational facilities, and so on. Since these universities recruit overwhelmingly from more affluent backgrounds, this truly is a case of 'to them that hath'. Yet a national higher education policy should surely reflect the needs of all the institutions, and the groups and interests they serve, and not just a subset. It is time to turn to the final part of this discussion, the policy responses that the UK experience since 1979 indicates are needed to achieve a suitable supply of public and private goods through the careful deployment of market-type mechanisms.

Marketisation policy responses

To begin with, it is necessary to be cautious about the claims made for or against the introduction or intensification of market-based reforms in higher education, especially ones based on ideology or something very close to it. Some of these have been referred to already.

Next, market or quasi-market competition should only be introduced gradually and after careful assessment of the effects before further changes are made. In particular:

- The objectives and benefits to be achieved should be stated as clearly and as specifically as possible.
- The assumptions and evidence on which the objectives and policy instruments are based should be stated and clearly set out.
- The potential impacts should be carefully modelled.
- There should be some statement of the costs and risks, and who will bear them.[4]

Of these various requirements, two stand out: impacts and costs.

Because of the interrelated nature of teaching, research and scholarship, impact assessments need to cover the effects on all university activities, and not just on the activity at which the policy is directed. The consistent failure to do this in relation to the RAE – on the frankly sophistical grounds that selectivity was only about improving research performance, and other impacts were irrelevant – is a serious blot on the Funding Council's stewardship of the sector since 1992. This wilful blindness continues in the fact that whilst the definition of 'impact' in the 2014 Research Excellence Framework is very widely drawn – 'economic, social, public policy, cultural and quality of life' – it does not include the impact on student learning. But what other justification can there be for conducting research in universities than the (potential) benefits to student learning?

However, the impact assessments need to go even wider. In Chapter 7 we noted that not only was increased stratification in higher education likely to intensify the pressure on middle-class parents to get their offspring into the 'right' secondary (and even primary) school, but increased competition in the schools would damage the cause of widening participation in higher education and effectively negate whatever efforts the universities were making to broaden their intakes, never mind government palliatives like the National Scholarship Programme. Similarly, in Chapter 8 we saw that changes in the sixth-form curriculum were regarded by many well-informed parties as one of the major causes of concern about academic standards in universities.

Turning to costs, we noted in Chapter 6 that no proper assessment of the benefits, costs and detriments of the additional information requirements on institutions since 2001 has ever been provided. Given the fundamental and unavoidable problems with information about educational quality, it seems clear that – like the

National Student Survey and summaries of external examiners' reports before it – the new Key Information Set will involve institutions in a lot of effort, with only marginal benefits to student learning. Similarly, in Chapter 8 we noted that the financial and other costs of institutional engagement in the RAE far outweighed the financial and other benefits. This is not to deny that there are gains in efficiency to be had from some degree of research selectivity and from a student/ graduate contribution to the cost of teaching (which is also justifiable on grounds of equity). But there are major provisos in each case.

In research, selectivity at department/unit level is a good way of galvanising the system to make best use of its resources, but diminishing returns set in as institutions learn to 'play the game'. After one or two rounds, selectivity should be confined to subjects or areas where research is disproportionately expensive to conduct, to new areas of the curriculum, and/or to subjects or areas where there are concerns about overall research quality, and where there is a clear case for creating a 'critical mass'; in other words, a selective approach to selectivity. There may also be ways of making the assessments more economically.[5]

In teaching, student/graduate contributions (assuming the existence of subsidised loans to cover fees) should be confined to no more than half of the average cost, with the remaining resources coming from grants to institutions. This is for several reasons.

First, no one can foretell the future: in this case, the 'best' combination of subjects and courses. It is therefore desirable to have as wide a range of inputs to decision making as possible, including not only institutions and students, but also employers and employer bodies, trades unions, professional bodies and associations and even the media, as well as government. In this context it is worth noting that as well as reducing the direct public contribution to teaching, the dominance of the student contribution to universities' income will downgrade still further the actual or potential business contribution.[6] Second, such a breakdown reflects the best estimate we currently have of the monetary value of the public and private benefits that we noted in Chapter 2 (McMahon, 2009). Third, there is a very clear risk that students will make decisions based on short-term factors that will be counterproductive to their own and other interests in the medium to longer run. To quote Gareth Williams again:

> Higher education provision determined solely by the wishes of large numbers of individual students would be unlikely to meet their real long-term needs, or those of society as a whole, as effectively as a system in which significant resource allocation authority is held by a democratic government, advised by expert agencies that can interpret the economic and social processes with which tertiary education interacts.
>
> (Williams, G., 1999, p. 149)[7]

Fourth, as we noted in Chapter 8, there is an obvious risk – seen on many US campuses – that in order to attract students, institutions will devote more resources to things like fitness centres, entertainment complexes, sports arenas, restaurants and shopping malls that take money away from teaching but have little bearing on student learning (Samuels, 2012). In the United States, college admissions is shifting from being a selection function aimed at finding a 'fit' between an applicant and an institution, to being a marketing function where the needs of the university as a business may take precedence over the educational needs of the consumer (Fallows, 2005). We can expect this to be increasingly true in Britain after 2012 as institutions develop their brands and other associated promotional activities.[8]

Finally, as well as posing a threat to institutional stability – bearing in mind the length of the 'product cycle' – a student-focussed funding scheme removes or limits the ability of institutions to cross-subsidise subjects or areas that are weaker in market terms, and thus offer what they would see as a balanced curriculum. This in turn, and ironically, reduces student choice rather than strengthens it. The business schools have already made a public statement objecting to continued subsidisation of 'weaker' subjects (Matthews, 2011b); we can surely expect similar plaints from other 'market-friendly' subject areas. At the same time, fears have been expressed about the future demand for STEM courses, given the continuing difficulties in recruiting students in some of these subjects and the rationalisation that has already occurred in subjects like physics and chemistry.[9]

There are in fact signs of a widespread culling of courses as institutions clear the decks for the new funding regime, on top of significant course reductions since 2006. A UCU (2012) survey found that the number of different undergraduate degree courses offered in UK universities had dropped by more than a quarter in the past six years, with one English region (the south west) seeing a fall of almost a half; the decline in England was much greater than in Scotland or Wales. In subject terms, the biggest falls were in arts and humanities provision for single subjects like French and German studies. There has also been a 12 per cent reduction in the number of separate courses for 2012 entry advertised through UCAS. However, some of this may simply be rationalisation: another analysis of UCAS data (Cunnane, 2010) found that between 2003 and 2008 a quarter of new undergraduate courses had not recruited, rising to half of all joint honours courses.

In short, there needs to be a balance in the funding arrangements for teaching if an appropriate balance in the production of public and private goods is to be secured. But it is also essential that there is an overall cap, a uniform level of fee, and a common system of student financial support; otherwise, institutions will just use status and reputation to introduce or increase differences in tuition or student aid that cannot be justified by any differences in educational quality.[10]

The basic message, therefore, is that some competition for students and research income leads to improvements in efficiency and responsiveness. But if this is carried too far it leads – ironically, given the justification for introducing competition in the first place – to waste and inefficiency. This further confirms the importance of identifying, monitoring and assessing impacts and costs. However, the UK experience since 1979 suggests three more pre-requisites if any significant degree of competition is to be introduced into student education or academic research without serious and disabling detriments.

Overall funding levels

First, to follow up the point made at the end of Chapter 8, market competition is no substitute for adequate levels of funding. On the research side, the blurring over time of the dual support system, as well as ever-increasing selectivity, was ultimately due to the insufficiency of core support even with the various efficiency gains and income diversification that were achieved. On the teaching side, it is virtually certain that quality declined as the growth in resources fell seriously behind the growth in student numbers, never mind the increasing shortfall in capital investment as capital grants fell and institutions were driven to rely more on borrowing, putting greater pressure on revenue flows and increasing still further the financial disparities between providers that we have already noted. It is therefore disappointing that neither the Browne Report, nor any subsequent government announcement has offered any estimate of the changes in the share of GDP that UK funding of higher education will represent as a result of the funding changes described in Chapter 5.

Moreover, such funding has to be sustainable, yet there are major question marks over this aspect of the new funding regime.

In their extensive critique of the 2011 White Paper, Thompson and Bekhradnia (2011) questioned the Government's published assumptions about the likely future cost to the taxpayer of the new loans regime. The issue is the relationship between the value of the repayments made and the established long-term cost, the Resource Accounting and Budgeting Charge or 'RAB'. If no repayments are made, the RAB is 100 per cent; if all loans are repaid at the required rate of interest, the RAB is zero. The Higher Education Policy Institute (HEPI) believes that the Government's RAB charge estimates (30 per cent) are lower than they should be, i.e. that the savings that will accrue to the Government will in reality be much lower than expected, and that far from a saving, there may well be a cost to the Government, i.e. the taxpayer (see also Thompson and Bekhradnia, 2012).

Another report (McGettigan, 2012) points to the inflationary impact of the increased fees and the consequential effect on the Government's finances. The analysis suggests that the projected fee increases could add 0.6 per cent to the Consumer Price Index (CPI) over the next three years. Since the CPI is used to determine changes in state pensions and certain other benefits, this could add £ 2.2 billion to the welfare budget. This would more than offset the estimated savings of £1 billion a year from higher education currently planned; it would be fascinating to know if this was picked up in Whitehall before the funding changes were announced (it does not appear in any of the official impact assessments).

If these calculations are correct, and the Government is not prepared to seek compensating reductions in expenditure elsewhere, its options are limited. It could make further reductions in HEFCE grants, although this would reduce its ability to 'steer' the system by protecting market-vulnerable subjects, widening participation, specialist colleges, etc. It could try to offload the liabilities by selling the loans, although any purchaser might well exact a large discount or a continuing subsidy (the Government is known to be pursuing this option). Finally, it could change the terms and conditions on which loans are provided, in order to obtain higher graduate repayments: subsidised loans that may be non-repayable can after all be seen as equivalent to an up-front grant.

Barr and Johnston (2011) argued that whilst increasing the interest rate on loans was an improvement on the post-2006 regime, the raising of the repayment threshold indexed to earnings means that the student funding regime continues to be fiscally expensive and thus restricts the number of places that can be 'afforded'. Cutting places may be inevitable anyway if the number of AAB+ students recruited in 2012 (or ABB+ students in 2013) exceeds plans: even before any students enrol in 2012, the Government has revised upwards its estimate of the number of students with AAB+ or equivalent qualifications (Willetts, 2012b), although it is now believed that then estimates may also be incorrect.

There is certainly a case for lowering the repayment threshold, and possibly other changes, as Barr and others have suggested, and without making it less progressive. After all, the personal tax regime that higher earners face today is far less onerous than it was in 1979 (Adam and Browne, 2011). However, the present funding crisis in higher education, and in most other activities that deliver substantial public goods, is ultimately a reflection of a governmental, and societal, choice of a low tax regime for the better off, together with a complaisant attitude towards tax avoidance and evasion. This necessarily constrains the scope for subsidising even highly valuable activities like education and research, at considerable social, cultural and economic cost, as McMahon (2009) has shown (see also Goldin and Katz, 2008).[11]

The regulation of quality

The second pre-requisite for any significant degree of competition is effective monitoring and regulation of quality.

We have noted the Government's belief, along with the Browne Committee, that the key to improving quality is empowering students. Armed with what are effectively vouchers, with enhanced information, and with greater leverage through charters, stronger complaints procedures, even the odd student-instigated institutional review, etc., student choices will force universities to 'raise their game' or go under. Unfortunately, this view reflects the most profound ignorance of how markets in higher education work: to follow Oscar Wilde on second marriages and call it the 'triumph of hope over experience' is altogether too kind.

There is simply no getting round the fundamental difficulties with consumer information that were set out in Chapter 7. Even if these problems could be overcome – and valid, reliable and accessible information about quality could be produced in time to be of use – what we know of consumer behaviour in general, and student decision making in particular (Brown, 2012c), gives little confidence that it would be used in a 'rational' manner:

> Research in consumer psychology has shown that consumer decisions are sel-dom the result of purely rational cost-benefit analysis based on a stable set of preferences. Instead, consumer decisions are highly complex and cannot be detached from the social and political contexts in which they take place. Indi-viduals may select a product or service on the basis of non-rational considera-tions ... an 'ideal type' consumer acting in a perfect market characterised by full information does not exist.
>
> (Jongbloed, 2006, p. 24)

The point about context is particularly relevant to higher education:

> The relationship between information and decision making appears much less straightforward than is assumed ... People having access to identical information about higher education may construct it to come to entirely different decisions about whether or not to apply to university. These reflect their perceptions of the providers of information, as well as a whole range of contextual and identity factors.
>
> (Hutchings, 2003, p. 98, quoted in Callender, 2006, p. 115)

Jongbloed put the issue very well:

> If individuals are fundamentally rational and the problems are [uncertainty, imperfect information], the potential role for policy would be to try to address these market imperfections by helping students make the decisions they want. If, on the other hand, students are fundamentally irrational then giving them more information or eliminating market imperfections will not necessarily improve outcomes. In the latter case there may not be a need to strengthen consumer choice in higher education, and it might be bet-ter to, for example, let educational authorities offer the programmes they deem best for students rather than let student preference drive programme selection.
>
> (Jongbloed, 2006, p. 25)

There is simply no evidential basis for supposing that the increased amounts of information that are being made available, and the proliferation in would-be interpreters of such information,[12] together with the other ways in which the Government is trying to give students greater leverage, will have more than a marginal impact on quality. There is, however, a very clear danger that, taken together with the new funding and market entry rules, the current reforms will damage quality by undermining the UK's 'controlled pluralism' (Watson, 1997, p. 9) without putting anything worthwhile in its place (this is in addition to the further push that the reforms will give to consumerisation, something which the publication of employment, earnings and loan repayments by course, which the Government is known to be interested in, would reinforce).[13]

To begin with, whatever happens to the overall level of resourcing, there will, through deliberate policy, be even greater resourcing differences between institutions than there are already. This will be bound to put strains on a quality assurance framework that, at least in principle but also for the most part in practice, has been 'resource blind'. This could well lead to a fragmentation in our quality assurance arrangements going well beyond that implied in a 'risk-based' approach. The *Times Higher* in 2010 reported that the Group of Eight universities (the Australian equivalent of the Russell Group) was discussing establishing a separate system of external examiners, although nothing seems to have come of this so far (THE, 2010). It can surely only be a matter of time before something similar happens here, and indeed the point has already been raised by Sir Steve Smith.[14]

Next, although the Government has not for the time being pursued its idea of giving the power to award degrees to organisations that neither teach nor do research, the encouragement it is giving private 'for profit' providers is deeply worrying. There is a fundamental difference between what can be expected from organisations that have as their main purpose the creation of value for their owners – their proprietors or shareholders – and what can be expected from those that aim to create value for their stakeholders – students, employers, etc. Some of these differences have been played out in the problems created in America by the 'for profit' private providers, where enrolment has had a much higher priority than retention, achievement or subsequent employment, leading to serious revenue losses to the Federal Government (Connelly and Angel, 2011). In the meantime, and referring to the Government's recent decision (DBIS, 2012c) to lower the numbers bar for university title, it is very hard to see how an institution with 750 or fewer degree-level students can provide a balanced curriculum if the staff are to be engaged in any worthwhile research and scholarship.

Third, there is the distortion of focus that these changes involve. This is not so much about the staffing and other costs involved, although that it is certainly a factor. It is more about the distraction it represents. To put it quite starkly, time that academic staff could be spending to improve the quality of student learning and achievement by benchmarking assessment practices (for example) is being used to chase up students (many already suffering from 'survey fatigue') to complete the latest NSS or other questionnaire. There is also the shift within quality assurance away from enhancement and towards reputation management. Even the usually compliant QAA was moved to complain of this aspect of the Government's reforms:

It is critical that in the concentration on risk and potential problems, the new system does not lose sight of the power of quality assurance to enhance and improve higher education and students' experiences. Quality assurance is not limited to reviews, however often they take place, it is also about promoting and encouraging good practice and supporting institutions in their development. We would welcome stronger recognition in the regulatory framework of the value of enhancement in protecting students' interests.

(QAA, 2011c, p. 2)

Finally, and most important of all, there is the threat that increased market competition poses to the peer review-based mechanisms that still represent the best means of safeguarding quality even in a mass system (Brown, 2004). In Chapter 6 we noted that through such devices as league tables, student surveys, information brokers and samizhdat websites, markets are beginning to challenge the view that professional academic staff are the best judges of quality and standards. In Chapter 8 we referred to a number of cases where institutional managers had intervened to alter or shape academic decisions. Without knowing more, it is impossible to say whether these are atypical outliers or the tip of an iceberg. What we can be sure of, however, is that they will grow in number as competitive pressures increase, whether for prestige in the case of the more selective universities, or for income in the case of the less selective ones.

These considerations lead inescapably to the conclusion that to protect peer review, and to preserve our international reputation for quality, a much stronger external regulatory regime is needed. Such a regime has to attend not only to the adequacy of resourcing, but also to the use that institutions make of those resources, including through governance, leadership and management (including especially the management and engagement of staff). It has to embrace all providers of higher education, however they are owned and financed.[15] It must ensure at least minimum standards of student learning and achievement (Brown, 2010d). Bearing in mind our discussion of what we know about the relationship between funding and quality in Chapter 8, this almost certainly implies some mechanism for equalising institutional resources, or at least controlling the variations, something completely contrary to both the letter and the spirit of the current reforms.

As well as increasing resourcing disparities between institutions, it is widely expected that the new funding regime will lead to substantial restructuring, as institutions that are performing poorly in financial terms go to the wall, and indeed the Funding Council has already anticipated this (HEFCE, 2012e). The regulatory regime should therefore incorporate powers to review proposed changes in institutional ownership and status (as noted in Chapter 3, the Government is keen to remove the barriers to private takeovers of HEFCE-funded institutions, in the meantime envisaging what is in effect a 'Dutch auction' of taught degree-awarding powers). Regulation should also define and keep under review the degree of diversity (and innovation) in the system. This could include a power to approve or reject mergers or takeovers, where diversity and student choice may be at serious risk (particularly vulnerable are less prestigious institutions serving a local or sub-regional community where there may be no alternative provider). This in turn suggests that while institutional autonomy should continue as one of the bed-rocks of policy, there may be occasions when a national agency – whether a funder or a regulator – should be able to intervene to protect the public interest in having a diverse, as well as a responsive and efficient, system. This may involve replacing the governing body and/or top management of an institution or institutions, as happened in 2009 with London Metropolitan University after two independent reports (Melville, 2009).[16]

The need for independence

In 2001 the author proposed that the existing regulatory functions of HEFCE, QAA and the Teacher Training Agency should be brought together in a Higher Education Audit Commission along the lines of the then Audit Commission (Brown, 2001a). Since then, the regulatory jungle has become even more thickly populated with the arrival of OFFA and OIA, not to mention the UK Border Agency. The final pre-requisite is the need for a new, streamlined regulator not only to have a wide remit – essentially, to advise and report on the value being obtained from all the resources invested in our universities, and how that value can be increased – but also to be completely independent – legally, financially and operationally – from government. This could be done by making the new regulator directly accountable to Parliament, as the Comptroller and Auditor-General is.

This would not of course render the regulator immune from political influence. But it would fill what is currently a crucial gap in our arrangements, the capability to provide a well-grounded and independent view of the system's performance and needs that is not unduly influenced by either the Government or the sector. As the author wrote in 2006:

> making [the regulatory agency] directly accountable to Parliament would reduce the susceptibility of the present regulatory agencies to influences, formal or informal, from government, if not from politics, whilst enabling a properly independent and credible view to be taken of quality across the sector, something which the sector and its representative bodies can never achieve however hard they try.
>
> (Brown, 2006b, p. 10)

These are some of the policy responses that are essential if we are to protect the supply of public goods, as well as producing an appropriate volume of private goods, from higher education.

Conclusion

The current Higher Education Minister, David Willetts, has described the Browne Report as a 'paradigm-shifting' publication, standing alongside the Robbins and Dearing reports (Willetts, 2011). This raises one last question, namely, whether the current higher education reforms do indeed represent such a shift, or whether there is more continuity with previous policies than the phrase implies. It may be useful here to refer to the theory of social learning developed by Hall (1993). Hall argued that public policy making is a process of 'social learning':

> a deliberate attempt to adjust the goals or techniques of policy in response to past experience and new information. Learning is indicated when policy changes as a result of such a process.
>
> (Hall, 1993, p. 278)[17]

He further argued that policy making usually involves three central variables:

> the overarching goals that guide policy in a particular field, the techniques or policy instruments used to attain those goals, and the precise settings of those instruments.
>
> (Hall, 1993, p. 278)

This was illustrated by reference to changes in macroeconomic policy in Britain between 1970 and 1989:

- Changes in the setting of policy instruments ('first order changes in policy') are exemplified by changes in interest rates or the fiscal stance (the balance between government spending and income).
- Changes in the techniques or policy instruments ('second order changes in policy') are exemplified by the introduction of monetary controls or the development of 'cash limits' for public expenditure.
- Changes in the overarching policy goals ('third order changes in policy') are exemplified by the shift from a broad Keynesian to a broad monetarist approach to economic regulation (Hall, 1993, pp. 278–279).

Under this framework, it could be argued that the earlier higher education policy changes since 1979 were first or second order changes, whereas what we have now is something far more radical. We may indeed have reached a 'tipping point'.

However, the picture is far from clear, as policy changes which, under Hall's model, fit into a higher order may trigger consequent changes at lower orders as well; an example of this would be increases in the amounts available as publicly-subsidised student loans ('second order'), which will be accompanied from 2012 by changes in the repayment terms for the resulting student debt ('first order'). Furthermore, as we have repeatedly seen, policies may have unintended consequences or have their roots in compromises, often driven by wider budgetary considerations, or political 'fixes'. That is to say that, in higher education as elsewhere, political decisions are not always the rational conclusion to a reasoned debate (for example, as we have seen, with the detailed conditions that surrounded the introduction of £3,000 undergraduate fees under the 2004 legislation).

Hall's categorisation does though still offer a useful framework within which to consider the extent to which any specific policy initiative may be evaluated; is it seeking to adjust detailed delivery, broad operational frameworks, or strategic objectives? The question then arises of the extent to which the declared objectives behind a policy – and thus the context in which it is to be assessed within Hall's framework – reflect political priorities and thinking, or are influenced by considerations of public or political acceptability. That is to say, how much is the presentation of that policy 'spun'?

The initial recourse to the presentation of policies in a market context appears to have been primarily a response to the need to accommodate the increased costs of the post-Robbins expansion within what was believed to be the available resource envelope, given the perceived or claimed limitations of the tax base. Hence references to markets and private benefits during the 1980s and most of the 1990s were largely rhetorical. In the 2000s and beyond, though, it is less obvious that this is the case – both the concentration of research funding and the move towards 'cost sharing' for undergraduate education were pursued so determinedly that what was earlier market rhetoric was becoming an ideological commitment (with, for example, Prime Minister Blair staking the credibility of his Government on defeating Parliamentary opposition to variable fees). As one distinguished critic wrote of the Government's response to Browne:

> It seeks to replace one model of higher education, a statist model, with an alternative one, that of a self-regulated market in which students rather than the state provide the dynamic that powers the higher education system.
>
> (Bogdanor, 2010, p. 14)

It seems clear from the available evidence that the Coalition Government really does believe that, as far as politically possible, higher education, or at least student education, should be organised as an economic market. As a result, higher education in England (and, to a more limited extent, in the other countries of the UK too) is now the subject of a 'real time' experiment which is being implemented without any 'control' or fallback position. This is in spite of the copious evidence from America, Australia and now Britain, summarised in this book and elsewhere (Brown, R., 2011a and b),[18] showing the very clear limitations of markets as a means of providing an effective, efficient and fair higher education system.

It will therefore be instructive to see how institutions, their students, staff and others with whom they engage respond to the changed circumstances in which teaching and research are to be conducted in the future. It will be particularly informative to see what the reaction of the politicians will be if and when their policies do not deliver what their beliefs and assumptions lead them to expect. Both extensive scholarship and 25 years' experience of policy making in higher education suggest that this point will come sooner rather than later. It would be nice to think that the narrative, analysis and recommendations in this book might play some part in the ensuing debate.

Notes

1 Introduction

1 Litwin (2009) argues that universities are actually engaged in three sets of markets:

- 'Core markets': student education and staff research (markets for students, research funds).
- 'Optional markets': intellectual property (research commercialisation, university presses); service provision (clinical trials, institutional consulting, faculty consulting, industry-related research).
- 'Resource markets' (to underpin the others: finance, personnel, real estate, ICT etc.).

For the corporatisation of university governance and the development of system-wide performance indicators, see Brown, 2012a and b.

2 A 'pure' educational voucher approach would involve the Government issuing students or parents with certificates (vouchers) that could be used at any approved provider after being redeemed by that provider. It is in other words a means of channelling public support for provision directly via the consumer rather than through a subsidy to the provider (Belfield and Levin, 2005; see also Bekhradnia and Massy, 2009).

3 Following the 1999 Bologna Declaration, the European Higher Education Area was launched in 2010. The main objective is to ensure more 'comparable, compatible and coherent systems' of higher education in Europe (European Higher Education Area, 2010, p. 1).

2 Markets and non-markets

1 Richard Bird was the Deputy Secretary for Higher and Further Education at the Department for Education and Science – the most senior civil servant concerned with higher education – until 1990.

2 Economists appear to disagree about whether distributional inequity – the failure of markets to allocate resources in accordance with socially accepted standards of fairness – is technically a market failure (for a discussion, see Wolf, 1993). But there does seem to be a consensus that markets are driven by economic efficiency rather than social equity; that equity requires some sort of state intervention; and that democratic societies are usually prepared to sacrifice some of the gains of efficiency for some measure of fairness, even if it is only about reducing excessive disparities in income or wealth.

3 Mongolia may be an exception (Johnstone and Marcucci, 2007).

3 The institutional pattern of provision

1 The other main proposals were improving information for students; requiring new professional standards for teachers; creating a new academy to develop and promote good professional practice (the Higher Education Academy); establishing Centres of Excellence (CETLs) to reward good teaching at departmental level; and increasing the scale of the National Teaching Fellowships Scheme (see Chapter 6).

2 Bath Spa, Canterbury Christ Church, Chester, Chichester, Liverpool Hope, Northampton, Roehampton, Southampton Solent, Winchester and Worcester.

3 Bolton (2005), Buckinghamshire New (2007), Cardiff Metropolitan (2011), Cumbria (2007), Edge Hill (2006), Glyndwr (2008), Highlands and Islands (2011), Queen Margaret, Edinburgh (2007), Swansea Metropolitan (2008), the University for the Creative Arts (2008), and York St John (2006).

4 Robinson (2007) argued that amongst post-war developments in UK higher education the development of the local authority colleges – first through the Colleges of Advanced Technology (the CATs) and then through the polytechnics policy – was in both scale and substance the most significant. The Oakes Committee (Working Group on the Management of Higher Education in the Maintained Sector, 1978) found that, excluding teacher training, the number of full time and sandwich students in public sector higher education had increased from 81,000 in 1969–70 to a planned figure of 181,000 in 1981–82.

5 Kogan and Hanney (2000) suggested that the UK followed the logic of development that seems to apply in many systems. The first step is to consolidate and enhance those parts of post-school education which both depend for their intellectual substance on disciplined inquiry and yet look toward the world of application. For a while they remain as the less 'noble' part of higher education. But increasingly, as the concepts of what constitutes advanced learning and inquiry become broader, and the non-university institutions seek to emulate universities in undertaking research, a natural process of convergence sets in. Hence it is only where the most determined efforts are made to sustain a viable non-university sector, as in California or with the German Fachhochschulen, that the division is sustained; thus the creation of single but differentiated patterns in America, Australia and Sweden. In fact, Britain had amongst the strongest cases for unification because (a) it accommodated a smaller proportion of each school-leaving age group than other countries, and (b) it assumed from the beginning that most of the higher education student body was capable of reaching degree standard, an assumption not shared by the 'broader gauge' binary systems in some other countries.

6 At a Chatham House-style seminar in 1991 to discuss the White Paper at which the author was present, the distinguished American student of higher education systems, Martin Trow, amused the audience by saying that until he arrived in England he hadn't realised that the document he had been sent to read was not the executive summary but the whole thing.

7 Watson and Bowden (1997, p. 22) made the point that the original title of the NAB was 'The Interim National Advisory Board'.

8 The four 'strategic aims' were widening participation and fair access, enhancing excellence in learning and teaching, enhancing excellence in research, and enhancing the contribution of higher education to the economy and society.

9 The Russell Group consists of 20 (from August 2012, 24) universities; it began as an association of nine English provincial universities with medical schools, which then merged with the Oxbridge Plus Group (Oxford, Cambridge, Imperial, UCL and Warwick, LSE and Edinburgh later being co-opted). The 1994 Group represents 20 (from August 2012, 16) universities: the core consists of several post-Robbins 'plate glass' institutions, a number of ex-CATs, and several former constituent colleges of the University of London. The University Alliance has 23 'business-engaged' members. These

include two ex-CATs (Bradford and Salford) together with the OU and 20 post-1992 universities. Million+ describes itself as a 'think tank which uses rigorous research and evidence-based policy to solve complex problems in higher education'. It has 26 members, all of them post-1992 institutions.

10 However, the recently (July 2012) published Further and Higher Education (Wales) Bill does not appear to contain the necessary powers (Frankel, 2012).

11 Mergers that don't fit this pattern include London Guildhall University and the University of North London to form London Metropolitan University (2002) and Manchester and University of Manchester Institute of Science and Technology (2004). There was also the Federal University of Surrey, involving the University of Surrey and Roehampton Institute, between 2000 and 2004.

12 However, the Government response to the consultation on the White Paper and the Technical Consultation Document (DBIS, 2012c) confirms its intention to bring all private providers within the overall student number controls and the national quality assurance framework, though it is not yet clear how this will be done. Nor is it yet clear what protection students will have where a provider fails or becomes insolvent.

4 The funding of research

1 Adams and Bekhradnia (2004) drew attention to the fact that the distinction between the two legs of dual support has become increasingly blurred; this they suggest is due mainly to deficiencies in the level of core grant. Indeed, by introducing a requirement on universities to recover Full Economic Costs (FEC) on research grants and contracts, as a means of supporting core research facilities, that blurring has been exacerbated.

2 Whilst this is only a surmise on the author's part, it is based on separate conversations that David Dill and the author had with Sir Peter Swinnerton-Dyer, the UGC Chief Executive, in the mid-1990s. It is consistent with the analysis and conversations reported in Kogan and Hanney (2000). Sir Peter also said that the RAE was originally intended to apply only to 'expensive' subjects like science and technology. But the humanities and social science academics on the Committee pressed for universal coverage, since otherwise their disciplines might lose money and kudos.

3 The RAE was initially called the Research Selectivity Exercise by the Funding Council.

4 Nevertheless, estimates (Sastry and Bekhradnia, 2006) suggest that the RAEs have been a significantly less costly method of allocating public funds to research than the competitive process of grant allocation used by the research councils. With the success rate for grant applications averaging under 30 per cent, the cost to institutions of such applications was estimated to amount to about 10 per cent of the funds ultimately allocated, whereas the cost to institutions of preparing submissions for the RAEs was closer to 1 per cent of the QR funds subsequently allocated.

5 It should be noted that in addition to the weightings based on grades achieved in the RAE, the funding formula also includes a multiplier to reflect the broad differences in costs of research in different subject groups: 1.7 or 1.6 for high cost laboratory and clinical subjects, 1.3 for intermediate cost subjects, and 1 for the rest. This has remained constant throughout the period.

6 There is some support for this argument in data collected for UUK (Evidence Ltd, 2007). This study compared research activity in 2000–1 with that in 2004–5 across six representative Units of Assessment; it found that, in all but one of the six, departments that had been rated 4 in the 2001 RAE were generating an increased share of the PhDs awarded nationally in their subject.

7 In its Impact Assessment of this change, HEFCE (2011a) expressed the opinion that:

> We do not have evidence to judge the likely sustainable development impacts of allocating funding more selectively on the basis of quality but we expect it is likely to be positive (or at least neutral) over the longer term because it will enable institutions if they so chose to target funding preferentially on research groups and institutions that undertake the highest quality research with demonstrable cultural, social and economic benefits.
>
> (HEFCE, 2011a, p. 4)

However, the same document noted that this change in funding will increase the proportion of male PGR students by 0.6 per cent and decrease the proportion of PGR students aged 28 or over by 1.5 per cent.

8 Most recently, an initiative begun by the ESPRC in 2009 to identify a limited number of settings in which it would found doctoral study, has spread to three further Councils (ESRC, BBSRC and, from 2014, NERC). While these include some of the Government research establishments, no post-1992 university is included in the ESRC or BBSRC's approved locations.

9 DevR was a comparatively small stream of funding allocated by HEFCE to support the development of research capability in institutions that were not research intensive. In 1996–7, for example, HEFCE total research budget was £638 million, of which £16 million was awarded as DevR grants (HEFCE, 1996c).

5 The funding of undergraduate education

1 Under the Government's original proposals some part-time students would have been required to begin repaying their loans prior to completing their studies if they were earning more than £21,000. The Government has now agreed (DBIS, 2012c) that part-time students will not be required to begin repaying until the April four years after the start of their course, or the April after they leave the course if this is sooner. This is one year later than first proposed.

2 For an account of how the UGC approached the cuts allocations, see Moore, 1987.

3 It is possible that Sir Keith was influenced by the debates that had been going on publicly and semi-publicly for some time about moving to a 'voucher' system for funding schools, whereby the entire costs of provision would be met through a voucher issued to each student, funded by some combination of public and private contributions (Friedman, 1962) Sir Keith's Higher Education Minister, Dr Rhodes Boyson, was known to be an advocate of this approach, but if there was any serious discussion within the Department about applying it to the universities, it was not widely reported at the time. Nor is there any reference, in Seldon's contemporaneous (1986) account of the development of British thinking on vouchers as a funding mechanism for schools, to their being contemplated for higher education (see also Salter and Tapper, 1994).

4 However, a senior civil servant who was involved at the time has provided another explanation for the changes. He recalls that the quinquennial system for funding universities (a form of deficit financing whereby universities had their funding 'guaranteed' for five-year periods) had ultimately foundered (in the mid-1970s) because of concerns about levels of public funding. The Government's public expenditure plans nevertheless continued to include 'non-cash limited' expenditure on higher education (as well as in some other spending) to allow especially for the inevitable variations in the numbers of undergraduate students admitted each year. In the late 1980s, there was a particular difficulty because of discrepancies in the respective expenditure plans for the universities and for the polytechnics (which were part of local government spending). The difficulty was solved by increasing (more than doubling) the notional fee for undergraduates (paid for from public funds), which had the effect of transferring local

authority spending to central spending. This was presented as an incentive to institutions to recruit students, which of course it was.

5 Sir Peter Swinnerton-Dyer (1991, pp. 226–227), described the UFC's methodology as 'the first attempt to bring in market forces'. He personally could not see how the Council's scheme could ever have been made to work. It wasn't just that universities were being asked to cost services to be provided several years later in terms of 1989–90 pounds, which would then be adjusted for inflation in a way never revealed. But the Council had committed itself to announcing the 1994–95 grants for each institution when it didn't even know how much money it would have in 1993–94.

6 For the subsequent history of student number controls, see Thompson and Bekhradnia, 2011.

7 Mayhew *et al.* (2004) noted that the UK decline since the early 1980s was much sharper, though from a higher starting point, than that of most other OECD countries.

8 Another important trigger was the November 1995 HEFCE analysis of institutions' finances showing that the sector could be in deficit in two years' time with a substantial minority of institutions at risk of failing to comply with their funding contract with the Council, the Financial Memorandum (HEFCE, 1995b; see also Taggart, 2004, p. 91). The author can personally testify to the concern on the part of the Government to which the Vice-Chancellors' revolt gave rise. As Chief Executive of the Higher Education Quality Council, he attended CVCP Main Committee meetings as an observer. He recalls a senior civil servant calling him just before the February 1996 meeting and asking him to note the positions of the various vice-chancellors who spoke.

9 Wagner (1998) pointed out that Dearing's estimate was actually a modest one, amounting in real terms to an average annual increase of 2 per cent, below not only the planned increases in education expenditure but also the economy's trend growth rate.

10 This led in 2004 to a report *Increasing Voluntary Giving to Higher Education* by a group chaired by Eric Thomas, Vice Chancellor of Bristol (Thomas, 2004). HEFCE subsequently funded a capacity-building scheme administered by UUK. Between 2008 and 2011 a matched funding scheme with total government funding of £200 million aimed to incentivise institutional schemes. Although the fund gave a useful boost to less selective institutions' efforts to raise money from donors, half the new funds raised in 2009–10 went to Oxford and Cambridge and a fifth of the rest went to other Russell Group universities (Matthews, 2011a). The Funding Council has subsequently announced a Review of Philanthropic Support for Higher Education in the UK (HEFCE, 2012f).

11 See also Clarke, 2010.

12 This is the question, first raised by the MP for West Lothian in Scotland, Tam Dalyell, of the ability of MPs from constituencies outside England to vote on matters that only affect England.

13 As well as efficiencies, DELNI has set the two universities a number of targets, ranging from the amount of money to be raised from intellectual property to improved retention rates every year to 2020 (Matthews, 2012e).

6 Quality assurance

1 In the author's opinion this remains as good a statement as any of the functions of a system-wide quality regulator in a mass higher education system.

2 Also relevant are the 'Policy for addressing unsatisfactory quality in institutions' operated by the Funding Councils; the development of the Higher Education Achievement Record (HEAR, which is designed to supplement or even in time replace degree classification); and the final report of the Student Charter Group (see Brown, 2011c for details and references).

3 'Subject providers' (i.e., institutions) were invited to include, in the annex to their self-assessments, data on four statistical indicators: student entry profile, progression and completion rates, student attainment, and post-graduation employment and further study. However, relatively little use was made of these in the assessors' judgements. Yorke (1998) noted that the Funding Council originally claimed that these indicators would help it to determine the quality of teaching in the unit being assessed but that they were subsequently downgraded (see also Note 5 below).

4 The publication of the evaluation report was also the occasion of an article highly critical of the scheme by the recently retired Chief Executive of the Higher Education Academy (Ramsden, P., 2012).

5 Yorke (1998) reviewed a range of 'performance indicators' relating to teaching, including entry and exit qualifications, value added, retention and completion, and placement in employment. He concluded that whilst some were reasonably trustworthy in the aggregate (at system level), all should be used with great care and circumspection at institutional or sub-institutional level, especially given their vulnerability to partiality in use.

6 As it currently stands, the NSS questionnaire has 22 attitude questions about: teaching on the course; assessment and feedback; academic support; organisation and management; learning resources; personal development; and overall satisfaction. As part of the new Key Information Set (KIS – see below) a further question about the impact of students' unions has been added this year (2012). There is also an open-ended question: 'Looking back on the experience, are there any particularly positive or negative aspects that you would like to highlight?' Individual institutions can also add questions of their own; about three-quarters do so. There is a 50 per cent response threshold as well as a requirement for a minimum of 23 student responses per item. Since 2011, institutions have been given a benchmark for their NSS 'performance' which takes account of their student population and subject mix (HEFCE, 2011e).

7 The consultants' findings about the small significance of the NSS results are echoed in other analyses. For example, Cheng and Marsh (2010) noted that whilst the ratings are highly reliable and stable over time, the differences are too small to provide meaningful information for comparative purposes (see also Marsh, 2007; Marsh and Cheng, 2008; Marsh et al., 2011). In fact, the differences between subjects are far greater than the differences between institutions (HEFCE, 2010f). The importance of taking entering features into account was emphasised in the very first evaluation of the survey by Paula Surridge:

> The need to take into account student profiles when making any comparisons using the NSS data, as 'raw' figures do not take into account the characteristics of students, their courses and the institutions in which they study may produce at best misleading and at worst invalid measures of teaching.
>
> (HEFCE, 2006a, p. 132)

Needless to say, these warnings do not appear in any of the publications that use this information, not even in official ones. The 2011 White Paper referred to the consultants' reports but did so in such a way as to imply that they actually supported the Government's proposals (DBIS, 2011a, paragraph 2.9, note 17).

8 The NSS does of course meet the publishers' need for quantitative indicators of teaching quality, something they have been bereft of since the demise of Teaching Quality Assessment /Subject Review. Sabri (submitted for review, p. 10) points out that, because the course is the chosen unit of analysis, the NSS occludes wider institutional and national forces that also structure students' experiences. And even within its own frame of reference the survey does not address some central issues such as the relationship with peers and curriculum design and content, both important areas for students. She also points to the resourcing implications for institutions:

For institutions the work involved is immense: it includes analysis of quantitative ratings and students' open comments, and making records at multiple levels (university, school, department, course, etc.) that record results, response, action, comparison with past years, and with other universities and comparable courses. These records and associated innumerable rankings add layers of meaning and emotion to the way that staff members experience the NSS. Sometimes highly charged discussions take place about culpability or credit, conflicting interpretations, and perceptions of validity. All of this can take place independently of any technical understanding of the statistics.

(Sabri, submitted for review, p. 15)

Sabri argues that the NSS has become a 'fact-totem' (de Santos, 2010) which has gained a legitimacy and a significance that far outweighs its validity or intended use; parallels with the RAE (Chapter 4) and AAB+ (Chapter 5) suggest themselves. This issue is explored further in Chapter 9.

9 The final version of the KIS is at http://www.hefce.ac.uk/whatwedo/It/publicinfo/kis. It may be worth recording the anonymous comment of one experienced university administrator:

the most significant departure which KIS represents seems to me to be the obligation to display such contentious, yet detailed, data in such a visually authoritative way, on HEIs' own webpages for more or less every single UG course they run. No amount of contextual data or explanatory text placed around, above or below the 'widget' will really be able to outweigh the target reader's perception that the widget contains nothing but unimpeachable fact: indeed attempts to explain or 'spin' the contents of the widget could well look like special pleading. It's a virtual cuckoo.

The widget is a link to information extracted from the KIS database.

10 It is possible that in future this information could include the projected income returns from attending different universities and studying specific subjects, using information collected by the Student Loans Company (Baker, 2011a).

11 Scotland's attachment to enhancement is also shown by the fact that whilst elsewhere the funding agencies still work to the remit of 'securing ... provision for the assessment of the quality of education', the Further and Higher Education Act (Scotland) 2005, which was primarily about merging the two previous separate funding councils for higher and further education, amended and extended the statutory responsibilities of the new Scottish Funding Council as follows:

The Council is to secure that provision is made for:

(a) assessing; and
(b) enhancing

the quality of fundable further education and fundable higher education provided by fundable bodies.

7 The impact of marketisation: efficiency, diversity and equity

1 In the US, whilst almost 100 institutions (all but one, private) charged $50,000 or more in 2010–11, most students were at institutions charging less than $12,000 ($£7,700$ at current – June 2012 – exchange rates), and many receive discounts (*The*

Chronicle of Higher Education, Almanack Issue, 26 August 2011). In Canada, average fees (2011–12 provisional) range from $Can 2,519 (Quebec) (£1,550) to $6,460 in Ontario (£4,000) (Statistics Canada, June 2012). In Australia, the maximum student contribution (2011) varies from $Aus 4,355 (£2,770) to 9,080 (£5,675) (Richard James, personal communication). In Japan, a leading private university charges Y1.1 million (£8,650), national and public universities typically charge Y818,000 (£6,542, including admission fees) (Futao Huang, personal communication). Fees are either low or non-existent across most of Europe. From 2012 the UK will be charging higher fees, and spending less of its national product on higher education, than almost any other comparable country.

2 The 1979–80 figure is the Age Participation Rate (API) for 18–19-year-olds; the 2011 figure is the Higher Education Initial Participation Rate (HEIPR) for 17–30-year-olds. These figures are for England, those for Scotland, Wales and Northern Ireland are broadly similar (Bruce, 2012). However, whilst the participation rate for women is 52 per cent, for men it is only 42 per cent. There has been a decline in the proportion of mature students, from 24 per cent of all full-time undergraduates in 1979–80 to 19 per cent in 2009–10).

3 The student-staff ratios are almost certainly an underestimate because the statistics count teaching and research academics as spending all their time on teaching, they do not weight the figures in any way (Stephen Court, personal communication). These ratios are anyway above those of most of our international competitors (OECD, 2011a, Table D2.2), as well as above those in our secondary schools, where the pupil-teacher ratio for state-funded institutions is 15.3 (Education and Training Statistics for the UK, December 2011, Table 1.7).

4 However, these are averages, based on how the economy has performed in the past. Also, it is well established that graduate earnings vary considerably by, inter alia, gender, subject studied, class of degree and type of institution (e.g., Hussain *et al.*, 2009). Moreover, these variations have widened in recent years (Thompson and Bekhradnia, 2011). Continuing high rates of return are of course an argument for greater investment (McMahon, 2009).

5 A survey for HEFCE, the British Council and the UK National Agency for Erasmus in 2010 (King *et al.*, 2010) gave estimates of 33,000 UK students studying abroad, compared with 370,000 foreign students in the UK.

6 While pointing out that exact comparisons are problematic, the HE-BCI survey also considers figures for US universities collected in the annual Association of Technology Managers Licensing Survey. Industrial research represents 7.4 per cent of activity within US universities, compared with 6.6 per cent in the UK; in the US, the research resource per patent granted is £10 million, whereas in the UK the figure is £8 million (HEFCE, 2012d).

7 However, if one is using population as a denominator, it is the Nordic countries that are the real stars in producing 'top-ranked' universities, as Gerritsen (2008) pointed out. Li *et al.* (2011) point out that conditional on the resources it has, the US is actually underperforming by about 4–10 per cent.

8 In the author's view, another important factor making for convergence has been the fact that the great majority of vice-chancellors appointed to post-1992 universities have come from positions in the pre-1992 institutions. By contrast, the number of pre-1992 universities that have appointed vice-chancellors from the post-1992 institutions can almost be counted on the fingers of one hand. Similarly, knighthoods for post-1992 vice-chancellors remain a comparative rarity, whereas they can be confidently anticipated for the heads of Russell Group institutions. There could hardly be better illustrations of the persistence of the reputational hierarchy described by Scott (2009) and Locke (2011).

9 For a similar conclusion, see Lucas (2006), Locke (2009) and Scott (2009). Kogan and Hanney (2000) argued that the leading universities were actually more secure

after 1992 because comparisons that were previously difficult to make were now much easier. Scott in fact argues that markets are incompatible with any serious degree of (horizontal) diversity:

> Functional differentiation, as determined by policy instruments, is compatible with the establishment of a stable hierarchy of institutions. Reputational differentiation, as determined by the market, is not. Even if the overall pattern of institutions remains broadly unchanged, the position of individual institutions can change substantially – and unpredictably because reputational criteria are both discretionary and subjective and consequently outcomes are more volatile. In short the market, however imperfect, has a systematic tendency to undermine carefully organized institutional categorization; in that sense it is the enemy of differentiation. In another sense, of course, the market promotes other (more superficial?) forms of differentiation as institutions seek to secure competitive advantage by occupying the most attractive market niches (and, if some niches are firmly occupied, they must try to occupy others).
>
> (Scott, 2009, p. 48)

10 Johnes and Taylor (1990) reckoned that 70 per cent of the differences between universities' costs could be accounted for by differences in subject mix. Even if one applies this 'deflator', though, Cambridge still has more than four times the income per student of Edge Hill. These resourcing differentials are even clearer when one looks at institutional wealth. Leaving aside specialist colleges, net assets (excluding pension liabilities) per FTE student range from £152.46 (Cambridge) to £4.27 (Roehampton). Moreover, this wealth is highly concentrated: the 24 members of the enlarged Russell Group together own 52 per cent of the sector's total net assets. It should also be noted that the Oxford and Cambridge figures do not include the colleges.

11 For 2012–13 the share of QR going to the existing 20 members of the Russell Group will increase to 71.3 per cent from the present (2011–12) 70.2 per cent. This is the result of the Government's decision that research rated 2* in the 2008 RAE will be excluded so that only 'internationally excellent' research (4* and 3*) will be funded. There will be an even bigger increase in the Group's share of total HEFCE funding for research students (Jump, 2012a).

12 They will also be able to borrow more and/or more cheaply than other institutions (McGettigan, 2011). Almost as soon as the new funding regime was announced, the credit rating agency Standard and Poors (2010) pointed out that one result would be a widening in universities' creditworthiness.

13 It should be noted that Northern Ireland has a higher, and Scotland and Wales, a lower rate of participation than England of higher education students from the National Statistics-Socio-Economic Classes 4–7. Northern Ireland and Wales have a lower rate of participation from low-participation neighbourhoods than England; there are no figures for Scotland (Bruce, 2012). It should also be borne in mind that this discussion deals with participation. It is well established that, as well as being clustered in mainly low-status institutions, students from the most disadvantaged backgrounds are (a) more likely to be living at home (which may mean them missing out on various extracurricular activities and networking); (b) more likely to be working while studying (with greater risk to their academic attainments – see below); (c) more likely to drop out; and (d) more likely to be studying less 'economically valuable' subjects (Brown, 2007b).

14 It is therefore unhelpful that the October 2011 Institute for Fiscal Studies analysis of the current Spending Review (Chowdry and Sibieta, 2011) indicates that planned

public spending on education in the UK will fall by 3.5 per cent per year in real terms between 2011 and 2015. IFS say that this would represent the largest cut in education spending over any four-year period since at least the 1950s. This includes cuts not only in outreach programmes like Aim Higher but also the abolition of Educational Maintenance Allowances for 16–18-year-olds in education or training, for which the new Learner Support Fund is a weak substitute (Exley, 2010). The Government has also withdrawn funding from Level 3 courses for those over 24 and from recognised Access Courses. This means that in future adults wishing to progress will have to pay much higher fees or take out private loans. This is bound to affect older students' progression to higher education. According to a recent poll conducted by the NUS and Million+, nearly two-thirds of mature applicants to undergraduate courses with Level 3 qualifications had completed them after the age of 24 (Million+ and NUS, 2012). Yet a recent official impact assessment estimates that nearly a third of FE loans will go unclaimed because older students are wary of taking on debt (Lee, 2012c). It is true that the Government has introduced the Pupil Premium for children from low-income families who are eligible for Free School Meals and for children who have been looked after continuously for more than six months. However, the amount of money allocated is well below the level of the overall cuts in funding and many schools are simply using it to offset cuts elsewhere.

15 The 2010 OFFA report on fair access stated:

> while young full-time entrants to English higher education as a whole increased by 16.1 per cent between 2003–4 and 2008–9, entrants to Russell Group institutions increased by 1.3 per cent over the same period. When coupled with the increase in the young population and the disproportionate increase in A level A and A* grades in selective schools, this has led to a significant increase in the relative competition for places at the most selective universities.
>
> (Harris, 2010, p. 25)

A recent analysis of UCAS data for the period 1996–2006 (Boliver, submitted for review) suggests that (a) UCAS applicants from 'lower class' backgrounds and state schools continued to be much less likely to apply to Russell Group universities than their comparably qualified counterparts from 'higher class' backgrounds and private schools, and (b) Russell Group applicants from state schools and from Black and Asian ethnic backgrounds continued to be less likely to receive offers of admission from Russell Group universities, in comparison with their equivalently qualified peers from private schools and from the White ethnic group. In other words, there continues to be discrimination, presumably unconscious, against these applicants in some prestigious institutions. However, there is also evidence of some state school teachers discouraging students from applying to the most selective universities (Sutton Trust, 2012).

8 The impact of marketisation: quality

1 The original purpose of the HEPI surveys was to track any changes in students' academic experience as a result of the additional income from variable fees; however, the 2012 report suggests that both contact time and class sizes have remained unchanged over the period, in spite of surveys consistently showing students asking for smaller group sizes and better academic facilities. While the HEPI surveys only go back to 2006, there is data from America that indicates that since the early 1960s the amount of time university students spend studying there has declined sharply (Babcock and Marks, 2011; see also Cote and Allahar, 2011). In a survey of the Australian first-year experience, James et al. (2010) found that between 2004 and 2009, both self-reported

contact and hours spent in private study declined. It was recently reported (Grove, 2012b) that the QAA was investigating a course in clinical hypnosis where students were complaining that teaching took place only on alternate Saturdays in classes of 30. If there has been a reduction in the amount of contact or study time it would be a serious matter because as a result of expansion and changes in the school curriculum (see below), many of today's students actually need more teaching rather than less.

2 Metcalf suggested that the financing system might lead to a polarised system, between institutions that facilitated term-time working and those that did not (the more prestigious ones). This would distort the university choice of those who needed to work during term-time, inhibiting access to more selective institutions, and lead to greater disadvantage amongst those who worked despite being at universities which made fewer allowances for term-time working.

3 Yorke (2009) hypothesised that one reason for the earlier increases in the Russell Group institutions might have been the concentration of resources following successive RAEs, one indirect result of which may have been to concentrate the most able students, as judged by entry qualifications, in the 'strongest' places, thus accentuating the rising trend of 'good honours degrees' there.

4 Callahan (2004) suggested that increased cheating was a direct consequence of increased marketisation and economic inequality. Universities might of course ask themselves how they can ask students not to cheat when they are themselves cheating, for example, in the preparation of RAE submissions (RAE2008), and in the supply of data to national agencies, not to mention the whole area of prospectus information, about which the OIA has explicitly warned institutions (Matthews, 2011c; see also Watson, 2008).

5 This is partly a question of power, but it hardly suits either HEFCE or UUK to question quality openly, the former because it is a government agency (so questions of adequacy or allocation of resourcing might arise), the latter because it could reflect badly on its members as well as upon the recruitment of the overseas students upon whose fees the sector relies so heavily.

6 The Chair of Council at University College London, Sir Stephen Wall, raised a number of eyebrows when reported as confirming that the institution would be using some of its income from £9,000 fees to 'fund the shortfall in government support for science and other research' (Baker, 2010a). However, even our most prestigious institutions have some way to go before emulating the University of California, Los Angeles where, according to Samuels (2009), only 3.5 per cent of the budget was spent on undergraduate education in 2007–8.

7 It should be noted that Marginson was referring to the introduction of research assessment in Australia in 1993.

8 Compare Brew and Lucas (2009, p. 5):

> government control is supported by implicit assumptions in these regimes that it is possible to 'manage' research by defining research outcomes in advance of doing the research, and to tie academics into a culture of ideas about what research is, and how to define it.

9 Mode 1 knowledge is held to be linear, disciplinary and university-centred, Mode 2 is a 'trans-disciplinary process in which academics cooperate with users and stakeholders to produce knowledge at the site of its application' (Jacob and Hellstrom, 2000, p. 2, quoted in Peters and Olssen, 2005, p. 43). Dill and van Vught (2010) argue that the Mode 1/2 debate has been overtaken by a perspective that emphasises the interactive character of the generation of ideas, scientific research and the development and introduction of new products and processes.

10 Compare the US Boyer Commission (1998):

> The liberal education model demands a commitment to the intellectual growth of individual students, both in the classroom and out, a commitment which is hard to accommodate to research productivity that brings research in universities recognition, professional advancement and financial security. Almost without realising it, research universities find themselves in the last half of the century operating large, often huge and extended undergraduate programmes as though they are sideshows to the main event. The numbers are there but the intention is elsewhere.

It is almost inevitable that in a regime where academic staff see research as their main, and teaching a secondary, concern, low priority will be given to developing expertise in the teaching process itself. For reviews of the literature on the relationship between research and teaching, see Jenkins, 2004 and Brown, 2010b.

11 Talib (2000) surveyed journal editors across a wide range of disciplines. Their view was that any improvement in quality that there had been (and they were not convinced) was not the result of the RAE.

12 Sharp and Coleman (2005) also raised the question of the representativeness of the panels, which is obviously crucial for fairness. Panel membership appeared to have had no direct effect on the 2001 RAE ratings. However, among universities not represented, pre-1992 universities were more favourably assessed than would have been expected on the basis of their 1996 ratings.

13 The two HEPI analyses inevitably prompt the question of what the 'research intensive' institutions have been doing with the moneys they have been receiving for research – from HEFCE, the research councils and other sources – since the mid-1980s. The author's strong suspicion – partially validated by some of McNay's evaluations – is that, at least in the earlier period (before the funding gradient steepened and the bottom rungs of the ladder were pulled off) much of this money was used to support less successful departments and units. There is in fact a strong case for saying that if research selectivity were concerned *only* with value for money, QR should first be given to the post-92 institutions and possibly the former Colleges of Advanced Technology (Geuna, 1997; Adams, 2005; Little, 2006; McNay, 2009; Million+, 2011).

14 Another case was that of Dr Aubrey Blumsohn of the University of Sheffield, who left its employment under a compromise agreement after alleging serious scientific misconduct in a drug study with a major pharmaceutical company (Baty, 2006).

9 Lessons from marketisation

1 See also Brennan and Patel, 2011.

2 In the market for 'standard' MBAs, fees currently range from £14,000 at Plymouth to £37,750 at Oxford (without a college fee) and £57,500 at the London Business School. There are similar differentials in the market for international students, as Dodds (2011) points out.

3 Filippakou *et al.* (2012) argue that the English (and indeed the British) model of higher education is better described as an increasingly differentiated network of sectors rather than as a system as such. However, as Watson (2007, pp. 26–27) wrote: 'It is important to recognise that even the most powerful institution can't really go it alone. At some stage, and for some important purposes, every institution is going to rely on the strength and reputation of the system as a whole'. The attempt by the UK Border Agency to limit visas for overseas students is a current case in point.

4 See also Brown, 2001b. The 2010 Independent Review of Higher Education Funding and Student Finance (the Browne Report) fulfilled none of these requirements.

There was no modelling of the potential impacts. There was no assessment of the risks. Little evidence was adduced to support the recommendations. There were no research underpinnings. The committee commissioned a single survey of student opinion costing a mere £68,000 (Morgan, 2011). This incidentally showed clear opposition to increased variable fees together with concern that variable fees might create or reinforce a two-tier system, where the differences between what were considered to be the 'best' courses and universities and the 'worst' courses and universities would be reinforced through differential pricing. It is not clear what weight the Committee gave to this information, and even to discover it required a Freedom of Information Act request.

5 Lucas (2006) and others have advocated making more use of metrics in science subjects where quantitative indicators may be more meaningful, and for high-performing departments where information on funding and citation counts may be appropriate, although there is HEPI work (Sastry and Bekhradnia, 2006) that indicates some of the problems with this. On the basis of their survey of national innovation policies, Dill and van Vught (2010, p. 24) commended the Dutch system of evaluation without funding. This involves institutions using external peers to review the quality, productivity, relevance and liability of their research: there is no direct link to funding (Jongbloed, 2010; see also Himanen et al., 2009).

6 The Government welcomed the announcement in January 2011 that the accountancy firm KPMG would pay tuition fees for its next intake of trainees, beginning with a degree course at Durham (BBC News, 2011a). However, such schemes, and employer sponsorship generally, are comparatively rare across the sector as a whole. Ironically, in view of government attempts over many years to link higher education more closely with the labour market, the main form of employment-focussed higher education – sandwich courses – is in terminal decline, while higher level Apprenticeships have still to take off. It has been estimated (Jenkins, 2011) that British companies are currently sitting on a £700 billion cash pile: it will be interesting to see how much of this will be invested in higher education.

7 For a slightly different view, see Watson, 2006b.

8 *The Chronicle of Higher Education* in 2006 (Farrell, 2006) carried a report of the annual conference of the National Association for College Admission Counselling. One of the main issues discussed was how competition for students and prestige was influencing colleges' recruitment practices. The report quoted Joanna Broda, Executive Director of Enrolment Management at Pace University:

> The current guiding principle in marketing colleges is attracting as many students as possible. We sell the sizzle but not the steak, and we market ourselves against our competitors instead of making students aware of the essential elements that distinguish our own college from other institutions.

9 In physics, the number of universities offering honours degrees dropped from around 72 in the mid-1980s to 47 or so in the mid-2000s. This was largely due to the combined effects of the RAE and reduced funding per student, although declining student demand was also a factor. More recently there has been a resurgence of interest and four new courses have either opened, or will open soon (Peter Main, personal communication). The fact that a significant proportion of the courses closed were at the 'applied' end of the subject shows yet again how the baleful influence of the RAE spread to university teaching.

10 The most important higher education system characterised by outright price competition is the US. Although it was only a minor factor, the US Department of Justice's decision in 1993 to restrict the extent to which the Ivy League institutions could coordinate their student aid practices, on top of the Congressional decision in 1972 to

channel funding for teaching through students rather than through formula-driven, enrolment-based grants to institutions (Dill and Beerkens, 2010), and the subsequent decision in 1978 to remove income limits on Guaranteed Student loans (Geiger, 2009), paved the way for the 'arms race' in institutional charges and funding, about which so many commentators (e.g. Winston, 1999) have written (in a 'pre-echo' of the Coalition Government's reforms, the 1972 decision was taken to enable the private colleges to compete more effectively with the public ones).

11 Meacher (2012) quotes £42 billion as the amount of tax estimated by Her Majesty's Revenue and Customs as having been lost last year through tax avoidance and evasion by multinational corporations and the super-rich. As Meacher points out, this is equivalent to a third of the current UK budget deficit.

12 The Consumers Association *Which?* has created a new website to provide information and advice for prospective students (*Which?*, 2012).

13 Our discussion hitherto has assumed that the key factor in student choice of course and institution is or should be educational quality – crudely, the quality of the educational 'programme' on offer. But there is a view that many students are already swayed more by employment and earnings considerations, which leads them to choose more prestigious providers, irrespective of educational quality, and that it is rational for them to do so, especially if leading employers do so as well (Morley and Aynsley, 2007; Watson, 2008). However, this is to reduce higher education to a 'screening' or 'sorting' role: if all universities are doing is acting as finishing schools for the offspring of the middle class, why should they receive any societal support or preference at all? So long as a reputational hierarchy persists, student choice is anyway unlikely to be much influenced by the various official or commercial sources of information, however authoritative and accessible, as Locke (2011) has pointed out.

14 On 23 March 2012 Sir Steve was reported as saying to a meeting of European university leaders:

> How do you guarantee quality for the lower end of the market when it costs £9,000 to go to Oxford but only £4,500 for a further education college?

He added:

> As soon as we damage quality at the lower end, we damage the whole brand.
>
> (Grove, 2012a)

This incidentally supports our earlier point (Note 3) about the need for the system to continue to exist as a meaningful entity.

15 In February 2012 a senior QAA official admitted that the agency had little or no knowledge of most of the private providers whose students were eligible for public funds via the Student Loans Company (Morgan, 2012b); as noted in Chapter 3, the Government has now confirmed its intention to bring all providers receiving public funding into a single regulatory framework (DBIS, 2012c).

16 For changes in institutional governance over the period, see Brown, 2012a. It would be preferable if the regulator, in conjunction with the funding agency, had the powers and resources to be more proactive in encouraging and enabling local institutional 'divisions of labour'. In *Higher Education and the Market* (Brown, 2011a), the author canvassed some of the US state systems as possible models for combining some degree of functional diversity with a minimum of reputational hierarchy. Even today, undergraduate tuition fees set centrally are common across all ten constituent campuses of the University of California. However, in California as in many other states, reduced state appropriations are placing great strains on system coherence and

integrity (Kelderman, 2012). One can never get away from the need for adequate levels of public funding if an adequate supply of public goods is to be assured; unfortunately, as the supply of public goods diminishes through lower state support, private contributors feel even less inclined to pay for them.

17 Brown, R. (2010c) points to the close parallels between scholarly inquiry and public policy analysis as learning processes.

Bibliography

Acton, E. (2011) *The UKBA's Proposed Restriction on Tier 4 Visas: Implications for University Recruitment of Overseas Students*. Oxford: HEPI.

Adam, S. and Browne, J. (2011) *A Survey of UK Tax System*. Briefing Note No. 9. London: Institute for Fiscal Studies.

Adams, J. (2005) Never mind the quality, feel the width, *Research Fortnight*, 28 September, 18–19.

Adams, J. (2006) *How Good is the UK Research Base?* Oxford: HEPI.

Adams, J. and Bekhradnia, B. (2004) *What Future for Dual Support?* Oxford: HEPI.

Adams, J. and Gurney, K. (2010) *Funding Selectivity, Concentration and Excellence – How Good is the UK's Research?* Oxford: HEPI.

Adams, J. and Smith, D. (2004) *Research and Regions: An Overview of the Distribution of Research in UK Regions, Regional Research Capacity and Links Between Strategic Research Partners*. Oxford: HEPI.

Adams, J., Cook, N., Law, G., Marshall, S., Mount, D., Smith, D. and Wilkinson, D. (2000) *The Role of Selectivity and the Characteristics of Excellence: Report to the Higher Education Funding Council for England: A Consultancy Study Within the Fundamental Review of Research Policy and Funding*. Leeds: Evidence Ltd.

Adnett, N. (2006) Student finance and widening participation in the British Isles: common problems, different solutions, *Higher Education Quarterly*, 60, 4, 296–311.

Advisory Board for the Research Councils (1987) *A Strategy for the Science Base*. London: HMSO.

Agasisti, T. (2011) Performances and spending efficiency in higher education: a European comparison through non-parametric approaches, *Education Economics*, 19, 2, 199–224.

Aghion, P., Dewatripoint, M., Hoxby, C., Mas-Collell, A. and Sapir, A. (2008) *Higher Aspirations: An Agenda for Reforming European Universities*. Bruegel Blueprint 5. Brussels: Bruegel.

Ainley, P. (2011) The fading dream. Review of *Low-Income Students and the Perpetuation of Inequality, Higher Education in America* by Gary A. Berg (Farnham: Ashgate Publishing Group), *Higher Education Review*, 44, 1, 99–101.

Alderman, G. (2008) Teaching Quality Assessment, League Tables and the Decline of Academic Standards in British Higher Education. Inaugural Professorial Lecture, University of Buckingham, 17 June.

Alderman, G. (2009) Defining and measuring academic standards: a British perspective, *Higher Education Management and Policy*, 21, 3, 9–21.

Alderman, G. (2010) Reflections: change, quality and standards in British higher education, *Journal of Change Management*, 10, 3, 243–252.

Alegre, M.A. and Ferrer, G. (2010) School regimes and education equity: some insights based on PISA 2006, *British Educational Research Journal*, 36, 3, 433–461.

Allen, F. (2011) Physics students 'unprepared for university', *TES*, 9 September, 11.

Altbach, P. (2004) The costs and benefits of world-class universities, *Academe Online*, http://www.aaup.org/AAUP/pubsres/academe/2004/JF/Feat/altb.htm (accessed 4 December 2011).

Anderson, C. (1960) *Grants to Students: Report of the Committee Appointed by the Minister of Education and the Secretary of State for Scotland*. Cmnd 1051. London: HMSO.

Archer, L. (2003) The 'value' of higher education. In Archer, L., Hutchings, M. and Ross, A. (Eds.) *Higher Education and Social Class: Issues of Exclusion and Inclusion* (pp. 119–136). London: RoutledgeFalmer.

Ashwin, P., Abbas, A. and McLean, M. (2011) A bad deal for 'consumers', *THE*, 17 November, 23.

Astin, A. and Oseguera, L. (2004) The declining equity of American higher education, *The Review of Higher Education*, 27, 3, 321–341.

Attwood, R. (2008a) Probe ordered into 'manipulation', *THE*, 28 February, 5.

Attwood, R. (2008b) Manchester social science contact time halved since 1988, report shows, *THE*, 24 April, 9.

Attwood, R. (2008c) Teaching quality under 'grave threat', *THE*, 15 May, 6.

Attwood, R. (2008d) 'Encouraging' survey reveals most students are satisfied with teaching, *THE*, 20 November, 7.

Attwood, R. (2009) Lecturers talk of students' 'shocking' abuse, *THE*, June 18, 10.

Babcock, P. and Marks, M. (2011) The falling time cost of college: evidence from half a century of time use data, *The Review of Economics and Statistics*, 93, 2, 468–478.

Baker, K. (1989) Higher education: the next 25 years. Speech by the Secretary of State for Education and Science, Rt Hon Kenneth Baker MP, University of Lancaster, 5 January 1989. London: DES.

Baker, K. (1993) *The Turbulent Years: My Life in Politics*. London and Boston: Faber and Faber.

Baker, S. (2010a) Research funding 'black hole'? Fill it with teaching cash, UCL chair advises, *THE*, 9 December, 6–7.

Baker, S. (2010b) Huge BPP write-off announced as Apollo prophesies bleak short-term future for private demand, *THE*, 18 November, 6–7.

Baker, S. (2011a) The jobs market has spoken? Employment data could be used to keep a lid on fees, *THE*, 26 May, 6–7.

Barker, I. (2010) Studying by day, pulling pints by night: trainees stem £20k debt, *TES*, 23 April, 8–9.

Barnett, R. (2000) *Realizing the University in an Age of Supercomplexity*. Buckingham and Philadelphia: SRHE and Open University Press.

Barr, N. (1989a) Alternative proposals for student loans in the United Kingdom. In M. Woodhall (Ed.) *Financial Support for Students: Grants, Loans or Graduate Tax?* (pp. 110–121). London: Kogan Page.

Barr, N. (1989b) *Student Loans: The Next Steps*. Aberdeen: University of Aberdeen Press.

Barr, N. (1989c) The White Paper on student loans, *Journal of Social Policy*, 18, 3, 409–417, reprinted in N. Barr and I. Crawford (2005) *Financing Higher Education: Answers from the UK* (pp. 66–75). London: Routledge.

Barr, N. and Johnston, A. (2011) *Saving Student Loans*, http://econ.lse.ac.uk/staff/nb/BarrJohnstonLoanThreshold110421.pdf (accessed 21 January 2012).

Barrett, R. (1996) On students as customers – some warnings from North America, *Higher Education Review*, 28, 3, 70–73.

Barrett, R. (2011) On students as customers: contesting the analogy, *Higher Education Review*, 43, 2, 65– 76.

Baty, P. (2000) V-c's 'plea for firsts' fuels quality fears, *THE*, 30 June, http://www.timeshighereducation.co.uk/story.asp?storyCode=152290&sectioncode=26 (accessed 27 June 2012).

Baty, P. (2004a) Poll reveals pressure to dumb down, *THE*, 19 November, http://www.timeshighereducation.co.uk/story.asp?sectioncode=26&storycode=192485 (accessed 27 June 2012).

Baty, P. (2004b) Caught in a vicious cycle of declining standards, *THE*, 19 November, http://www.timeshighereducation.co.uk/story.asp?sectioncode=26&storycode=192504 (accessed 27 June 2012).

Baty, P. (2005) Government considered £5000 fee, *THE*, 25 March, 7.

Baty, P. (2006) Payout in P & G drug data row, *THE*, 7 April, http://www.timeshighereducation.co.uk/story.asp?storycode=202393 (accessed 27 May 2012).

BBC News (2010) Universities in Wales told to 'adapt or die', *BBC News, Wales Politics*, 3 December, http://www.bbc.co.uk/news/uk-wales-politics-11911375?print=true (accessed 23 April 2012).

BBC News (2011a) *KPMG Offers to Pay Tuition Fees for Trainees*, 13 January 2011. http://www.bbc.co.uk/news/education-12181643 (accessed 13 January 2011).

BBC News (2011b) Fee Move for Non-Scots University Students, 29 June 2011, http://www.bbc.co.uk/news/uk-scotland-13951685 (accessed 8 July 2012).

Bekhradnia, B. (2003) *Widening Participation and Fair Access: An Overview of the Evidence*. Oxford: HEPI.

Bekhradnia, B. (2006) *The Academic Experience of Students at English Universities: 2006 Report*. Oxford: HEPI.

Bekhradnia, B. (2007) *The Academic Experience of Students at English Universities: 2007 Report*. Oxford: HEPI.

Bekhradnia, B. (2009) *The Academic Experience of Students at English Universities: 2009 Report*. Oxford: HEPI.

Bekhradnia, B. (2012) *The Academic Experience of Students at English Universities: 2012 Report*. Oxford: HEPI.

Bekhradnia, B. & Massy, W. (2009) *Vouchers as a Mechanism for Funding Higher Education*. Oxford: HEPI.

Belfield, C. and Levin, H.M. (2005) Vouchers and public policy: when ideology trumps evidence, *American Journal of Education*, 111, 548–567.

Bence, V. and Oppenheim, C. (2005) The evolution of the UK's research assessment exercise: publications, performance and perceptions, *Journal of Educational Administration and History*, 37, 2, 137–155.

Bettinger, E.P. and Terry Long, B. (2006) The increasing use of adjunct instructors at public institutions: are we hurting students? In R.G. Ehrenberg (Ed.) *What's Happening to Public Higher Education? The Shifting Financial Burden* (pp. 51–71). Baltimore: Johns Hopkins University Press.

Bird, R. (1994) Reflections on the British Government and higher education, *Higher Education Quarterly*, 48, 2, 73–85.

Birnbaum, R. (1983) *Maintaining Diversity in Higher Education*. San Francisco: Jossey-Bass.

Blair, T. (1999) Speech at the Labour Party Conference, Bournemouth, 28 September.

Blair, T. (2001) Speech at the Labour Party Conference, Brighton, 2 October.

Blose, G.L., Porter, J.D. and Kokkelenberg, E.C. (2006) The effect of institutional funding cuts on Baccalaureate graduation rates in public higher Education. In R.G. Ehrenberg (Ed.) *What's Happening to Public Higher Education? The Shifting Financial Burden* (pp. 71–83). Baltimore: The Johns Hopkins University Press.

Blumenstyk, G. (2011) Data show wider gaps in spending on students, *The Chronicle of Higher Education*, 23 September, A1, A12.

Blunkett, D. (2000) Speech on Higher Education at the University of Greenwich, 15 February 2000.

Boden, R. and Epstein, D. (2006) Managing the research imagination? Globalisation and research in higher education, *Globalisation, Societies and Education*, 4, 2, 223–236.

Bogdanor, V. (2010) Can we afford *not* to spend more? *THE*, 28 October, 35–39.

Boliver, V. (Submitted for review) How fair is access to more prestigious universities?

Bone, J. and McNay, I. (2006) *Higher Education and Human Good*. Bristol: Tockington Press.

Boulton, G. and Lucas, C. (2008) *What Are Universities For?* League of European Research Universities, http://www.leru.org/file.php?type=download&id=1323 (accessed 23 December 2008).

Bound, J. and Turner, S. (2007) Cohort crowding: How resources affect collegiate attainment, *Journal of Public Economics* 91, 877–899.

Bound, J., Lovenheim, M. F. and Turner, S. (2010) Why have college completion rates declined? An analysis of changing student preparation and collegiate resources, *American Economic Journal: Applied Economics 2 (July 2010)*, 129–157.

Boyer Commission on Educating Undergraduates in the Research University (1998) *Reinventing Undergraduate Education: A Blueprint for America's Research Universities*. Stony Brook: State University of New York at Stony Brook.

Brennan, J. (2004) The social role of the contemporary university: contradictions, boundaries and change. In *CHERI Ten Years On: Changing Higher Education in a Changing World*. London: Centre for Higher Education Research and Information.

Brennan, J. (2007) Submission to the House of Commons Education and Skills Select Committee inquiry into the future sustainability of the higher education sector.

Brennan, J. and Patel, K. (2011) Up-market or down-market? Shopping for higher education in the UK. In P.N. Teixeira and D.D. Dill (Eds.) *Public Vices, Private Virtues? Assessing the Effects of Marketization in Higher Education* (pp. 315–326). Rotterdam: Sense.

Brew, A. and Lucas, L. (Eds.) (2009) *Academic Research and Researchers*. Maidenhead: SRHE and Open University Press.

Brewer, D. J., Gates, S. M. and Goldman, C. A. (2002) *In Pursuit of Prestige: Strategy and Competition in US Higher Education*. Somerset, NJ: Transaction.

Broadfoot, P. (1998) Quality, standards and control in higher education, *International Studies in Sociology of Education*, 8, 2, 155–180.

Brown, N. and Ramsden, B. (2006) Measuring the prosperity of UK higher education institutions. (Unpublished research commissioned by HEPI).

Brown, N. and Ramsden, B. (2009) *Variable Tuition Fees in England: Assessing their Impact on Students and Higher Education Institutions. A Fourth Report*. London: UUK.

Brown, R. (2001a) Accountability in higher education: the case for a higher education audit commission. *Higher Education Review*, 33, 2, 5–20.

Brown, R. (2001b) Evidence based policy or policy based evidence? The case of quality assurance in higher education. Inaugural Lecture given on 11 December at City University, London.

Brown, R. (2004) *Quality Assurance in Higher Education: the UK Experience since 2004*. London and New York: RoutledgeFalmer.

Brown, R. (2006a) League tables – do we have to live with them? *perspectives* 10, 2, 33–38.

Brown, R. (2006b) Protecting quality and diversity in a market driven system. *Higher Education Review*, 39, 1, 3–16.

Brown, R. (2007a) Accountability in higher education: too much of the wrong sort and too little of the right sort? In M. Gokulsing (Ed.) *A Different Future? The New Shape of Higher Education in England* (pp. 86–104). Lewiston, Queenston, Lampeter: Edwin Mellen Press.

Brown, R. (2007b) Reeking hypocrisy? New Labour and widening participation in higher education, *perspectives*, 11, 1, 97–102.

Brown, R (2007c) *The Information Fallacy*. Oxford: HEPI.

Brown, R. (2009a) Effectiveness or economy? In J. Huisman (Ed.) *International Perspectives on the Governance of Higher Education – Frameworks for Coordination*. New York and London: Routledge.

Brown, R. (2009b) Quality assurance and the market. In J. Newton, and R. Brown (Eds.) *The Future of Quality Assurance*. Amsterdam: European Association for Institutional Research.

Brown, R. (2010a) The current brouhaha about standards in England, *Quality in Higher Education*, 16, 2, 129–137.

Brown, R. (2010b) Research-informed teaching or inquiry based education? *Pedagogical Research in Maximising Education (PRIME)*, Liverpool Hope University, 4, 1, 3–19.

Brown, R. (2010c) Challenging ideology: could a better understanding of academic enquiry lead to better public policy making? *Higher Education Review*, 42, 2, 46–58.

Brown, R. (2010d) *Comparability of Degree Standards*. Oxford: HEPI.

Brown, R. (Ed.) (2011a) *Higher Education and the Market*. New York and London: Routledge.

Brown, R. (2011b) The march of the market. In M. Molesworth, R. Scullion and E. Nixon (Eds.) *The Marketisation of Higher Education and the Student as Consumer* (pp. 11–24). London and New York: Routledge.

Brown, R. (2011c). The new English quality assurance regime, *Quality in Higher Education*, 17, 2, 213–230.

Brown, R. (2011d) The coalition government's higher education reforms: raising quality or 'nonsense on stilts'? Professorial lecture at the University of West London 14 December 2011, http://www.uwl.ac.uk/instil/Events.jsp. (accessed 18 March 2012).

Brown, R. (2011e) *Lessons from America?* Oxford: HEPI.

Brown, R. (2011f) What do we do about university governance – Part 1, *perspectives*, 15, 2, 53–58.

Brown, R. (2011g) What do we do about university governance – Part 2, *perspectives*, 15, 3, 87–91.

Brown, R. (2012a) *The Corporatisation of University Governance*. London: University of West London, http://www.uwl.ac.uk/instil/research/Occasional_pages.jsp.

Brown, R. (2012b) *The Development of System-wide Performance Indicators*. London: University of West London, http://www.uwl.ac.uk/instil/research/Occasional_pages. jsp.

Brown, R. (2012c) *The Myth of Student Choice. VISTAS: Education, Economy and Community*. London: University of West London.

Brown, R. (submitted for review) Mutuality meets the market: analysing changes in the governance of quality in UK higher education, 1980–2012.

Brown, R. and Alderman, G. (2012) When owners change, keep check on powers, *THE*, 26 April, 30.

Brown, R., Carpenter, C., Collins, R. and Winkvist-Noble, L. (2007) Recent developments in information about programme quality in the UK, *Quality in Higher Education*, 13, 2, 173–186.

Bruce, T. (2012) *Universities and Constitutional Change in the UK: the Impact of Devolution on the Higher Education Sector*. Oxford: HEPI.

Burke, J. and Associates (2005) *Achieving Accountability in Higher Education: Balancing Public, Academic and Market Demands*. San Francisco: Jossey-Bass.

Calhoun, C. (2006) The university and the public good, *Thesis Eleven*, 84, 7–43.

Callahan, D. (2004) *The Cheating Culture*. Orlando, FL: Harcourt.

Callender, C. (2003) Student financial support in higher education: access and exclusion. In M. Tight (Ed.) *Access and Exclusion* (pp. 127–158). Kidlington: Elsevier.

Callender, C. (2006) Access to higher education in Britain: the impact of tuition fees and financial assistance. In P.N. Teixeira, D.B .Johnstone, M.J. Rosa and H. Vossensteyn (Eds.) *Cost-Sharing and Accessibility in Higher Education: A Fairer Deal?* (pp. 105–132). Dordrecht: Springer.

Callender, C. (2009a) Institutional aid in England: promoting widening participation or perpetuating inequalities? In J.Knight (Ed.) *Financing Equity and Access in Higher Education* (pp. 127–149). Rotterdam: Sense.

Callender, C. (2009b) The impact of term-time employment on higher education students' academic attainment and achievement, *Journal of Education Policy*, 23, 4, 359–377.

Callender, C. (2010) Bursaries and institutional aid in higher education in England: do they safeguard and promote fair access? *Oxford Review of Education*, 36, 1, 45–62.

Callender, C. (2011) UK: Government reforms will decrease social mobility, *University World News*, 4 December 2011, http://www.universityworldnews.com/article.php?story=20111202221307320 (accessed 6 December 2011)

Callender, C. and Jackson, J. (2005) Does fear of debt deter students from higher education? *Journal of Social Policy*, 34, 4, 509–540.

Callender, C. and Jackson, J. (2008) Does the fear of debt constrain choice of university and subject of study? *Studies in Higher Education*, 33, 4, 405–429.

Carasso, H. (2010) *Implementing the Financial Provisions of the Higher Education Act (2004) – English Universities in a New Quasi-market*. DPhil thesis, University of Oxford. (access via http://tinyurl.com/3c28luh) (accessed 18 March 2012).

Carey, K. (2011) A college education for all, free and online, *The Chronicle of Higher Education*, 15 July, A72.

Carpentier, V. (2010) Public–private substitution in higher education funding and Kondratiev cycles: the impacts on home and international students. In E. Unterhalter, and V. Carpentier (Eds.) *Global Inequalities and Higher Education: Whose Interests Are We Serving?* (pp. 142–171). Basingstoke and New York: Palgrave Macmillan.

Cave, M., Hanney, S., Henkel, M. and Kogan, M. (2000) *The Use of Performance*

Indicators in Higher Education: The Challenge of the Quality Movement. London: Jessica Kingsley.

Centre for Higher Education Research and Information (2009) *Diversity in the Student Learning Experience and Time Devoted to Study: A Comparative Analysis of The UK and European Evidence*, http://www.hefce.ac.uk/pubs/rereports/year/2009/diversity-inthestudentlearningexperience/name,64092,en.html (accessed 10 June 2012).

Centre for Higher Education Research and Information and London South Bank University (2005*) Survey of Higher Education Students' Attitudes to Debt and Term-Time Working and Their Impact on Attainment*. London: UUK.

Centre for Higher Education Research and Information and Hobsons Research (2008) *Counting What is Measured or Measuring What Counts? Report to the Higher Education Funding Council for England*. Bristol: HEFCE.

Centre for Learning and Life Chances in Knowledge Economies and Societies (2011) *Education, Opportunity and Social Cohesion*. London: Institute of Education. http://www.llakes.org/wp-content/uploads/2011/06/Socialcohesion_webversion.pdf (accessed 18 May 2012).

Chancellor of the Duchy of Lancaster (1993) *Realising Our Potential: A Strategy for Science, Engineering and Technology*. Cm 2250. London: HMSO.

Chapman, B. (2006) Income related student loans: concepts, international reforms and administrative challenges. In P.N. Teixeira, D. Bruce Johnstone, M.J. Rosa and H. Vossensteyn (Eds.) *Cost-sharing and Accessibility in Higher Education: A Fairer Deal?* (pp. 79–104). Dordrecht: Springer.

Cheng, J.S. and Marsh, H.W. (2010) The National Student Survey: are differences between universities and courses reliable and meaningful? *Oxford Review of Education*, 36, 6, 693–712.

Cheng, S.C. and Gorard, S. (2010) Segregation by poverty in secondary schools in England 2006–2009: a research note, *Journal of Education Policy*, 25, 3, 415–418.

Chester, J. and Bekhradnia, B. (2009) *Oxford and Cambridge: How Different Are They?* Oxford: HEPI.

Chowdry, H. and Sibieta, L. (2011) *Trends in Education and Schools Spending*, Briefing Note BN 121. London: Institute for Fiscal Studies.

Chowdry, H., Crawford, C., Dearden, L., Goodman, A. and Vignoles, A. (2011) *Widening Participation in Higher Education: Analysis Using Linked Administrative Data*. IFS Working Paper W10/04. London: Institute for Fiscal Studies.

Clark, B.R. (1983) *The Higher Education System*. Berkeley and Los Angeles: University of California Press.

Clark, T. (2009) The impact of reforms on the quality and responsiveness of universities in the United Kingdom, *Higher Education Management and Policy*, 21, 2, 1–16.

Clarke, C. (2010) *Submission from Rt Hon Charles Clarke MP to the Browne Enquiry into Higher Education Funding*, http://www.webarchive.nationalarchives.gov.uk/+/hereview.independent.gov.uk/hereview/2010/03/submissions-to-the-first-call-for-evidence (accessed 11 July 2012)

Clarke, M. (2005) Quality assessment lessons from Australia and New Zealand, *Higher Education in Europe*, 30, 2, 183–197.

Coate, K., Barnett, R. and Williams, G. (2001) Relationships between teaching and research in higher education in England, *Higher Education Quarterly*, 55, 2, 158–174.

College of Law (2012) College of Law change of ownership: interview with Nigel Savage, CEO of the College of Law, *The College of Law*, 19 April 2012, http: www.college-of-law.co.uk/About-the-College/Interview-with-Nigel-Savage,-CEO-of-The-College-of-Law/ (accessed 19 April 2012)

Collini, S. (2010) Browne's Gamble, *London Review of Books*, 18 October, http://www.lrb.co.uk/v32/n21/stefan-collini/brownes-gamble/print (accessed 27 June 2011).

Collins, R. (2002) Credential inflation and the future of universities. In S. Brint (Ed.) *The Future of the City of Intellect* (pp. 23–47). Stanford, CA: Stanford University Press.

Committee on Higher Education (Robbins Committee) (1963) *Higher Education*. (Cmnd. 2154. London: HMSO.

Connelly, T. and Angel, D. (2011) Is the bloom off the rose? *Inside HigherEd*, September 30 2011, http://www.insidehighered.com/layout/set/print/views/2011/9/30/connelly_angel_essay_on_for_profit_colleges_putting_future_at_risk (accessed 3 October 2011).

Cooper, P. (2007) Knowing your 'lemons': quality uncertainty in UK higher education, *Quality in Higher Education*, 13, 1, 19–29.

Cote, J.E. and Allahar, A.L. (2011) *Lowering Higher Education: The Rise of Corporate Universities and the Fall of Liberal Education*. Toronto: University Press.

Council for Industry and Higher Education (2006) *International Competitiveness: Businesses Working With UK Universities*. London: Council for Industry and Higher Education.

Council for Scientific Policy (1967) *Second Report on Science Policy*. Cmnd 3420. London: HMSO.

Court, S. (1999) Negotiating the research imperative: the views of UK academics on their career opportunities, *Higher Education Quarterly*, 53, 1, 65–87.

Crespi, G. and Geuna, A. (2006) *The Productivity of UK Universities*. Science Policy Research Unit Electronic Working Paper Series No 147. University of Sussex: Science Policy Research Unit.

Cunnane, S. (2010) i-Map finds too many weeds in the portfolio garden, *THE*, 8 December, 6–7.

Cuthbert, R. (2010) Students as customers? *Higher Education Review*, 42, 3, 3–25.

CVCP (1986) *Academic Standards in Universities*. London: CVCP.

CVCP (1987) *Academic Standards in Universities*. London: CVCP.

CVCP (1988) *Academic Standards in Universities*. London: CVCP.

CVCP (1996) *Review of the Teaching Funding Method: CVCP Comments*. London: CVCP.

CVCP (1997) *CVCP Submission to HEFCE on Funding Method for Teaching from 1998–99*. N/97/51. London: CVCP.

CVCP (1992) *Annual Report of the Director 1990/91* Academic Audit Unit. London: CVCP.

Davies, P., Slack, K., Hughes, A., Mangan, J. and Vigurs, K. (2008) *Knowing Where to Study? Fees, Bursaries and Fair Access*. Stoke-on-Trent: Institute for Educational Policy Research and Institute for Access Studies, Staffordshire University.

DBIS (2009) *Higher Ambitions: The Future of Universities in a Knowledge Economy*. London: DBIS.

DBIS (2010) *Progressive Plans for Higher Education*, 3 November, http://nds.coi.gov.uk/content/Detail.aspx?ReleaseID=416343&NewsAreaID=2 (accessed 4 November 2010).

DBIS(2011a) *Higher Education. Students at the Heart of the System*. Cmnd 8122. London: DBIS.

DBIS (2011b) *A New Fit-For-Purpose Regulatory Framework for the Higher Education Sector. Technical Consultation*. London: DBIS. http://bis.gov.uk/assets/biscore/higher-education/docs/n/11-1114-new-regulatory-framework-f (accessed 6 August 2011).

DBIS (2012a) Higher education funding 2012–13. Letter dated 25 January 2012 from the Secretary of State, Vince Cable MP, and the Minister for Universities and Science, David Willetts MP, to Tim Melville-Ross, Chair of the Higher Education Funding Council for England.

DBIS (2012b) *International Comparative Performance of the UK Research Base – 2011*, http://www.bis.gov.uk/assets/biscore/science/docs/i/11/-p123-international-comparative-performance-UK-research-base-2011.pdf (accessed 21 May 2012).

DBIS (2012c) *Government Response. Consultations on 1. Students at the Heart of the System 2 A New Fit For Purpose Regulatory Framework for the Sector June 2012*, http://www.bis.gov.uk/assets/biscore/higher-education/docs/g/12-890-government-response-students-and=regulatory-framework-higher-education. (accessed 12 June 2012).

Deer, C.M.A. (2002) *Higher Education in England and France since the 1980s*. Oxford: Symposium Books.

DELNI (2011) *Update to Independent Review of Variable Fees and Student Finance Arrangements*. Belfast: DELNI.

Denham, A. and Garnett, M. (2001) *Keith Joseph*. Chesham. Acumen.

Denham, J. (2008) Education (Student Support) Regulations. *Hansard*, 29 October, Cols 32–33WS.

De Santos, M. (2010) Fact-totems and the statistical imagination: the public life of a statistic in Argentina 2001, *Sociological Theory*, 27, 4, 466–489.

DES (1972) *Education: A Framework for Expansion*. Cmnd 5174. London: HMSO.

DES (1978) *Report of the Working Group on the Management of Higher Education in the Maintained Sector (Chaired by Gordon Oakes)*. Cmnd 7130. London: HMSO.

DES (1985a) *The Development of Higher Education into the 1990s*. Cmnd 9524. London: HMSO.

DES (1985b) *Academic Validation in Public Sector Higher Education: Report of the Committee of Inquiry (Lindop Report)*. Cmnd 9501. London: HMSO.

DES (1987) *Higher Education. Meeting the Challenge*. Cm 114. London: HMSO.

DES (1988a) *Top-Up Loans for Students* Cm. 520. London: HMSO.

DES (1988b) *Letter Dated 31 October 1988 from Rt Hon Kenneth Baker MP to Lord Chilver, Chairman of the Universities Funding Council*. London: DES.

DES (1988c) *Letter Dated 31 October 1988 from Rt Hon Kenneth Baker MP to Sir Ron Dearing, Chairman of the Polytechnics and Colleges Funding Council*. London: DES.

DES (1989) *Shifting the Balance of Public Funding of Higher Education to Fees*. Consultation Paper. London: DES.

DES (1991) *Higher Education: A New Framework*. Cm 1541. London: HMSO.

DES (1992) *Letter Dated 2 June 1992 from Rt Hon John Patten MP to Sir Ron Dearing*. London: DES.

DES (1993) Education spending to rise by £670 million. Press Release (393/93) 30 November 1993.

DES (1995) Departmental expenditure in 1996–97: written reply by the Secretary of State, Mrs Gillian Shephard, 28 November.

DFEE (1998) *Higher Education for the 21st Century: Response to the Dearing Report*. London: DFEE.

DFES (2003) *The Future of Higher Education*. Cm 5735. London: The Stationery Office Limited.

Dickie, V. Dunker, K. and Saxena, V. (2012) The role, responsibilities and remuneration of graduate teaching assistants in Scotland. *Scottish Educational Review*, 44, 2, 24–44.

Dill, D. D. (2007) Will market competition assure academic quality? An analysis of the UK and US experience. In D.F. Westerheijden, B. Stensaker and M.J. Rosa (Eds.) *Quality Assurance in Higher Education: Trends in Regulation, Translation and Transformation* (pp. 47–72). Dordrecht: Springer.

Dill, D.D. and Beerkens, M. (2010) Introduction. In D.D. Dill and M. Beerkens (Eds.) *Public Policy for Academic Quality* (pp. 1–19). Rotterdam: Sense.

Dill, D.D. and Soo, M. (2005) Academic quality, league tables and public policy: a cross-national analysis of university ranking systems, *Higher Education*, 49, 4, 495–533.

Dill, D.D. and van Vught, F.A. (Eds.) (2010) *National Innovation and the Academic Research Enterprise*. Baltimore: The Johns Hopkins University Press.

DiMaggio, P.J. and Powell, W.W. (1983) The iron cage revisited: institutional isomorphism and collective rationality in organizational fields, *American Sociological Review*, 48, 2, 147–160.

Dodds, A. (2011) The British higher education funding debate: the perils of 'talking economics', *London Review of Education*, 9, 3, 317–331.

Dorling, D. (2012) Raising equality in access to higher education. In Dorling, D. *Fair Play. A Daniel Dorling Reader on Social Justice* (pp. 170–186). Bristol: The Policy Press.

Easton, D. (1965) *A Systems Analysis of Political Life*. New York and London: Wiley.

Ederer, P., Schuller, P. and Willms, S. (2008) *University Systems Ranking: Citizens and Society in the Age of Knowledge*. Policy Brief. Brussels: The Lisbon Council.

Ehrenberg, R.G. and Zhang, L. (2006) Do tenured and tenure-track faculty matter? In R.G. Ehrenberg (Ed.) *What's Happening to Public Higher Education? The Shifting Financial Burden* (pp. 37–51). Baltimore: The Johns Hopkins University Press.

Equality Challenge Unit (ECU) (2011) *Equality in Higher Education: Statistical Report 2011*. London: ECU.

European Higher Education Area (2010) *Bologna Process – European Higher Education Area*, http://www.ehea.info (accessed 27 June 2012).

Evidence Ltd (2002) *Maintaining Research Excellence and Volume. A Report by Evidence Ltd to the Higher Education Funding Councils for England, Scotland and Wales and to UniversitiesUK*. Leeds: Evidence Ltd.

Evidence Ltd (2003) *Funding Research Diversity*. London: UUK.

Evidence Ltd (2005) *Impact of Selective Funding of Research in England, and the Specific Outcomes of HEFCE Research Funding*. Bristol: HEFCE.

Evidence Ltd (2007) *Monitoring Research Diversity: Changes Between 2000 and 2005*. London: UUK.

Evidence Ltd. (2008) *International Comparative Performance of the UK Research Base. A report to the Department of Innovation, Universities and Skills*, http://www.dius.gov.uk/science/science_funding/science_budget/uk_research_base.

Evidence Ltd. (2011) *Funding Research Excellence: Research Group Size, Critical Mass and Performance*. London: University Alliance.

Exley, S. (2010) EMA replacement is at least '£200m short', *TES*, 17 December, 17.

Fallows, J. (2005) College admissions: a substitute for quality? In R. Hersh and J. Merrow (Eds.) *Declining by Degrees: Higher Education at Risk* (pp. 39–47). New York and Basingstoke: Palgrave Macmillan.

Farrell, E.F. (2006) At college counsellors' conference, debate swirls over test scores and early admissions, *The Chronicle of Higher Education*, 20 October, A15.

Ferlie, E., Ashburner, L., Fitzgerald, L. and Pettigrew, A. (1996) *The New Public Management in Action*. Oxford: University Press.

Filippakou, O., Salter, B. and Tapper, T. (2012) Higher education as a system: the English experience, *Higher Education Quarterly*, 66, 1, 106–122.

Forsyth, A. and Furlong, A. (2000) *Socio-economic Disadvantage and Access to Higher Education*, http://www.jrf.org.uk/knowledge/findings/socialpolicy/n110.htm (accessed 28 November 2000)

Foskett, N. (2011) Markets, government, funding and the marketisation of higher education. In M. Molesworth, R. Scullion and E. Nixon (Eds.) *The Marketisation of Higher Education and the Student as Consumer* (pp. 25–38). London and New York: Routledge.

Frank, R. and Cook, P.J. (1997) *The Winner-Take-All Society*. New York: Martin Kessler Books, The Free Press.

Frankel, M. (2011) Coalition higher education policy is just a repair mechanism: Labour's Gareth Thomas in pre-emptive strike on David Willetts, *Research Fortnight*, 3766, 27 September, 13–14.

Frankel, M. (2012) Is university autonomy under threat in Wales? *Research Fortnight*, 11 July, 1.

Friedman, M. (1962) *Capitalism and Freedom*. Chicago: Chicago University Press.

Furedi, F. (2009) Now is the age of the discontented, *THE*, 4 June, 30–35.

Furedi, F. (2012) Satisfaction and its discontents, *THE*, 8 March, 36–40.

Furlong, J., Barton, L., Miles, S., Whiting, C. and Whitty, G. (2000) *Teacher Education in Transition: Re-forming Professionalism?* Buckingham: SRHE and Open University Press.

Geiger, R.L. (2004) Market coordination of higher education: the United States. In P. Teixeira, B. Jongbloed, D. Dill and A. Amaral (Eds.) *Markets in Higher Education: Rhetoric or Reality?* (pp. 161–183). Dordrecht: Kluwer Academic Publishers.

Geiger, R.L. (2009) Markets and the end of the current era in US higher education. Paper presented to the *CHER 22nd Annual Conference*, Porto 10–12 September.

Gerritsen, J. (2008) The real Shanghai Jiao Tong winners. *University World News* 31 August, http://www.universityworldnews.com/article.php?story=200808281503333 16 (accessed 25 March 2009)

Geuna, A. (1997) Allocation of funds and research output: the case of UK universities, *Revue d'Economie Industrielle*, 79, 1, 143–162.

Geuna, A. (2001) The changing rationale for European university research funding: are there negative unintended consequences? *Journal of Economic Issues*, XXXV, 3, 607–632.

Geuna, A. and Martin, R.R. (2003) University research evaluation and funding: an international comparison, *Minerva*, 41, 277–304.

Gibbs, G. (2010) *Dimensions of Quality*, http://www.heacademy.ac.uk/assets/York/documents/ourwork/evidence-informed-practice/Dimensions_of_Quality.pdf (accessed 25 October 2010).

Gibbs, G. (2012) Will chasing the market really result in an increase in quality? *THE*, 16 February, 28–29.

Gill, J. (2008a) Spending spree on RAE stars may spark cash crisis, *THE*, 10 January, 9.

Gill, J. (2008b) Keep it stupid, simple, *THE*, 23 October, 32–37.

Gill, J. (2008c) Despair over home students' grasp of English, *THE*, 11 December, 11.

Gill, J. (2009) Lecturers hit back at efforts to discredit grade-inflation claims, *THE*, 19 March, 11.

Gill, J. (2010) *Cable: Elite Held Gun to Our Heads*, 16 November, http://www.times-highereducation.co.uk/story.asp?sectioncode=26&storycode=41430 (accessed 16 November 2010).

Glatter, R. (2010) Changing organisational structures: will we never learn? Paper presented at the British Educational Leadership, Management and Administration Society Annual Conference, Wokefield Park, Reading, 9 July 2010.

Glenn, D. (2008) Keep adjuncts away from intro courses, report says, *The Chronicle of Higher Education*, 4 April 2008, pp. A1, A10.

Goldin, C. and Katz, L.F. (2008) *The Race Between Education and Technology.* Cambridge, MA and London: Harvard University Press.

Gorard, S. (2008) Who is missing from higher education? *Cambridge Journal of Education*, 38, 3, 421–437.

Gorard, S., Smith, E., May, H., Thomas, L., Adnett, N. and Slack, K. (2006) *Review of Widening Participation Research: Addressing the Barriers to Participation in Higher Education. A Report to HEFCE by the University of York, the Higher Education Academy and the Institute for Access Studies.* Bristol: HEFCE.

Greenaway, D. (1995) *The Economic Impact of International Students in UK Higher Education.* London: CVCP.

Greenaway, D. and Haynes, M. (2000) *Funding Universities to Meet National and International Challenges.* Nottingham: School of Economics Policy Report, University of Nottingham.

Greenbank, P. (2007) Higher education and the graduate labour market: the 'class factor', *Tertiary Education and Management*, 13, 4, 365–376.

Greenberg, D.S. (2007) *Science for Sale: the Perils, Rewards and Delusions of Campus Capitalism.* Chicago and London: University of Chicago.

Griffiths, R. (2004) Knowledge production and the research-teaching nexus: the case of the built environment disciplines, *Studies in Higher Education* 29, 6, 709–726.

Grove, J. (2012a) *Low-quality teaching detrimental to 'brand UK'*, *THE*, 29 March, 12.

Grove, J. (2012b) Complaints over standards on hypnosis course earn QAA scrutiny, *THE*, 12 April, 11.

Haldane (1918) *Report of the Machinery of Government Committee under the Chairmanship of Viscount Haldane of Cloan.* London: HMSO.

Hall, P.A. (1993) Policy paradigms, social learning and the state, *Comparative Politics*, 25, 3, 275–296.

Halsey, A.H. (1995) *Decline of Donnish Dominion: The British Academic Professions in the Twentieth Century* (2nd Edition). Oxford: Clarendon Press.

Hamlin, A. (1994) Regulation, rent-seeking and reform in higher education, *Financial Accountability and Management*, 10, 4, 291–304.

Hannan, A. and Silver, H. (2000) *Innovating in Higher Education: Teaching, Learning and Institutional Cultures.* Buckingham: SRHE and Open University Press.

Harding, D.W. (2009) *Talking Up, Dumbing Down*, http://www.dwharding.com/dumbingdown.html. (accessed 7 June 2009).

Hare, P.G. (2002) Constraints and incentives in the UK university system. Discussion paper in economics 2000/3. School of Management, Heriot-Watt University.

Harris, M. (2010) *What More Can be Done to Widen Access to Highly Selective Universities?* Bristol: OFFA.

Harris, R. (1990) The CNAA, accreditation and quality assurance, *Higher Education Review*, 22, 3, 34–54.

Harrison, N. (2011) Have the changes introduced by the 2004 Higher Education Act made higher education admissions in England wider and fairer? *Journal of Education Policy*, 26, 3, 449–468.

Hazelkorn, E. (2011) *Rankings and the Reshaping of Higher Education: The Battle for World Class Excellence*. Basingstoke: Palgrave Macmillan.

HEA and the Genetics Education Networking for Innovation and Excellence (GENIE) CETL, University of Leicester (2009) *Reward and recognition in higher education: Institutional policies and their recognition*. York: HEA.

Hearn, A. (2008) 'Through the looking glass' The promotional university 2.0. In M. Aroczyk and D. Powers (Eds.) *Blowing up the Brand: Critical Perspectives on Promotional Culture* (pp. 197–219). New York: Peter Lang.

HEFCE (1993a) *Assessment of the Quality of Education*. Circular 3/93. Bristol: HEFCE.

HEFCE (1993b) *Funding for 1994–5: Preliminary Decisions*. 47/93. Bristol: HEFCE.

HEFCE (1994) *1996 Research Assessment Exercise*. Circular RAE96 1/94. Bristol: HEFCE.

HEFCE (1995a) *Report on Quality Assessment. 1992–1995*. M18/95. Bristol: HEFCE.

HEFCE (1995b) *Analysis of 1995 Strategic Plans and Financial Forecasts*. Circular 28/'95. Bristol: HEFCE.

HEFCE (1996a) *Funding Method for Teaching*. Consultation 1/96. Bristol: HEFCE.

HEFCE (1996b) *Review of Postgraduate Education*. M 14/96. Bristol: HEFCE.

HEFCE (1996c) *Recurrent Grants for 1996–97*. Bristol: HEFCE.

HEFCE (1997) *Funding Method for Research from 1997–98*. 4/97. Bristol: HEFCE.

HEFCE (1999) *Awards Herald New Era for State of the Art Laboratories*, http://www.hefce.ac.uk/news/hefce/1999/jif1105.htm (accessed 31 August 2011).

HEFCE (2000) *Review of Research*. 00/37. Bristol: HEFCE.

HEFCE (2001a) *Quality Assurance in Higher Education: Proposals for Consultation*. 01/45. Bristol: HEFCE.

HEFCE (2001b) *Wider Benefits of Higher Education*. 01/46. Bristol: HEFCE.

HEFCE (2001c) *Information on Quality and Standards of Teaching and Learning. Proposals for Consultation*. 01/66. Bristol: HEFCE.

HEFCE (2001d) *2001 Research Assessment Exercise: The Outcome*. RAE 4/01. Bristol: HEFCE.

HEFCE (2002a) *Recurrent Grants for 2002–03*. 02/11 Bristol: HEFCE.

HEFCE (2002b) *Information on Quality and Standards in Higher Education. Final Report of the Task Group*. 02/15. Bristol: HEFCE.

HEFCE (2003a) *HEFCE Strategic Plan 2003–08 Consultation*. 2003/12. Bristol: HEFCE.

HEFCE (2003b) *Consultation by the UK Funding Bodies on the Review by Sir Gareth Roberts*. 2003/22. Bristol: HEFCE.

HEFCE (2003c) *Review of Research Funding Method*. 2003/38 Bristol: HEFCE.

HEFCE (2003d) *Recurrent Grants for 2003–04*. 03/10 Bristol: HEFCE.

HEFCE (2004a) *Centres for Excellence in Teaching and Learning: Invitation to Bid for Funds*. 2004/05. Bristol: HEFCE.

HEFCE (2004b) *Recurrent Grants for 2004–05*. 14/12 Bristol: HEFCE.

HEFCE (2005) *Review of the Quality Assurance Framework Phase One Outcomes*. 2005/35. Bristol: HEFCE.

HEFCE (2006a) *The National Student Survey 2005: Findings – Main Report. Report to HEFCE by Paula Surridge*. Bristol: HEFCE.

HEFCE (2006b) *Recurrent Grants for 2006–07*. 2006/08. Bristol: HEFCE.

HEFCE (2006c) *Review of the Quality Assurance Framework Phase Two Outcomes.* 2006/45. Bristol: HEFCE.

HEFCE (2007) *Funding Higher Education in England. How HEFCE Allocates its Funds.* 2007/20. Bristol: HEFCE.

HEFCE (2008) *The Sustainability of Learning and Teaching in English Higher Education. A Report prepared for the Financial Sustainability Strategy Group by JM Consulting.* Bristol: HEFCE.

HEFCE (2009) *Recurrent Grants for 2009–10* 2009/08. Bristol: HEFCE.

HEFCE (2010a) *Review of the Teaching Funding Method. Consultation on Key Principles and Features.* 2010/10. Bristol: HEFCE.

HEFCE (2010b) *Future Arrangements for Quality Assurance in England and Northern Ireland: Outcomes of Consultation.* 2010/17. Bristol: HEFCE.

HEFCE (2010c) *National Student Survey. Findings and Trends 2006 to 2009.* 2010/18. Bristol: HEFCE.

HEFCE (2010d) *Understanding the Information Needs of Users of Public Information About Higher Education. Report to HEFCE by Oakleigh Consulting and Staffordshire University.* Bristol: HEFCE.

HEFCE (2010e) *Enhancing and Developing the National Student Survey. Report to HEFCE by the Centre for Higher Education Studies at the Institute of Education.* Bristol: HEFCE.

HEFCE (2010f) *Public Information about Higher Education. Consultation on Changes to Information Published by Institutions.* 2010/31. Bristol: HEFCE.

HEFCE (2011a) *Consultation on Allocation Method for Postgraduate Research Funding from 2012–13.* 2011/09 Bristol: HEFCE.

HEFCE (2011b) *Provision of Information about Higher Education. Outcomes of Consultation and Next Steps.* 2011/18. Bristol: HEFCE.

HEFCE (2011c) *Teaching Funding and Student Number Controls. Consultation on Changes to be Implemented in 2012–13.* June 2011/20. Bristol: HEFCE.

HEFCE (2011d) *REF 2014. Assessment Framework and Guidance on Submissions* Bristol: HEFCE.

HEFCE (2011e) *Eight Out of 10 Higher Education Students Give Their Courses Top Marks.* Press release 17 August, http://www.hefce.ac.uk/news/hefce/2011/nss.htm (accessed 3 January 2012).

HEFCE (2011f) *PhD Study – Trends and Profiles 1996–7 to 2009–10.* Bristol: HEFCE.

HEFCE (2011g) *Student Number Controls for 2012–13 Invitation to Bid for Student Places.* October 2011/30. Bristol: HEFCE.

HEFCE (2011h) *HEFCE Business Plan 2011–15 Principles, Priorities and Practices.* 2011/34. Bristol: HEFCE.

HEFCE (2011i) *Sector Impact Assessment (RDPQR)* Bristol: HEFCE.

HEFCE (2012a) *Financial Health of the Higher Education Sector* 2012/05. Bristol: HEFCE.

HEFCE (2012b) *Recurrent Grants and Student Number Controls for 2012–13.* 2012/08. Bristol: HEFCE.

HEFCE (2012c) *A Risk-Based Approach to Quality Assurance.* 2012/11. Bristol: HEFCE.

HEFCE (2012d) *Higher Education-Business and Community Interaction Survey,* 23 May, http://www.hefce.ac.uk/whatwedo/kes/measureke/hebci (accessed 9 June 2012).

HEFCE (2012e) *Collaborations, Alliances and Mergers in Higher Education. Consultation on Lessons Learned and Guidance for Institutions.* 2012/12. Bristol: HEFCE.

HEFCE (2012f) *Review of Philanthropic Support for Higher Education,* 23 May, http://www. hefce.ac.uk/news/newsarchive/2012/name,73009,en.html (accessed 26 May 2012).

HEFCE (2012g) *HEFCE has Allocated 20,000 Student Places for 2012–13 Through the Margin Process,* http://www.hefce.ac.uk/news/newsarchive/2012/name,69551,en. html (accessed 11 July 2012).

HEFCW (2003) *The Higher Education Quality Assurance and Standards Framework for Wales.* W03/08HE. Cardiff: HEFCW.

HEFCW (2009) *Recommendations for the Institutional Review: Wales from 2009/10.* W09/01HE. Cardiff: HEFCW.

HEFCW (2011a) *Consultation on Amendments to the Institutional Review: Wales.*W11/ 18HE. Cardiff: HEFCW.

HEFCW (2011b) *Future Structure of Universities in Wales. Confidential Advice to the Minister for Education and Skills 29 June 2011,* http://wales.gov.uk/docs/dcells/ Consultation/110711futureofunihefcwen.pdf (accessed 21 July 2011).

Heller, D.E. (2007) Financing public research universities in the United States: the role of students and their families. In R.L. Geiger, C.L. Colbeck, R.L. Williams, and C.K. Anderson (Eds.) *The Future of the American Public Research University.* Rotterdam and Taipei: Sense.

Hemsley-Brown, J. (2011) Market heal thyself: the challenges of a free market in higher education, *Journal of Marketing for Higher Education,* 21, 2, 115–132.

Hencke, D. (1978) *Colleges in Crisis: The Reorganisation of Teacher Training 1971–1977.* Harmondsworth: Penguin.

Henkel, M. (2000) *Academic Identities and Policy Change in Higher Education.* London: Jessica Kingsley.

Henkel, M. and Kogan, M. (2010) The United Kingdom. In D.D. Dill and F.A. van Vught (Eds.) *National Innovation and the Academic Research Enterprise* (pp. 337–386). Baltimore: The Johns Hopkins University Press.

Henkel, M. & Little, B. (1999) Introduction. In M. Henkel and B. Little (Eds.) *Changing Relationships Between Higher Education and the State* (pp. 9–22). London: Jessica Kingsley.

HMI (1989) *Quality in Higher Education: A Report on an HMI Invitation Conference.* London: HMI.

HMT (1979) *The Government's Expenditure Plans for 1980/81.* Cmnd 7746. London: HMSO.

HMT (1981) *The Government's Expenditure Plans 1981–82 to 1983–84.* Cmnd. 8175. London: HMSO.

HMT, Department of Health, DES, and DTI (2006) *Science and Innovation Investment Framework 2004–14 – Next Steps.* Norwich: HMSO.

Hicks, D. (2008) *Evolving Regimes of Multi-university Research Evaluation.* Georgia Institute of Technology School of Public Policy Working Paper #27. Atlanta: Georgia Institute of Technology.

Hicks, D. (2009) Evolving regimes of research evaluation, *Higher Education,* 57, 393–404.

Himanen, L., Auranen, O., Puuska, H-M. and Nieminen, M. (2009) Influence of research funding and science policy on university research performance: a comparison of five countries, *Science and Public Policy,* 36, 6, 419–430.

Hirsch, F. (1976) *Social Limits to Growth.* Cambridge, MA: Harvard University Press.

Horta, H., Huisman, J. and Heitor, M. (2008) Does competitive research funding encourage diversity in higher education? *Science and Public Policy*, 35, 3, 146–158.

Hotson, H. (2011) Don't look to the Ivy League, *London Review of Books*, 19 May, 20–22.

House of Commons Science and Technology Committee (2002) *Report on the Research Assessment Exercise. Second Report.* London: HMSO.

Huisman, J., Kaiser, F. and Vossensteyn, H. (2000) Floating foundations of higher education policy, *Higher Education Quarterly*, 54, 3, 217–238.

Hundley, K. (2011) Billionaire's role in hiring decisions at Florida State University raises questions, *tampabay.com*, 9 May, http://www.tampabay.com/news/business/billionaires-role-in-hiring-decisions-at-florida-state-university-raises/1168680 (accessed 28 May 2012).

Hunt, L.H. (Ed.) (2008) *Grade Inflation: Academic Standards in Higher Education.* Albany, NY: State University of New York Press.

Hussain, I., McNally, S. and Telhaj, S. (2009) *University Quality and Graduate Wages in the UK.* Centre for Education and Employment Discussion Paper 99. London: London School of Economics.

Hutchings, M. (2003) Information, advice and cultural discourses of higher education. In L. Archer, M. Hutchings and A. Ross (Eds.) *Higher Education and Social Class: Issues of Exclusion and Inclusion* (pp. 97–118). London: RoutledgeFalmer.

Independent Review of Higher Education Funding and Student Finance (Browne Report) (2010) *Securing a Sustainable Future for Higher Education*, http:webarchive.nationalarchives.gov.uk/+/hereview.independent.gov.uk/hereview (accessed 11 July 2012).

Independent Study into the Devolution of the Student Support System and Tuition Fee Regime in Wales (The Rees Review) (2005) *Fair and Flexible Funding: A Welsh Model to Promote Quality and Access in Higher Education.* Cardiff: Welsh Assembly Government.

IUSSC (2009) *Students and Universities Eleventh Report of Session 2008–09.* HC 170–1. London: The Stationery Office Limited.

Jack, I. (2008) After 1998 students didn't need to begin essays with a blank screen, *The Guardian*, 28 June, 28.

Jackman, R.W. and Siverson, R.M. (1996) Rating the rating: an analysis of the National Research Council's appraisal of political science programs, *Political Science and Politics*, 29, 2, 155–160.

Jacob, M. and Hellstrom, T. (Eds) (2000) *The Future of Knowledge Production in the Academy*, Buckingham: SRHE and Open University Press.

James, R., Krause, K.-L., and Jennings, C. (2010) *The First Year Experience in Australian Universities: Findings from 1994 to 2009.* Melbourne: Centre for the Study of Higher Education.

Jenkins, A. (1995) The Research Assessment Exercise, funding and teaching quality, *Quality Assurance in Education*, 3, 2, 4–12.

Jenkins, A. (2004) *A Guide to the Research Evidence on Teaching-Research Relations.* York: HEA.

Jenkins, S. (2011) Without a growth plan, the EU faces a financial Waterloo, *The Guardian*, 28 September, 33.

Jenkins, S.P., Micklewright, J. and Schnepf, S.V. (2006) *Social Segregation in Secondary Schools: How does England Compare with Other Countries?* University of Essex: Institute for Social and Economic Research.

JM Consulting Ltd (2000) *Interactions Between Research, Teaching and Other Activities: Report for HEFCE*. Bristol: JM Consulting Ltd.

JM Consulting Ltd (2001) *Study of Science Research Infrastructure – A Report for the Office of Science and Technology*. Bristol: JM Consulting Ltd

JM Consulting Ltd (2002) *Arts and Humanities Research Infrastructure – A Report to the HEFCE (2002/35)*. Bristol: HEFCE.

Johnes, G. (1992) Bidding for students in Britain – why the UFC auction 'failed', *Higher Education*, 23, 173–182.

Johnes, J. and Taylor, J. (1990) *Performance Indicators in Higher Education: UK Universities* Buckingham: SRHE and Open University Press.

Johnson, N. (1994) Dons in decline: who will look after the cultural capital? *Twentieth Century British History*, 5, 3, 370–385.

Johnston, R. (2008) On structuring subjective judgements: originality, significance and rigour in RAE 2008, *Higher Education Quarterly*, 62, 1/2, 120–147.

Johnston, R., Currie, J., Grigg, L., Martin, B., Hicks, D., Ling, N. and Skea, J. (1993) *The Effects of Research Concentration on Research Performance*. Commissioned Report No 25. National Board of Employment, Education and Training. Canberra: Australian Publishing Service.

Johnstone, D.B. (1986) *Sharing the Costs of Higher Education. Student Financial Assistance in the United Kingdom, the Federal Republic of Germany, France, Sweden and the United States*. New York: College Examination Board.

Johnstone, D.B. and Marcucci, P. (2007) *Worldwide Trends in Higher Education Finance: Cost-Sharing, Student Loans, and the Support of Academic Research*. Paper commissioned by the UNESCO Forum on Higher Education, Research and Development, http://www.gse.buffalo.edu/org/IntHigherEdFinance/project_publications.html (accessed 4 October 2009).

Jones, G. (2006) 'I wish to register a complaint': the growing complaints culture in higher education, *perspectives*, 10, 3, 69–73.

Jones, G. and Philp, C. (2011) Challenging student behaviour, *perspectives*, 15, 1, 19–23.

Jones, S. (1984) Reflections on a capped pool, *Higher Education Review*, 17, 1, 5–18.

Jongbloed, B. (2006) Strengthening consumer choice in higher education. In P.N. Teixeira, D.B. Johnstone, M.J. Rosa, and H. Vossensteyn (Eds.) *Cost-Sharing and Accessibility in Higher Education: A Fairer Deal?* (pp. 19–50). Dordrecht: Kluwer.

Jongbloed, B. (2010) The Netherlands. In D. Dill and F.A. van Vught (Eds.) *National Innovation and the Academic Research Enterprise*. (pp. 286–336). Baltimore: The Johns Hopkins University Press.

Jump, P. (2011) We can't afford to be too choosy, *THE*, 11 August, 7.

Jump, P. (2012a) Elite powers of concentration, *THE*, 29 March, 7.

Jump, P. (2012b) Elite institutions predicted to fall short on research student qualifications, *THE*, 17 May, 6–7.

Kelderman, E. (2012) Fault lines form among campuses as finances strain U. of California, *The Chronicle of Higher Education*, 17 February, A26.

Kells, H.R. (1992) *Self-Regulation in Higher Education*. London and Philadelphia: Jessica Kingsley.

Kenber, B. and Taylor, M. (2010) Students 'pressed to be positive' in university survey, *The Guardian*, 27 April, 4.

Kezar, A. (2004) Obtaining Integrity? Reviewing and examining the charter between higher education and society, *The Review of Higher Education*, 27, 4, 429–459.

King, D.A. (2004) The scientific impact of nations: what different countries get for their research spending, *Nature*, 430, 15 July 2004, 311–316.

King, R., Findlay, A. and Ahrens, J. (2010) *International Student Mobility Review. Report to HEFCE, and Co-funded by the British Council, UK National Agency for Erasmus*, http://www.hefce.ac.uk/media/hefce/content/pubs/2010/rd2010/rd20_10.pdf. (accessed 30 June 2012).

Kirp, D.L. (2003) No brainer, *The Nation*, October 23, 1–3.

Kirp, D.L. (2005) This little student went to market. In R.J. Hersh and J. Merrow (Eds.) *Declining by Degrees: Higher Education at Risk* (pp. 113–130). New York and Basingstoke: Palgrave Macmillan.

Kogan, M. and Hanney, S. (2000) *Reforming Higher Education*. London: Jessica Kingsley.

Krimsky, S. (2005) *Science in the Public Interest: Has the Lure of Profits Corrupted Biomedical Research?* New York and Oxford: Rowman and Littlefield.

Kuh, G.D. and Pascarella, E.T. (2004) What does institutional selectivity tell us about educational quality? *Change*, September/October, pp. 52–58.

Kupfer, A. (2011) Towards a theoretical framework for the comparative understanding of globalisation, higher education, the labour market and inequality, *Journal of Education and Work*, 24, 1, 185–208.

Lane, J. (2005) Politics of mission creep: A framework for understanding the phenomenon. Paper prepared for the *30th Annual Conference of the Association for the Study of Higher Education*, Philadelphia, Pa, November 17–19 2005.

Lawson, N. (1992) *The View from No 11: Memoirs of a Tory Radical*. London: Bantam Books.

Le Grand, J. (1987) The middle-class use of the British social services. In R.E. Goodin and J. Le Grand (Eds.) *Not Only The Poor: The Middle Classes and the Welfare State* (pp. 91–107). London: Allen and Unwin.

Le Grand, J. and Bartlett, W. (1993) *Quasi-Markets and Social Policy*. Basingstoke: Macmillan.

Leathwood, C. (2004) A critique of institutional inequalities in higher education (or an alternative to hypocrisy for higher educational policy), *Theory and Research in Education* 2, 1, 31–48.

Leathwood, C. and O'Connell, P. (2003) 'It's a struggle': the construction of the 'new student' in higher education, *Journal of Education Policy* 18, 6, 597–615.

Lederman, D. (2011) The rapid rise of merit aid. *Inside Higher Ed*, October 19, http://www.insidehighered.com/news/2011/10/19/rapid-rise-merit-aid (accessed 19 December 2011).

Lee, D. (2006) *University Students Behaving Badly*. Stoke-on-Trent: Trentham Books.

Lee, J. (2012a) A degree of difference: sixth-form colleges go into HE for first time, *TES*, 9 March 2012, 48–49.

Lee, J. (2012b) Collaboration gives way to dog eat dog at the HE funding bowl, *TES*, 16 March 2012, 48–49.

Lee, J. (2012c) Nearly a third of loans could go unclaimed by students afraid of debt, *TES*, 22 June, 52–53.

Leon, P. (2001) Working students focus on marks, *THE*, 7 December, 4.

Li, M., Shankar, S. and Tang, K.K. (2011) Why does the USA dominate university league tables? *Studies in Higher Education*, 36, 8, 923–937.

Lindblom, C.E. (2001) *The Market System: What It Is, How It Works, and What to Make of It*. New Haven, CT: Yale University Press.

Little, Arthur D. (2006) *The Social and Economic Impact of Publicly Funded Research in 35 Participating Universities.* Cambridge: Arthur D. Little Limited.

Litwin, J.M. (2009) The segments of higher education – a Canadian context, *Higher Education Management and Policy*, 21, 3, 91–108.

Locke, W. (2004) Integrating research and teaching strategies: implications for institutional management and leadership in the United Kingdom, *Higher Education Management and Policy*, 16, 3, 101–120.

Locke, W. (2009) Higher education policy in England: missed opportunities, unintended consequences and unfinished business, *Journal of Access Policy and Practice*, 5, 2, 180–204.

Locke, W. (2011) False economy? Multiple markets, reputational hierarchy and incremental policymaking in UK higher education. In R. Brown (Ed.) *Higher Education and the Market*. New York and London: Routledge.

London Economics (2011) *The Returns to Higher Education Qualifications*. London: DBIS.

Lovelock, C.H. (1983) Classifying services to gain strategic marketing insights, *Journal of Marketing*, 47, 9–20,

Lucas, L. (2006) *The Research Game in Academic Life*. Maidenhead: McGraw-Hill.

Luettger, L. (2008) Brands speak beyond images: reflect lifestyle, students, *Rochester Business Journal*, 24, 18.

Macdonald, S. (2011) Seducing the goose: a review of patenting by UK universities, *Intellectual Property Quarterly*, 4, 323–344.

Major, J. (1999) *John Major: The Autobiography*. New York: Harper Collins.

Mansell, W. (2010a) A-level reforms could trigger 'collapse' in maths take-up, *TES*, 30 July, 4.

Mansell, W. (2010b) 'Spoonfed' students lack confidence at Oxbridge, *TES*, 10 December, 13.

Marcus, J. (2006) Students who pay the piper may call the tune, *THE*, 18 August, 13.

Marcus, J. (2008) Stiff competition for places in the US has led potential students to enlist the help of parents and consultants to give their application an edge, *THE*, 14 August, 35.

Marginson, S. (1997) Steering from a distance: power relations in Australian higher education, *Higher Education*, 34, 1, 63–80.

Marginson, S. (2004) Competition and markets in higher education: a 'glonacal' analysis, *Policy Futures in Education*, 2, 2, 175–244.

Marginson, S. (2007) The public/private divide in higher education: a global revision, *Higher Education*, 53, 307–333.

Marginson, S. (2011a) Higher education and public good, *Higher Education Quarterly*, 65, 4, 411–433.

Marginson, S. (2011b) Higher education and public good. Presentation to the British Educational Research Association, London, 6 September.

Marginson, S. (2012) The 'public' contribution of universities in an increasingly global world. In B. Pusser, K. Kempner, S. Marginson and I. Orderika (Eds.) *Universities and the Public Sphere: Knowledge Creation and State Building in the Era of Globalization* (pp. 7–26). New York and London: Routledge.

Marginson, S. (Submitted for review) The limits of market reform in higher education.

Marks, D. (2007) The unsettled meaning of undergraduate education in a competitive higher education environment, *Higher Education in Europe*, 32, 2/3, 173–83.

Marsh, H.W. (2007) Students' evaluations of university teaching: dimensionality, reliability, validity, potential biases, and usefulness. In R.T. Perry and J.C. Smart (Eds.) *The Scholarship of Teaching and Learning in Higher Education: An Evidence-based Perspective* (pp. 319–383). Dordrecht: Springer.

Marsh, H.W. and Cheng, J.H.S. (2008) *NSS: Dimensionality, Multilevel Structure, and Differentiation at the Level of University and Discipline,* http: www.heacademy.ac.uk/ assets/York/documents/outwork/research/nss/NSS_herb_marsh_28.08.08.pdf (accessed 13 April 2012).

Marsh, H.W., Ginns, P., Morin, A.J.S. and Nagengast, B. (2011) Use of student ratings to benchmark universities: multilevel modelling of responses to the Australian course experience questionnaire (CEQ), *Journal of Educational Psychology,* 103, 3, 733–748.

Massy, W. (2003) *Honoring the Trust – Quality and Cost Containment in Higher Education.* Bolton, MA: Anker Publishing Company.

Matthews, D. (2011a) Hefce gift-matching ends with a flurry, *THE,* 4 August, 9.

Matthews, D. (2011b) Business schools object to scale of cross-subsidisation, *THE,* 6 October, 14.

Matthews, D. (2011c) Full-throttle hype could crash: OIA, *THE,* 27 October, 12.

Matthews, D. (2011d) £58m boost to close grants 'gap', *THE,* 22–29 December, 8.

Matthews, D. (2012a) Boom and bust. *THE,* 5 January, 31–37.

Matthews, D. (2012b) Double bind and binary line menace for Welsh post-92s, *THE,* 2 December, 12.

Matthews, D. (2012c) Core and margin plan tests the limits of collegial behaviour, *THE,* 16 February, 16–17.

Matthews, D. (2012d) Welsh funding council 'forces through' 20 per cent in places, *THE,* 10 April, http://www.timeshighereducation.co.uk/story.asp?sectioncode=26& storycode=419598&c=1 (accessed 11 April 2012).

Matthews, D. (2012e) Have it our way, NI tells sector, *THE,* 3 May, 12.

Matthews, D. (2012f) If they don't succeed, don't let them try, try again. Teesside dean criticised for email guidance on 'maximising performance', *THE,* 31 May, 8.

Mayhew, K., Deer, C. and Dua, M. (2004) The move to mass higher education in the UK: many questions and some answers, *Oxford Review of Education,* 30, 1, 65–82.

McGettigan, A. (2011) Borrowing greatness, *Research Fortnight,* 5 October, 1–4.

McGettigan, A. (2012) *False Accounting? Why the Government's Higher Education Reforms Don't Add Up.* London: Intergenerational Foundation.

McMahon, W.W. (2009) *Higher Learning, Greater Good: The Private and Social Benefits of Higher Education.* Baltimore: The Johns Hopkins University Press.

McNay, I. (1997a) *The Impact of the 1992 RAE on Institutional and Individual Behaviour in English Higher Education: The Evidence From a Research Project.* M5/97. Bristol: HEFCE.

McNay, I. (1997b) The impact of the 1992 Research Assessment Exercise in English universities, *Higher Education Review,* 29, 2, 34–43.

McNay, I. (1999) The paradoxes of research assessment and funding. In M. Henkel and B. Little (Eds.) *Changing Relationships between Higher Education and the State* (pp. 191–203). London and Philadelphia: Jessica Kingsley.

McNay, I. (2003) Assessing the assessment: an analysis of the UK Research Exercise, 2001, and its outcomes, with special reference to research in education, *Science and Public Policy,* 30, 1, 47–54.

McNay, I. (2007) Research assessment; learner autonomy. In C. Kayrooz, G.S. Akerlind and M. Tight (Eds.) *Autonomy in Social Science Research: The View from UK and Australian Universities. International Perspectives on Higher Education Research, Volume 4.* Oxford: Elsevier.

McNay, I. (2009) Research quality assessment – objectives, approaches, responses and consequences. In A. Brew and L. Lucas (Eds.) *Academic Research: Policy and Practice* (pp. 35–53). Maidenhead: McGraw-Hill.

McNay, I. (2010) Research quality assessment. In P. Peterson, E. Baker and B. McGaw (Eds.) *International Encyclopedia of Higher Education, Vol. 4* (pp. 307–315). Oxford: Elsevier.

McNay, I. (2011a) From global to local: research quality and assessment and education. Proceedings of the *Canadian International Conference on Education*, Toronto, April 2011.

McNay, I. (2011b) Research assessment: work in progress, or *la lutta continua.* In Saunders, Trowler and Bamber (Eds.) *Reconceptualising Evaluation in Higher Education* (pp. 51–57). Maidenhead: SRHE and Open University Press.

McPherson, M.S. and Winston, G.C. (1993) The economics of cost, price and quality in US higher education. In M.S. McPherson, M.O Schapiro and G.C. Winston (Eds.) *Paying the Piper: Productivity, Incentives and Financing in US Higher Education* (pp. 15–34). Ann Arbor: University of Michigan Press.

Meacher, M. (2012) Letter in *The Guardian,* 28 June, 35.

Melville, D. (2009) *London Metropolitan University. An Independent Review into the Circumstances and Issues Associated with the Clawback of Significant Funds in 2009.* London: London Metropolitan University.

Merrison, A. (1982) *Report of a Joint Working Party on the Support of University Scientific Research.* Cmnd. 8567. London: HMSO.

Metcalf, H. (2003) Increasing inequality in higher education: The role of term-time working, *Oxford Review of Education,* 29, 3, 315–329.

Middleton, C. (2000) Models of state and market in the 'modernisation' of higher education, *British Journal of Sociology of Education,* 21, 4, 537–554.

Milburn, A. (2012) *Fair Access to Professional Careers. A Progress Report by the Independent Reviewer on Social Mobility and Child Poverty,* http://www.cabinetoffice.gov.uk/sites/default/files/resources/IR_FairAccess_acc2.pdf (accessed 3 June 2012).

Million+ (2011) *Research that Matters.* London: Million+.

Million+ and NUS (2012) *Never Too Late to Learn: Mature Students in Higher Education.* London: Million+.

Minogue, K (1986) Political science and the gross intellectual product, *Government and Opposition,* 21, 4, 396–405.

Molesworth, M., Nixon, E. and Scullion, R. (2009) Having, being and higher education: the marketisation of the university and the transformation of the student into consumer, *Teaching in Higher Education,* 14, 3, 277–287.

Molesworth, M., Scullion, R. and Nixon, E. (Eds.) (2011) *The Marketisation of Higher Education and the Student as Consumer.* London and New York: Routledge.

Moore, P.G. (1987) University financing 1979–86, *Higher Education Quarterly,* 41, 1, pp. 25–42.

Morgan, J. (2011) Now that's research impact: 'paradigm-shifting' Browne drew on a single opinion survey, *THE,* 6 January, 6–7.

Morgan, J. (2012a) Holding pattern for bill may simply take plans under radar, *THE,* 26 January, 6–7.

Morgan, J. (2012b) QAA in the dark on 63 of 94 private providers, *THE*, 23 February, 6–7.

Morgan, J. (2012c) Russell Group 'a more natural fit', *THE*, 15 March, 7.

Morgan, J. (2012d) Private bodies saddle up for state subsidies, *THE*, 12 July, 6–7.

Moriarty, P. (2008) Reclaiming academia from post-academia, *Nature Nanotechnology*, 3, February 2008, 60–62.

Moriarty, P. (2011) Science as a public good. In J. Holmwood (Ed.) *A Manifesto for the Public University* (pp. 56–73). London: Bloomsbury Academic.

Morley, L. (2003) Reconstructing students as consumers: power and assimilation? In M. Slowey and D. Watson (Eds.) *Higher Education and the Lifecourse* (pp. 79–92). Buckingham: SRHE and Open University Press.

Morley, L. and Aynsley, S. (2007) Employers, quality and standards in higher education: shared values and vocabularies or elitism and inequalities? *Higher Education Quarterly*, 61, 3, 229–249.

Morris, E. (2001) Key challenges of the next decade. Speech given at London Guildhall University, 22 October.

Muzaka, V. (2009) The niche of graduate teaching assistants (GTAs): perceptions and reflections, *Teaching in Higher Education*, 14, 1, 1–12.

Naidoo, R. (2008) The competitive state and the mobilised market: higher education policy reform in the United Kingdom (1980–2007), *Critique Internationale*, 39 (April/June), Presses de Sciences Po: 47–65.

Naidoo, R. and Jamieson, I. (2005) Knowledge in the marketplace: the global commodification of teaching and learning. In P. Innes, and M. Hellsten (Eds.) *Internationalising Higher Education: Critical Explorations of Pedagogy and Policy* (pp. 37–53). Comparative Education Research Centre, The University of Hong Kong: Springer.

Naidoo, R., Shankar, A. and Veer, E. (2011) The consumerist turn in higher education: Policy aspirations and outcomes, *Journal of Marketing Management*, 27, 11–12, 1142–1162.

NAO (2002) *Improving Student Achievement in English Higher Education*. London: NAO.

NAO (2007) *Staying the Course: The Retention of Students in Higher Education*. London: NAO.

NAO (2008) *Widening Participation in Higher Education*. London: NAO.

National Committee of Inquiry into Higher Education (Dearing Committee) (1997) *Higher Education in the Learning Society: Report of the Main Committee*. London: HMSO.

Naylor, R. (2007) *Whose Degree is it Anyway? Why, How and Where Universities are Failing Our Students*. London: Pencil-Sharp.

Neave, G. (2005) The supermarketed university: reform, vision and ambiguity in British higher education, *perspectives*, 9, 1, 17–22.

Newby, H. (1999) Higher education in the 21st century: some possible futures. Paper VC/99/5. CVCP Main Committee 5 March 1999.

Newman, M. (2008) Students urged to inflate national survey marks to improve job options, *THE*, 15 May, 7.

NUS (2012) *The Pound in your Pocket – Survey Results*. London: NUS.

OECD (2008) *Growing Unequal? Income Distribution and Poverty in OECD Countries*. Paris: OECD.

OECD (2011a) *Education at a Glance*. Paris: OECD.

OECD (2011b) *Economic Survey of the United Kingdom 2011*. Paris: OECD.

OFFA (2011) *OFFA Announces Decisions on Revised 2012–13 Access Agreements*. News release Friday 2nd December 2011, http://www.offa.org.uk/press-releases/offa-announces-decisions-on-revised-2012-13-access-agreements. (accessed 6 June 2012).

OIA (2012) *Annual Report 2011*. Reading: OIA.

Okun, A. (1975) *Equality and Efficiency-the Big Trade-Off*. Washington, DC: Brookings Institution Press.

Ovens, P. (In preparation) The real crisis in higher education: student learning.

Oxford, E. (2008) The American dream, *THE*, 17 April, 40–42.

Palfreyman, D. (2010) HE's 'get-out-of-jail' card. The future of judicial deference to the exercise of expert academic judgement, *perspectives*, 14, 4, 113–119.

Parkinson, S. (2011) *Science and the Corporate University in Britain*. Open Democracy, 16 December 2011, http://opendemocracy.net/print/63214 (accessed 30 April 2012).

Pascarella, E. (2001) Identifying excellence in undergraduate education, *Change*, 33, 3, 19–23.

Pascarella, E.T. and Terenzini, P.T. (2005) *How College Affects Students. Volume 2. A Third Decade of Research* San Francisco: Jossey-Bass.

Pascarella, E.T., Cruce, T., Umbach, P.D., Wolniak, G.C., Kuh, G.D., Carini, R.M., Hayek, J.C., Gonyea, R.M., and Zhao, C-M. (2006) Institutional selectivity and good practices: how strong is the link? *Journal of Higher Education* March/April, 251–285.

Pearce, N. (2004) *Review of the Week – 16 January 2004*, http://www.ippr.org.uk/articles/archive.asp?id=356&fID=54 (last accessed 15 February 2009).

Pennell, H. and West, A. (2005) The impact of increased fees on participation in higher education in England, *Higher Education Quarterly*, 59, 2, 127–137.

Peters, M.A. and Olssen, M. (2005) 'Useful knowledge': redefining research and teaching in the learning economy. In R. Barnett (Ed.) *Reshaping the University: New Relationships between Research, Scholarship and Teaching* (pp. 37–48). Maidenhead: SRHE and Open University Press.

Potts, M. (2005) The consumerist subversion of education, *Academic Questions*, 18, 22, 3, 54–65.

Powell, S and Green, H. (2006) The national funding of doctoral training: warnings from the English experience, *Journal of Higher Education Policy and Management*, 28, 3, 263–275.

Pratt, J. (1997) *The Polytechnic Experiment, 1965–1992*. Buckingham: SRHE and Open University Press.

Pratt, J. (1999) Policy and policy making in the unification of higher education, *Journal of Education Policy*, 14, 3, 257–269.

Pratt, J. and Burgess, T. (1974) *Polytechnics: A Report*. London: Pitman.

PriceWaterhouseCooper and UUK (2007) *Research Report: The Economic Benefits of a Degree*. London: UUK.

Pritchard, R.O. (1994) Government power in British higher education, *Studies in Higher Education*, 19, 3, 253–265.

QAA (2003) *Handbook for Enhancement-Led Institutional Review: Scotland*. Glasgow: QAA, Scottish Office.

QAA (2004) *Code of Practice for the Assurance of Academic Quality and Standards: Section 1. Postgraduate*. Gloucester: QAA.

QAA (2006) *Outcomes From Institutional Audit: Academic Guidance, Support and Supervision, and Personal Support and Guidance*. Gloucester: QAA.

QAA (2009) *Kingston University: Special Review of the Circumstances Surrounding the Amendments to an External Examiner's Report*, http://www.qaa.ac.uk/Complaints/causesforconcern/Kingston09.pdf (accessed 12 June 2012).

QAA (2011a) *Institutional Review of Higher Education for Institutions in England and Northern Ireland. Operational Description*. Gloucester: QAA.

QAA (2011b) *Changes to the Academic Infrastructure: Final Report*. Gloucester: QAA.

QAA (2011c) *Response to BIS Technical Consultation – A New Fit-For-Purpose Regulatory Framework for the Higher Education Sector*, http://www.qaa.ac.uk/Newsroom/Press-Releases/Documents/BIS_Technical_Consultation_QAA_response.pdf (accessed 18 November 2011).

RAE2008 (2008) *RAE2008: the Outcome* 01/2008, http://www.rae.ac.uk/pubs/2008/01 (accessed 9 July 2012).

RAE2008 (2009) *RAE2008 Subject Overview Reports January 2009*, http://www.rae.ac.uk/pubs/2009/ov (accessed 29 June 2012).

Raffe, D., Croxford, L., Iannelli, C., Shapira, M. and Howieson, C. (2006) *Social Class Inequalities in Education in England and Scotland*. Edinburgh: Centre for Educational Sociology, University of Edinburgh.

Rammell, B. (2007) Higher Education (Loans, Charters and Fees). *Hansard*, 2 July, Col. 42WS.

Ramsden, B. (2012) *Institutional Diversity in UK Higher Education*. Oxford: HEPI.

Ramsden, B. and Brown, N. (2002) *The Internal Economy of UK Higher Education Institutions*. London: UUK.

Ramsden, P. (1991) A performance indicator of teaching quality in higher education: the course experience questionnaire, *Studies in Higher Education*, 16, 2, 129–150.

Ramsden, P. (2012) A poor policy poorly managed leaves little to show for £315m, *THE*, 15 March, 32–33.

Ranson, S. (1993) Markets or democracy for education? *British Journal of Education Studies*, XXXXI, 4, 333–352.

Reay, D., Crozier, G. and Clayton, J. (2010) 'Fitting in' or 'standing out': working-class students in UK higher education, *British Educational Research Journal*, 36, 1, 107–124.

Reay, D., David, M. and Ball, S. (Eds.) (2005) *Degrees of Choice: Social Class, Race and Gender in Higher Education*. London: Trentham Books.

Rhoades, G. (2007) Distinctive choices in intersecting markets: seeking strategic niches. In R.L. Geiger, C.L. Colbeck, R.L. Williams, and C.K. Anderson (Eds.) *Future of the American Public Research University*. Rotterdam and Taipei: Sense.

Richard, A. (2006) The well-educated undergraduate. Annual address to the Regent House, 2 October.

Riesman, D. (1958) *Constraint and Variety in American Education*. New York: Doubleday & Company (Anchor edition).

Ro, H.K., Terenzini, P.T. and Yin, A.C. (Submitted for review) Between-college effects on students reconsidered.

Roberts, G. (2002) *SET for Success: The Report of Sir Gareth Roberts' Review*. London: Her Majesty's Treasury.

Roberts, G. (2003) *Review of Research Assessment*, http://www.raereview.ac.uk/reports/roberts.asp (accessed 12 July 2012).

Roberts, G. (2006) The duel over dual support, *Research Fortnight*, 21 June, 16–17.

Roberts, K. (2010) Expansion of higher education and the implications for demographic class formation in Britain, *21st Century Society*, 5, 3, 215–228.

Robinson, E. (2007) 1966 and all that: a revolution in higher education that is yet incomplete, *Higher Education Review*, 39, 3, 45–58.

Rolfe, H. (2002) Students' demands and expectations in an age of reduced financial support: the perspectives of lecturers in four English universities, *Journal of Higher Education Policy and Management*, 24, 2, 171–182.

Rolfe, H. (2003) University strategy in an age of uncertainty: the effect of higher education funding on old and new universities, *Higher Education Quarterly*, 57, 1, 24–47.

Rowland, S. (2000) *The enquiring university teacher*. Buckingham: SRHE and Open University Press.

Royal Society (2003) *Keeping Science Open*. London: Royal Society.

Russell Group (2012) *Russell Group of Universities Agrees to Expand*, http://www.russellgroup.ac.uk/.../5216-russell-group-of-universities-agrees-to-expand (accessed 20 March 2012).

St. Aubyn, M., Pina, A., Garcia, F. and Pais, J. (2009) *Study on the Efficiency and Effectiveness of Public Spending on Tertiary Education*. Economic Papers 390. Brussels: European Commission.

Sabri, D. (Submitted for review) Student evaluations of teaching as 'fact-totems': The case of the UK National Student Survey.

Salter, B. and Tapper, T. (1994) *The State and Higher Education*. London: Woburn Press.

Samuels, B. (2009) *Only 3.5% of the UCLA Budget is Spent on Undergraduates: Where Does the Rest Go?* 14 December, http://changinguniversities.blogspot.co.uk/2009/12/only-35-of-ucla-budget-is-spent-on (accessed 6 July 2012).

Samuels, B. (2012) *How Universities Became Hedge Funds*, 1 March, http://www.renewal.org.uk/articles/how-universities-became-hedge-funds (accessed 9 May 2012).

Samuelson, P. (1954) The pure theory of public expenditure, *Review of Economics and Statistics*, 36, 4, 387–389.

Sandler, T. (1999) Intergenerational public goods: strategies, efficiency and institutions. In I. Kaul, I. Grunberg, and M. Stern (Eds.) (1999) *Global Public Goods: International Cooperation in the 21st Century* (pp. 20–51). New York: Oxford University Press.

Sastry, T. and Bekhradnia, B. (2006) *Using Metrics to Allocate Research Funds – A Short Analysis of Alternatives to the RAE*. Oxford: HEPI.

Schmidt, P. (2008) Use of part-time instructors tied to lower student success, *The Chronicle of Higher Education*, 14 November, A1, 8–10.

Scientists for Global Responsibility (2009) *Science and the Corporate Agenda: The Detrimental Effects of Commercial Influence on Science and Technology*, http://www.sgr.org.uk/SciencePolicy/SGR_corp_science_full.pdf (accessed 13 October 2009).

Scott, P. (1995) *The Meanings of Mass Higher Education*. Buckingham: SRHE and Open University Press.

Scott, P. (2001) Conclusion: triumph and retreat. In D. Warner and D. Palfreyman (Eds.) *The State of UK Higher Education: Managing Change and Diversity* (pp. 186–204). Buckingham: SRHE and Open University Press.

Scott, P. (2005) Mass higher education – ten years on, *perspectives*, 9, 3, 68–73.

Scott, P. (2009) Structural changes in higher education: the case of the United Kingdom. In D. Palfreyman and T. Tapper (Eds.) *Structuring Mass Higher Education: The Role of Elite Institutions* (pp. 35–56). New York and Abingdon: Routledge.

Scott, P. (2011) All change or no change? Evolution of the pattern of institutions in

English higher education. Paper given at a conference 'The 2011 Higher Education White Paper – Prospects for the Sector', Centre for Higher Education Studies, Institute of Education, University of London, 29 March 2011.

Scott, P. (2012) Opinion 'AAB: result, happiness. AAC: result, misery', *The Guardian*, 7 February, 35.

Scott, S.V. (1999) The academic as service provider: is the customer always right? *Journal of Higher Education Policy and Management*, 21, 2, 193–202.

Scottish Government (2011) *Putting Learners at the Centre: Delivering Our Ambitions for Post-16 Education*. Edinburgh: Scottish Government.

Seldon, A. (1986) *The Riddle of the Voucher*. London: Institute of Economic Affairs.

Sharp, S. (2004) The Research Assessment Exercises 1992–2001: patterns across time and subjects *Studies in Higher Education*, 29, 2, 201–218.

Sharp, S. and Coleman, S. (2005) Ratings in the Research Assessment Exercise 2001 – the patterns of university status and panel membership, *Higher Education Quarterly*, 59, 2, 153–171.

Shattock, M. (1994) *The UGC and the Management of British Universities*. Buckingham: SRHE and Open University Press.

Shattock, M. (2008) The change from private to public governance of British higher education: its consequences for higher education policy making 1980–2006, *Higher Education Quarterly*, 62, 3, 181–203.

Shattock, M. and Rigby, G. (Eds.) (1983) *Resource Allocation in British Universities*. Guildford: SRHE.

Shavit, Y., Arum, R. and Gamoran, A. (2007) *Stratification in Higher Education: A Comparative Study*. Stanford, CA: Stanford University Press.

SHEFC (2001) *Update on Quality Issues*. Circular 55/01. Edinburgh: SHEFC.

SHEFC (2007) *Evaluation of the Higher Education Quality Enhancement Framework: Final Report*. Circular 11/07. Edinburgh: SHEFC.

SHEFC (2008) *Council Guidance to Higher Education Institutions on Quality*. Circular 30/08. Edinburgh: SHEFC.

Shepherd, J. (2008) What happened to the love? Students aren't passionate about their subjects any more, say lecturers. All they care about is job prospects, *The Guardian*, 4 March, 23.

Shepherd, J. (2011) School leavers falling behind with maths skills, says report, *The Guardian*, 14 June, 8.

Shepherd, J. (2012a) Academies form majority of state secondary schools, *The Guardian*, 6 April, 5.

Shepherd, J. (2012b) A-level exams have become easier, says regulator, *The Guardian*, 2 May, 9.

Smith, A. (2012) Making an impact: when science and politics collide, *The Guardian*, 1 June, http://www.guardian.co.uk/science/2012/jun/01/making-impact-scientists/ print (accessed 1 June 2012).

Smith, D.M. (1986) UGC research ratings: pass or fail? *Arena*, 18, 3, 247–250.

Smith, D.P., Scott, P. and McKay, L. (1993) Mission impossible? Access and the dash for growth in British higher education, *Higher Education Quarterly*, 47, 4, 334–356.

Smith, T. (1987) The UGC's research rankings exercise, *Higher Education Quarterly*, 41, 4, 303–316.

Soin, K. and Wheatley, S. (Submitted for review) Risk management in higher education: an action nets perspective.

SRHE (1983) *The Leverhulme Report. Excellence in Diversity. Towards a New Strategy for Higher Education*. Guildford: SRHE.

SQW Ltd (1996) *Selective Allocation of Research Funds: a Report to HEFCE*. Cambridge: SQW Ltd.

SQW Ltd (1999) *Providing Public Information on the Quality and Standards of Higher Education Courses*. HEFCE ref 99/61. Bristol: HEFCE.

SQW Ltd (2011) *Summative Evaluation of the CETL Programme. Final report by SQW to HEFCE and DEL December 2011*, http://www.hefce.ac.uk/pubs/rdreports/2011/rd11_11/rd11_11.pdf (accessed 4 June 2012).

Standard and Poors (2010) Tuition fee reforms set to widen gap in creditworthiness between strongest and weakest U.K. universities. *Global Credit Portal*, 7 December 2010.

Steenhart, K. and Newton, J. (2012) *2012 Applicants Survey: How Have Higher Tuition Fees Affected the Decision-Making Process of 2012 Applicants?* London: OpinionPanel.

Stewart, W. (2011) Attack of the clones: plagiarism by university applicants soars, *TES*, 18 February, 9.

Stewart, W. (2012a) Exam board head: Ofqual wanted me to adjust marks. Former exam boss says he now accepts standards have dropped, *TES*, 2 March, 14–15.

Stewart, W. (2012b) World rankings and exam results just don't add up, says exam boss, *TES*, 18 May, 8–9.

Stratton, A. (2012) Michael Gove wants universities to create new A-levels. *BBC News* 3 April, http://www.bbc.co.uk/news/education-17588292?print=true (accessed 24 June 2012).

Sutton Trust (2012) Less Than Half of State School Teachers Would Advise Their Most Able Pupils to Apply to Oxbridge. News release, 27 April 2012, http://www.sutton-trust.com/news/less-than-half-of-state-teachers-oxbridge (accessed 10 June 2012).

Sweeting, W. (2011) Offa's strike against bursaries not work of fair-access champion, *THE*, 8 December, 28–29.

Swinnerton-Dyer, P. (1991) Policy on higher education: the Rede lecture, 1991, *Higher Education Quarterly*, 45, 3, 204–218.

Taggart, G.J. (2004) A critical review of the role of the English Funding Body for higher education in the relationship between the State and Higher Education in the period 1945–2003. A dissertation submitted to the University of Bristol in accordance with the requirements of the degree of Doctor of Education in the Graduate School of Education, Faculty of Social Sciences and Law.

Tahir, T. (2007) Fees blamed for bad behaviour. *THE*, September 14, 7.

Talib, A.A. (2000) The RAE and publications: a view of journal editors, *Higher Education Review*, 33, 1, 32–46.

Tapper, T. (2007) *The Governance of British Higher Education: The Struggle for Control*. Dordrecht: Springer.

Tapper, T. and Salter, B. (1992) *Oxford, Cambridge and the Changing Idea of the University: The Challenge to Donnish Domination*. Buckingham: SRHE and Open University Press.

Taylor-Gooby, P. and Straker, G. (2011) The coalition programme: a new vision for Britain or politics as usual? *The Political Quarterly* 82 (1): 8–18.

Technopolis (2009) *Science Research Investment Fund: a Review of Round 2 and Wider Benefits*. Brighton: Technopolis Ltd.

Teichler, U. (2006) Changing structures of higher education systems: the increasing complexity of underlying forces, *Higher Education Policy*, 19, 4, 447–461.

Tennant, P. and Duggan, F. (2008) *Academic Misconduct Benchmarking Research Project: Part II*. York: HEA and JISC.

THE (2006) *Threat to Students' Demands for 8 Hours Contact*, 17 March, 8.

THE (2010) *Light Touch for Top Rankers*, 30 September, 18.

Thomas, E. (2004) *Increasing Voluntary Giving to Higher Education: Task Force Report to Government*, http://bit.ly/ThomasReport (accessed 6 June 2012).

Thomas, E. (2007) The future of research assessment. In H. de Burgh, A. Fazackerley and J. Black (Eds.) *Can the Prizes Still Glitter? The Future of British Universities in a Changing World*. Buckingham: The University of Buckingham Press.

Thompson, J. and Bekhradnia, B. (2011) *Students at the Heart of the System. An Analysis of the Higher Education White Paper*, http://www.hepi.ac.uk/455-1987/Higher-Education-Students-at-the-Heart-of-the-System.An-Analysis.html. (accessed 25 August 2011).

Thompson, J. and Bekhradnia, B. (2012) *The Cost of the Government's Reforms of the Financing of Higher Education*. Oxford: HEPI.

Thornton, M. (2012) *Privatising the Public University: The Case of Law*. Abingdon and New York: Routledge.

Thrupp, M. (1999) *Schools Making a Difference: Let's Be Realistic!* Buckingham: Open University Press.

TLRP (2008) *What Is Learned at University? The Social and Organisational Mediation of University Learning*. Teaching and Learning Research Briefing No. 32, March, http://www.tlrp.org/pub/documents/Brennan/020RB%2032%20FINAL.pdf (accessed 31 May 2012).

Trow, M. (1974) Problems in the transition from elite to mass higher education. In *Policies for Higher Education* from the General Report on the Conference on Future Structures of Post Secondary Education (pp. 55–101). Paris: OECD.

Trow, M. (1984) The analysis of status. In B.R. Clark (Ed.) *Perspectives on Higher Education – Eight Disciplinary and Comparative Views* (pp. 132–164). Berkeley, Los Angeles and London: University of California Press.

Turner, D. and Pratt, J. (1990) Bidding for funds in higher education, *Higher Education Review*, 23, 3, 19–33.

UCAS (2011) *End of Cycle Report 2010/2011* Cheltenham: UCAS.

UCAS (2012) *How Have Applications for Full-time Undergraduate Higher Education in the UK Changed in 2012?* http://www.ucas.ac.uk/about_us/media_enquiries/media_releases/2012/2012applicationsanalysis (accessed 9 July 2012).

UCU (2012) *Choice Cuts: How Choice Has Declined in Higher Education*, http://www.ucu.org.uk/media/pdf/d/k/Choice_cuts.pdf (accessed 23 February 2012).

UGC (1984) *A Strategy for Higher Education into the 1990s*. London: HMSO.

UGC (1985) *Planning for the Late 1980s: the Resource Allocation Process*. Circular 22/85. London: UGC.

UGC (1987) *The Oxburgh Report on the 'Size of Earth Science departments'*. London: UGC.

UUK (2001) *New Directions for Higher Education funding. Funding Options Review Group. Final report*. London: UUK.

UUK (2009) *Monitoring Research Concentration and Diversity: Changes Between 1994 and 2007*. London: UUK.

UUK (2011) *Efficiency and Effectiveness in Higher Education: A Report by the Universities UK Efficiency and Modernisation Group*. London: UUK.

Usher, A. and Medow, J. (2010) *Global Higher Education Rankings 2010. Affordability and Accessibility in Comparative Perspective* Toronto: Higher Education Strategy Associates.

Van Vught, F. (2008) Mission diversity and reputation in higher education, *Higher Education Policy*, 21, 2, 151–174.

Vasagar, J. (2010) Students seek private tuition, *The Guardian*, 30 December, 2.

Vasagar, J. (2012) The UK threat to academic independence, *The Guardian2*, 22 May, 11.

Vignoles, A. (2008) *Widening Participation in Higher Education: A Quantitative Analysis.* ESRC Teaching and Learning Research Programme, http://www.tlrp.org/pub/documents/Vignoles%20RB%2039%20Final.pdf (accessed 18 May 2012).

Vincent-Lancrin, S. (2006) What is changing in academic research? Trends and future scenarios, *European Journal of Education*, 41, 2, 169–202.

Wagner, L. (1993) The teaching quality debate, *Higher Education Quarterly*, 47, 3, 274–285.

Wagner, L. (1998) How spending review can be a win/win situation, *THE*, 26 June 1998, p 13

Wakeling, P. (2010) Inequalities in postgraduate education. In G. Goastellec (Ed.) *Understanding Inequalities in, through and by Higher Education* (pp. 61–74). Rotterdam: Sense.

Wales, P. (2012) Access all areas? The impact of fees and background on student demand for postgraduate education in the UK. Paper presented at the Royal Economic Society.

Walford, G. (1988) The privatisation of British higher education, *European Journal of Education*, 23, 1/2, 47–64.

Walne, J.C. (1973) Analysis of university costs at the UGC. *Higher Education*, 2, 2, 228–235.

Washburn, J. (2005) *University Inc.: The Corporate Corruption of Higher Education*. New York: Basic Books.

Watson, D. (1997) Quality, standards and institutional reciprocity. Paper for the QSC conference on changing conceptions of academic standards. London, 12 March.

Watson, D. (1998) The limits to diversity. In D. Jary and M. Parker (Eds.) *The New Higher Education: Issues and Directions for the Post-Dearing University* (pp. 65–82). Stoke-on-Trent: Staffordshire University Press.

Watson, D. (2006a) How to think about widening participation in UK higher education. Discussion paper for HEFCE by David Watson, Institute of Education, University of London. Bristol: HEFCE.

Watson, D. (2006b) UK higher education: the truth about the student market, *Higher Education Review* 38, 3, 3–16.

Watson, D. (2007) *Whatever Happened to the Dearing Report?* London: Institute of Education, University of London.

Watson, D. (2008) Universities behaving badly? *Higher Education Review*, 40, 3, 3–14.

Watson, D. and Bowden, R. (1997) *Ends without Means: the Conservative Stewardship of UK Higher Education 1979–1997*. Brighton: Education Research Centre, University of Brighton.

Watson, D. and Bowden, R. (1999) Why did they do it? The Conservatives and mass higher education, 1979–1997, *Journal of Education Policy*, 14, 3, 243–256.

Watson, D. and Bowden, R. (2001) *'Can we be Equal and Excellent Too?' The New Labour*

Stewardship of UK Higher Education, 1997–2001. Brighton: Education Research Centre, University of Brighton.

Watson, D. and Bowden, R. (2002) *The New University Decade: 1992–2002*. Brighton: Education Research Centre, University of Brighton.

Watson, D. and Bowden, R. (2005) *The Turtle and the Fruit Fly: New Labour and Higher Education 2001–2005*. Brighton: University of Brighton Education Research Centre.

Weimer, D. L. and Vining, A. R. (1992) *Policy Analysis: Concepts and Practice*. Englewood Cliffs, NJ: Prentice-Hall.

Wellings, P. and Winzer, R. (2011) *Mapping Research Excellence: Exploring the Links between Research Excellence and Research Funding Policy*. London: 1994 Group.

Wellman, J. (2008) Spending more, getting less, *Change*, November/December, 19–25.

Welsh Government (2011) *Strong, Sustainable and Successful – Proposals for the Future Shape of HE in Wales*, http://wales.gov.uk/newsroom/educationandskills/2011/111129universities/?lang (accessed 2 December 2011).

Welsh Government (2012) *Higher Education Funding Council for Wales Remit Letter 2012–13, 16 March 2012*, http://www.hefcw.ac.uk/documents/about_he_in_wales/wag_priorities_and_policies/Remit%202012_13.pdf (accessed 22 March 2012).

Westerheijden, D.F. (2007) States and Europe and quality of higher education. In D.F. Westerheijden, B. Stensaker and M.J. Rosa (Eds.) *Quality Assurance in Higher Education: Trends in Regulation, Translation and Transformation* (pp. 73–98). Dordrecht: Springer.

Which (2012) *NUS Supports New University Service from Which?* 4 July, http:www.which.co.uk/news/2012/07/nus-supports-new-university-service-from-which-290203 (accessed 6 July 2012).

White, N. (2007) 'The customer is always right?': student discourse about higher education in Australia, *Higher Education*, 54, 4, 593–604.

Whiteley, P. (2009) Should Research Funds be Concentrated? RAE Performance and Institutional Size. Personal communication by email, 19 March 2009.

Willetts, D. (2011) *Speech to UniversitiesUK Spring Conference 2011*, http://www.bis.gov.uk/news/speeches/david-willetts-uuk-spring-conference2011 (accessed 6 June 2012).

Willetts, D. (2012a). Higher Education Student Finance for the 2013–14 Academic Year. Written Ministerial Statement 8 March 2012.

Willetts, D. (2012b) Speech to HEFCE Annual Conference 2012 London, Royal College of Music, 18 April 2012.

Williams, B. (1987) *Universities' Responses to Research Selectivity*. University of London Institute of Education Centre for Higher Education Studies Occasional Paper No 2.

Williams, G. (1992) *Changing Patterns of Finance in Higher Education*. Buckingham: SRHE and Open University Press.

Williams, G. (1995) The 'marketisation' of higher education: reforms and potential reforms in higher education finance. In D.D. Dill and B. Sporn (Eds.) *Emerging Patterns of Social Demand and University Reform: Through a Glass Darkly* (pp. 170–193). Oxford: Pergamon Press.

Williams, G. (1997) The market route to mass higher education: British experience 1979–1996, *Higher Education Policy*, 10, 3/4, 275–289.

Williams, G. (1999) Financing of higher education. An overview of theoretical and empirical issues. In M. Henkel and B. Little (Eds.) *Changing Relationships between Higher Education and the State* (pp. 142–161). London and Philadelphia: Jessica Kingsley.

Williams, G. (2004) The higher education market in the United Kingdom. In P. Teixeira, B. Jongbloed, D. Dill and A. Amaral (Eds.) *Markets in Higher Education: Rhetoric or Reality?* (pp. 98–112) Dordrecht: Kluwer.

Williams, G. and Filippakou, O. (2010) Higher education and UK elite formation in the 20th century, *Higher Education*, 59, 1, 1–20.

Williams, J. (2011) Constructing consumption: what media representations reveal about today's students. In M. Molesworth, R. Scullion and E. Nixon (Eds.) *The Marketisation of Higher Education and the Student as Consumer* (pp. 170–182). London and New York: Routledge.

Williams, J. (2012) *Consuming Higher Education: Why Learning Can't Be Bought* London: Continuum.

Williams, L. (1987) Overseas students in the United Kingdom: some recent developments, *Higher Education Quarterly*, 41, 2, 107–118.

Williams, P. (Ed.) (1981) *The Overseas Student Question: Studies for a Policy.* London: Heinemann for the Overseas Students Trust.

Williams, P. (1984) Britain's full-cost policy for overseas students, *Comparative Education Review*, 28, 2, 258–278,

Williams, Z. (2012) I don't see a plan at all, Lampl says, *THE*, 3 May 2012, p. 11.

Willmott, H. (2003) Commercialising higher education in the UK: the state, industry and peer review, *Studies in Higher Education*, 28, 2, 129–141.

Winston, G.C. (1999) Subsidies, hierarchy and peers: the awkward economics of higher education, *Journal of Economic Perspectives*, 13, 1, 13–36.

Wolf, C. (1993) *Markets or Governments: Choosing between Imperfect Alternatives.* Cambridge, MA.: Massachusetts Institute of Technology Press.

Woodhall, M. and Richards, K. (2006) Student and university funding in devolved governments in the United Kingdom. In, P.N. Teixeira, D. Bruce Johnstone, M.J. Rosa, and H. Vossensteyn (Eds.) *Cost-Sharing and Accessibility in Higher Education: A Fairer Deal?* (pp. 189–212) Dordrecht: Springer.

Working Group on the Management of Higher Education in the Maintained Sector (1978) *The Oakes Report.* Cmnd 7130. London: HMSO.

Yorke, M. (1998) Performance indicators relating to student achievement: can they be trusted? *Quality in Higher Education*, 4, 1, 45–61.

Yorke, M. (2008) *Grading Student Achievement in Higher Education.* London and New York Routledge.

Yorke, M. (2009) *Trends in Honours Degree Classifications, 1994–95 to 2006–7, for England, Wales and Northern Ireland,* http://heacademy.ac.uk/resources/detail/publications/trends_in_honours_degree_classifications (accessed 10 October 2009).

Yorke, M. and Alderman, G. (1999) 'Money talks' mentality is taking its toll, *Guardian Higher*, 15 June, ii–iii.

Zemsky, R. (2005) The dog that doesn't bark: why markets neither limit prices nor promote educational quality. In J. Burke and Associates *Achieving Accountability in Higher Education: Balancing Public, Academic and Market Demands* (pp. 275–295). San Francisco: Jossey-Bass.

Index